**Conversations with
Ben Okri**

Literary Conversations Series
Monika Gehlawat
General Editor

Conversations with Ben Okri

Edited by Vanessa Guignery

University Press of Mississippi / Jackson

The University Press of Mississippi is the scholarly publishing agency of
the Mississippi Institutions of Higher Learning: Alcorn State University,
Delta State University, Jackson State University, Mississippi State University,
Mississippi University for Women, Mississippi Valley State University,
University of Mississippi, and University of Southern Mississippi.

www.upress.state.ms.us

The University Press of Mississippi is a member
of the Association of University Presses.

Copyright © 2024 by University Press of Mississippi
All rights reserved

∞

Library of Congress Cataloging-in-Publication Data

Names: Guignery, Vanessa, editor.
Title: Conversations with Ben Okri / Vanessa Guignery.
Other titles: Literary conversations series.
Description: Jackson : University Press of Mississippi, 2024. | Series:
    Literary conversations series | Includes bibliographical references and index.
Identifiers: LCCN 2023043132 (print) | LCCN 2023043133 (ebook) |
    ISBN 9781496851550 (hardback) | ISBN 9781496851567 (trade paperback) |
    ISBN 9781496851574 (epub) | ISBN 9781496851581 (epub) | ISBN 9781496851598
    (pdf) | ISBN 9781496851604 (pdf)
Subjects: LCSH: Okri, Ben—Interviews. | Authors, Nigerian—Interviews. |
    Poets, Nigerian—Interviews. | Screenwriters—Nigeria—Interviews.
Classification: LCC PR9387.9.O394 C668 2024 (print) | LCC PR9387.9.O394
    (ebook) | DDC 823/.914—dc23/eng/20231221
LC record available at https://lccn.loc.gov/2023043132
LC ebook record available at https://lccn.loc.gov/2023043133

British Library Cataloging-in-Publication Data available

Books by Ben Okri

Novels

Flowers and Shadows, Harlow, Longman, 1980.
The Landscapes Within, Harlow, Longman, 1981.
The Famished Road, London, Jonathan Cape, 1991.
Songs of Enchantment, London, Jonathan Cape, 1993.
Astonishing the Gods, London, Weidenfeld & Nicholson, 1995.
Dangerous Love, London, Weidenfeld & Nicholson, 1996.
Infinite Riches, London, Weidenfeld & Nicholson, 1998.
In Arcadia, London, Weidenfeld & Nicholson, 2002.
Starbook, London, Rider & Co, 2007.
The Age of Magic, London, Head of Zeus, 2014.
The Freedom Artist, London, Head of Zeus, 2019.
Every Leaf a Hallelujah, London, Head of Zeus, 2021.
The Last Gift of the Master Artists, London, Head of Zeus, 2022.

Short Fiction

Incidents at the Shrine, London, Heinemann, 1986.
Stars of the New Curfew, London, Secker & Warburg, 1988.
Tales of Freedom, London, Rider & Co, 2009.
The Magic Lamp: Dreams of Our Age, in collaboration with painter Rosemary Clunie, London, Head of Zeus, 2017.
The Comic Destiny (previously *Tales of Freedom*), London, Head of Zeus, 2019.
Prayer for the Living, London, Head of Zeus, 2019.

Poetry

An African Elegy, London, Jonathan Cape, 1992.
Mental Fight, London, Weidenfeld & Nicholson, 1999.
Wild, London, Rider & Co, 2012.

A Fire in My Head: Poems for the Dawn, London, Head of Zeus, 2021.
(as editor) *Rise Like Lions: Poetry for the Many*, London, Hodder & Stoughton, 2018.

Plays

The Outsider (L'Étranger) by Albert Camus. Adapted for the stage by Ben Okri. London, Oberon Books, 2018.
Madame Sosostris, the Wisest Woman in Europe, 2020 (unpublished).
Changing Destiny, London, Bloomsbury, 2021.

Scripts

N: The Madness of Reason. Film by Peter Kruger, 2014.
Moby Dick, at last Queequeg speaks. Musical play directed by Gorges Ocloo, 2020 (unpublished).

Nonfiction

Birds of Heaven, London, Phoenix House, 1996.
A Way of Being Free, London, Weidenfeld & Nicholson, 1997.
A Time for New Dreams, London, Rider & Co, 2011.

Other Collections

The Mystery Feast: Thoughts on Storytelling, West Hoathly, Clairview, 2015 (essays, poem and stoku).
Tiger Work: Stories, essays and poems about climate change, London, Other Press, 2023.

Contents

Introduction   xi

Chronology   xix

Ben Okri   3
    Jane Wilkinson / 1986 and 1990

An Interview with Ben Okri   19
    Pietro Deandrea / 1990 and 1992

An Interview with Ben Okri   47
    Carolyn Newton / 1992

Whisperings of the Gods: An Interview with Ben Okri   52
    Delia Falconer / 1996

An Interview with Ben Okri   60
    Charles H. Rowell / 2005

"The Book of Laughter and Forgetting": An Interview with Ben Okri   70
    Nana Yaa Mensah / 2008

Points of Enchantment   83
    Sarah Fulford / 2008

Interview with Ben Okri   88
    Rosemary Gray / 2011

Ben Okri: Interview   94
    Saskia Vogel / 2011

The Mysteries of the Word: A Conversation with Ben Okri   98
Anderson Tepper / 2011

Ben Okri in Conversation   107
Vanessa Guignery and Catherine Pesso-Miquel / 2012

Painter of Secrets   118
Anupama Raju / 2012

Lookin Back: James Ogude in Conversation with Ben Okri   125
James Ogude / 2014

An Interview with Ben Okri   135
Vanessa Guignery / 2015

Ben Okri Q&A: "I Can't Live without Good Conversation, Or Love"   148
New Statesman / 2018

Ben Okri on His "Unavoidably" Political Poems   150
Ushnota Paul / 2019

Ben Okri Interview: We Can Ascend Mountains   155
Marc-Christoph Wagner / 2019

The Past Is a Changing Entity   163
Isabelle Rüf / 2020

"Courage Is a Luxury"   167
Katrien Steyaert / 2020

Ben Okri on Perception and Illusion   171
Deborah Treisman / 2021

Ben Okri: "Nations Like Ours Have a Hard Time Looking Back Truthfully"   174
Dorian Lynskey / 2021

In Conversation with Ben Okri   178
Rosemary Gray / 2021

"Write with New Urgency": A Conversation with Ben Okri   185
Anderson Tepper / 2022

Ben Okri on the Ambiguity of Reality   190
Deborah Treisman / 2022

Ben Okri or the Aesthetics of Suspicion   193
Vanessa Guignery / 2022

Ben Okri on Manipulating Reality   212
Katherine Hu / 2023

Index   217

Introduction

"I am addicted to dialogues," Ben Okri writes at the beginning of a 2020 essay entitled "Conversations Between Souls." He insists on the necessity to preserve the vitality and energy of dialogues in the third millennium which is "a time of monologues, soliloquies, solipsistic speech in twittersphere, [...] a time in which we talk from our solitudes." For him, a genuine exchange between two people depends on the collaboration between a sensitive and attentive interlocutor and "a central thinker who responds to questions with generosity and truthfulness," "one with whom we would like to engage in conversation about the great and the small things of life."[1] Such a description could apply to Ben Okri himself who is adept at the art of dialogue and conversation, whether discussing the texture of dreams, the value of myth or the food he is about to order in a restaurant. An interview is a more formal exercise, but the Nigerian writer would probably agree with Graham Swift that "the best interview is the one that forgets it is an interview and becomes a conversation."[2]

When Ben Okri gives an interview, he is very generous with his time, thereby ensuring that the conversation can be free-flowing and unobstructed by external constraints. This live moment of exchange is a unique and rich experience, where the writer is fully engaged, attentive to the way questions are formulated, precise and rigorous in his answers, sometimes playful and mischievous. When I discussed with him the possibility of publishing a collection of his interviews for the Literary Conversations Series at the University Press of Mississippi, he enthusiastically embraced the project, calling it "another adventure of the mind and spirit," "one that traverses time, to the beginnings of the work and peering into the future."[3] Although Ben Okri has given many interviews throughout the years, he rarely reads them after they are printed and when I sent him an early draft of the volume, he confessed to having had "a mild panic at the project," struck by the impression that he did not hear himself in some of the interviews. He remarked: "Perhaps the interview is an unnatural medium. It catches one in a mode of formality."[4] A few months later, his misgivings had not abated:

"I have come to realize now something of the inadequacies of the interview form. One tends to give an unsatisfactory answer on the spot to questions that require a lot more thought."[5] Despite these persistent doubts, the interviews collected in this volume reveal a writer who is passionate about his art and willing to share his views on the miracle of the human spirit, the fundamental freedom of imagination or the different modalities of invisibility.

As this collection shows, the interview is a polymorphous genre whose form varies according to the circumstances in which it is held and then made available, with inevitable repercussions on the answers provided by the author. The interview can be conducted privately with one interviewer (whom the writer knows more or less well) or in front of a live audience. It may serve a promotional agenda to mark the publication of a new book or be unrelated to such a temporality and provide room for discussion of a larger body of work and ideas. The interview can then be made available as a video or audio file online or published in a written form, thereupon transforming a live event into a fixed record. The interview may be lightly or heavily edited and the choices made during the editorial process (by the interviewer or/and the interviewee) about what to include and what to exclude concern not only form but also content. The author is not always involved in the editing stage and therefore may not have the opportunity to correct misunderstandings. An interview becomes another literary genre when it is transformed into an article in which only part of the author's answers is included or paraphrased rather than directly quoted. All these various options produce very different types of interviews in terms of content, length and format, and the present volume proposes a selection of these with the aim of illuminating Ben Okri's creative process, art, and interests from a multiplicity of angles over a period of thirty-seven years.

This long period of time has been deliberately chosen to offer a glimpse of the various phases of Okri's life and career, from his childhood (spent first in Nigeria and then in England between the ages of two and seven) and his upbringing in Nigeria (which he left in the autumn of 1978 at the age of nineteen to move permanently to England), followed by the publication of his early short stories and novels in the early 1980s up to his most recent literary production and artistic collaborations in the 2020s. The first parts of two long interviews by Jane Wilkinson and Pietro Deandrea were conducted before Ben Okri was awarded the Booker prize for his third novel *The Famished Road* in 1991 and can therefore dwell at length on his early readings in Nigeria (folktales, Greek, Roman and African myths, Western classics) and on his first steps as a writer. The two interviews discuss Okri's early production which consisted of articles on social inequalities and injustices in Nigeria (the very first of which was published in 1976 when Okri was seventeen), short stories (the early ones appeared in women's journals and evening papers in Nigeria), and his first two novels published in England by Longman in their "Drumbeat" series, *Flowers and Shadows* (1980) and *The Landscapes Within* (1981). In several interviews Okri explains that after publishing his second novel, he went through a crisis in his writing life as he realized that the naturalistic form of narration common in the West did not correspond to the way in which he perceived reality. He turned to myth, to African philosophy, riddles and storytelling, and looked for new ways of capturing the multidimensionality of reality, experimenting with this in his collections of short stories, *Incidents at the Shrine* (1986) and *Stars of the New Curfew* (1988), and subsequently in *The Famished Road*.

What is remarkable about the early interviews is that Okri's assured tone is already perceptible as he does not hesitate to gently but firmly refute an interpretation or hypothesis proposed by the interviewer or by reviewers who "misunderstood" or "ignored" some essential aspects of his literary production. Over the years, several interviewers have suggested comparisons with the work of other Nigerian writers (Wole Soyinka or Chinua Achebe in particular) and have wondered whether Okri's writing may be placed within the context of postcolonial debates or along the lines of magical realism (Deandrea, Newton, Falconer, Tepper, Ogude). Okri has patiently but systematically explained why the latter label does not correspond to his mode of writing or to West African conceptions of the real, and he has repeatedly questioned the tendency to try and identify influences among his Nigerian (or Western) predecessors. He prefers to say that he finds inspiration in "the invisible books of the spirit" (Wilkinson) as well as in music, nature or paintings (Fulford). He has also constantly fought against critics' temptation to narrow down his work and the African aesthetic by defining them along national or ethnic lines. "We have to declassify," he insists (Fulford), pointing out that his stories are "relevant everywhere" (Deandrea) and his context universal (Rowell, Ogude). This explains why he claims that the awarding of the Booker Prize to *The Famished Road* (Okri was then the first Black African writer and, at the age of thirty-two, the youngest to receive it) was for him "a triumph for the imagination" and not only for the African novel (Newton).

This award immediately granted Ben Okri great visibility and the book was the subject of many interviews over the years, sometimes to the detriment of other parts of the writer's production, especially as a poet, essayist, playwright, and short-story writer. This volume includes interviews that probe his most well-known novel at length, the significance of the spirit-child's dual consciousness, the centrality of myth, suffering, and history (Wilkinson, Deandrea, Guignery, and Pesso-Miquel) but it also comprises discussions that address Ben Okri's publications in a wide variety of genres (poetry, short stories, novels, stokus—a genre he invented which mixes the story and the haiku—plays, fables, and poetic essays). When the writer is asked how he knows which genre he will select for a specific text, he answers that "the impulse chooses the form" (Falconer) and refers to the mystery of the "pre-creative state" before an idea takes a specific form (Vogel, Paul). He also points to his tendency to blend and blur genres (Guignery and Pesso-Miquel) and not see strong demarcations between essay and poetry (Raju, Gray 2021).

The most recent interviews in the volume discuss literary genres that Okri more particularly experimented with in the last few years: his three plays *The Outsider* (adapted from Camus's novel in 2018), *Madame Sosostris, the Wisest Woman in Europe* (2020) and *Changing Destiny* (2021) as well as his script for the musical play *Moby Dick, at last Queequeg speaks* (2020) directed by Gorges Ocloo and his 2021 environmental fable *Every Leaf a Hallelujah* (Rüf, Steyaert, Guignery 2022). Okri's collaborations with other artists (painters, dancers, musicians, filmmakers) have intensified in the last decade and the writer talks about the exhilarating process of writing the poetic script for *N: The Madness of Reason* (2014), a film by Peter Kruger which oscillates between Western rationality and African spirituality (Guignery 2015). The volume also includes three interviews (by Deborah Treisman and Katherine Hu) that examine short stories published in the *New Yorker* and *The Atlantic* between 2021 and 2023, thus giving the author an opportunity to talk about the detail of these individual pieces.

Some conversations go deep into the structural, stylistic, and narratological specificities of certain short stories or novels, for instance when the author evokes the starlike structure of *Starbook* (Yaa Menshah) or explains the technique of echo-writing he employed for *The Famished Road* (Guignery and Pesso-Miquel). They also explore the expressive power of brevity in the poetic essays published in the cubist volume *A Time for New Dreams* (Vogel) and the economy or "atomization" of form found in Twitter poetry (collected in *Wild*) or in the stokus of *Tales of Freedom* and *Prayer for the Living* (Tepper 2011, Guignery 2015, Treisman 2021). Other conversations are more philosophical and metaphysical (Rowell, Gray) and Okri's philosophical trains of thoughts are sometimes so complex as to slightly disconcert the interviewer, leading for instance Charles Rowell to ask Okri for "a little more simplicity" and to "kindly explicate [his] explanation." At other times, his tone is prophetic as in some of his creative writing, for example when he claims that "[a]n accelerated awakening has to take place" (Wagner) and that "[w]e need a new consciousness to make a new future" (Tepper 2022). What comes out of the interviews is Okri's visceral belief in "the resilience of the spirit, the great dreaming capacities" (Wilkinson) which justify the persistence of our "desire for an Arcadia" (Rowell) and the hope for regeneration in the midst of the current chaos, unrest, and suffering. This endless quest for a better inner and outer world is regularly highlighted in Okri's poems and essays but also in such novels as *In Arcadia* (2002) and *The Age of Magic* (2014) while *The Freedom Artist* (2019) points to the necessity of freeing ourselves from the various prisons we harbor (Wagner).

The conversations address a wide range of issues and several common themes run through them, including the importance of dreams, myths and spirituality, the role of memory, history, loss and suffering, or the significance of magic, freedom and humor in Okri's work. A recurrent topic of conversation relates to the role of the writer. To Okri, the artist is "a questioner, an expander of consciousness, a widener of perception," whose role is "to re-dream our lives," "decode reality better" (Deandrea) and "extend the boundaries" (Gray 2011) rather than be hindered by self-imposed limitations. The writer repeatedly probes what constitutes reality, how one perceives and constructs it, and he interrogates the modalities through which the artist captures and conveys not one but several levels or layers of reality (Tepper 2011, Wagner). He is more interested in the "magic of things" than in their realism (Yaa Mensah) and argues that "[t]he future of the novel is the end of realism as we have known it" (Fulford).

Okri also discusses his conception of the social and political role of the writer in several interviews. His very first articles addressed social injustices in Lagos but in 1992, he described "Africa's limitation by political writing as a one-colour painting" (Newton). He argued that the duty of the artist was to "plant delayed detonations" rather than lead revolts and go to war as the poet Christopher Okigbo did (Deandrea). Three decades later, he defended the value of political poetry (Guignery 2022), of which his 2021 collection *A Fire in my Head* is emblematic, more specifically his poems "Grenfell Tower, June 2017" (discussed in Paul and Lynskey), "Breathing the Light" (a response to the death of George Floyd) and "Boko Haram." His most recent interviews and creative work regularly address questions relating to climate change and the environmental crisis, which has led him to develop what he calls "existential creativity,"[6] a creativity which speaks the truth of our environmental catastrophe. He implements this approach in his written work but also in his collaboration with Scottish painter Rosemary Clunie as evidenced by their 2023 exhibition *Firedreams* at the Bomb Factory in London.

The volume comprises twenty-six interviews of varied lengths and formats, some published in scholarly journals or volumes, others in newspapers, magazines, or on the Internet. The selection aims to reflect the international resonance of Ben Okri's work by including interviews conducted in Great Britain and the United States, but also in South Africa, India, Italy, France, Denmark, Switzerland, and Belgium. The interviewers come from diverse backgrounds in journalism or academia, thereby offering a wide range of approaches to Ben Okri's work. The selected interviews reveal Okri's faithfulness in his friendships and working relationships, as a few interviewers make two or three appearances, having conversed with the writer several times over the years (Rosemary Gray in 2011 and 2021, Anderson Tepper in 2011 and 2022, Deborah Treisman in 2021 and 2022, myself in 2012, 2015, and 2022).

When given the opportunity to edit interviews before their publication (which is often not possible), Ben Okri does so thoroughly and very carefully, rewriting, deleting, or adding whole sentences. This was my experience for the interviews I conducted with him over a period of ten years. For this volume, Ben Okri told me early on that he wanted to edit some of the interviews he had not been able to read prior to their publication in order to clarify a few things. This meticulousness comes as no surprise from an author who rewrote two of his novels some fifteen years after their original publication: in 1996, he issued a revised version of his second novel *The Landscapes Within* under the new title *Dangerous Love* (discussed in Falconer), and in 2022, he published *The Last Gift of the Master Artists*, a revised version of his 2007 novel *Starbook* (discussed in Guignery 2022). For previously published interviews, we limited the editing process to two of them (that by Pietro Deandrea and a 2011 interview with Rosemary Gray), choosing to preserve the others in their original form.

Thanks to their diversity, the interviews in this collection offer insights into Ben Okri's writing process, craft and philosophy, with the aim of creating a space where his thoughts and ideas may resonate. When giving an interview, the writer does not wish to provide clear and definitive interpretations on his literary production but on the contrary invites the reader to look for "the luminous hidden little scripts" (Falconer) in "the magic space" (Raju) he is creating and be open to a multiplicity of meanings. This volume therefore not only proposes dialogues between writer and interviewer but also hopes to extend the conversation to the reader who is encouraged to share in the philosophical reflections, meditations and dreaming.

I would like to express my warm thanks to all the people who helped me complete the project, in particular Mary Heath at the University Press of Mississippi who has always been very responsive and supportive. I am very grateful to all the interviewers and editors who granted me permission to republish their work and to Alice de la Barre de Nanteuil who assisted me for parts of the work. My deepest gratitude goes to Ben Okri, whom I cannot thank enough for his dedication to the project, his infinite patience, generosity, and truthfulness. We spent many hours discussing the interviews in person in London, through videoconference and in emails, and I am extremely grateful for his time and commitment to this "adventure of the mind and spirit."

VG

Notes

1. Ben Okri, "Conversations Between Souls," in *Justice and Love: A Philosophical Dialogue* by Mary Zournazi and Rowan Williams (London: Bloomsbury Academic), 2020.
2. Donald P. Kaczvinsky, "Introduction," in *Conversations with Graham Swift*, edited by Donald P. Kaczvinsky (Jackson: University Press of Mississippi, 2020), x.
3. Email correspondence with the editor, November 10, 2021.
4. Email correspondence with the editor, June 26, 2022.
5. Email correspondence with the editor, October 9, 2022.
6. Ben Okri, "Artists must confront the climate crisis—we must write as if these are the last days." *The Guardian*, November 12, 2021. https://www.theguardian.com/commentisfree/2021/nov/12/artists-climate-crisis-write-creativity-imagination

Chronology

1959	Ben Okri born on March 15 in Minna, Nigeria, to an Ika Igbo mother and Urhobo father, Grace and Silver Okri.
1961	The family moves to London.
1963	Attends primary school in Peckham.
1966	The family moves to Lagos, Nigeria, where Okri's father sets up a law practice.
1973	Finishes secondary school with the aim of studying physics and becoming a scientist but is deemed too young for university.
1974	Reads his way through his father's library and discovers his true vocation as a writer.
1976	First piece of writing published in the *Evening Times* (Lagos) and first short story published in a women's magazine.
1978	Staff reporter for *Afriscope Magazine* (Lagos). Moves to England to study journalism and literature, taking with him the manuscript of first novel, *Flowers and Shadows*.
1979	Works in a bookshop.
1980	Studies Comparative Literature at the University of Essex with a grant from the Nigerian government. Writes, directs, and performs in first play, *A Blighted Silence*, at the University of Essex theatre. Publishes first novel *Flowers and Shadows*.
1981	Writes and directs second play *Looking for the Room* at the University of Essex theatre.
1982	Publishes *The Landscapes Within*. Leaves university after grant from Nigeria runs out.
1983	Poetry editor of *West Africa* magazine (to 1986) and regular contributor to the BBC World Service (to 1985).
1984	"Disparities" chosen by Peter Ackroyd for his PEN anthology of short stories.
1985	"Laughter Beneath the Bridge" published in Penguin's *Firebird* anthology.
1986	Publishes *Incidents at the Shrine*.

1987	Wins the Commonwealth Writer's Prize (Africa Region, Best Book) for *Incidents at the Shrine* and the Paris Review Aga Khan Prize for Fiction for "The Dream-Vendor's August."
1988	Publishes *Stars of the New Curfew*.
1991	Wins the Booker Prize for *The Famished Road*, the youngest ever prize winner at age thirty-two. Appointed Fellow Commoner in Creative Arts at Trinity College Cambridge (to 1993).
1992	Publishes *An African Elegy* (poetry collection).
1993	Publishes *Songs of Enchantment*. Wins the Chianti Ruffino-Antico Fattore International Literary Prize for *The Famished Road*.
1995	Publishes *Astonishing the Gods*. Receives Crystal Award (World Economic Forum).
1996	Publishes *Dangerous Love* and *Birds of Heaven* (essays). Contributor to the BBC's *Brain's Trust* and *Great Railway Journeys* ("London to Arcadia").
1997	Awarded an Honorary Doctorate from the University of Westminster; publishes *A Way of Being Free* (essays). Appointed Vice President of English Centre for International PEN.
1998	Publishes *Infinite Riches*.
1999	Publishes *Mental Fight* (epic poem for the new millennium).
2000	Wins the Premio Palmi (Italy) for *Dangerous Love*.
2001	Awarded an OBE (Order of the British Empire).
2002	Publishes *In Arcadia*. Awarded an Honorary Doctor of Literature, University of Essex.
2004	Receives an Honorary Doctorate of Literature, University of Exeter.
2007	Publishes *Starbook*.
2008	Travels to America to cover the election of President Obama for *The Times*. Wins the International Literary Award, the Novi Sad, and the Premio Grinzane Cavour (African Mainstream Prize).
2009	Publishes *Tales of Freedom* (invents the form of the stoku, a cross between a haiku and short story). Receives an Honorary Doctor of Utopia, Universiteit voor het Algemeen Belang (University for the Common Good), Belgium.
2010	Receives an Honorary Doctor of Letters, SOAS, and an Honorary Doctor of Arts, University of Bedfordshire.
2011	Publishes *A Time for New Dreams* (poetic essays).
2012	Publishes *Wild* (poetry collection). Visiting Professor at Leicester University (to 2014).

2014 Publishes *The Age of Magic*. Writes script for *N: The Madness of Reason*, a film by Peter Kruger. Appointed an Honorary Fellow of Mansfield College, Oxford. Receives an Honorary Doctor of Literature, University of Pretoria, South Africa.

2015 Publishes *The Mystery Feast: Thoughts on Storytelling* (Clairview Books) and previously unpublished texts in a special issue of *Callaloo* devoted to him.

2016 Starts a creative collaboration of poetry and dancing with Charlotte Jarvis: "Ballet of the Unseen" performed in Tramway, Glasgow, in June. Birth of his daughter, Mirabella Grace.

2017 Okri's poem about the Grenfell Tower disaster published in the *Financial Times* and read aloud on Channel 4. Publishes *The Magic Lamp* (a collaboration with artist Rosemary Clunie).

2018 Publishes *Rise Like Lions* (anthology of political poems). Writes the adaptation of Camus's *The Outsider* performed at The Coronet, London (receives an Offies Award for Best Theatre Production).

2019 Publishes *The Freedom Artist* and *Prayer for the Living* (short stories and stokus). BBC's "100 Novels That Shaped Our World" for *Astonishing the Gods*. With Charlotte Jarvis, performs "Our lives; an infinite improvisation" at the Edinburgh Festival (poetry and dancing).

2020 *Madame Sosostris* first performed at Pulloff Theatre, Lausanne, Switzerland, in February. Writes the libretto for the opera *Moby Dick, at last Queequeg speaks*, an adaptation of Herman Melville's *Moby-Dick* by the Ghanaian-Belgian director Gorges Ocloo, performed at De Singel Theaterstudio in Antwerp in March. Receives an Honorary Doctor of Literature, Nelson Mandela University, South Africa.

2021 Publishes *Every Leaf a Hallelujah*, illustrated by Diana Ejaita (children's book), *A Fire in My Head* (poems) and "A Wrinkle in the Realm" (short story, the *New Yorker*). Poetic collaboration with Afrobeat legend Tony Allen and Damon Albarn on Allen's last recorded song, "Cosmosis." With Ackroyd & Harvey, realises "On the Shore," an installation and performance work in two acts at the Tate Modern, London. *Changing Destiny* performed at the Young Vic in London in July. With Charlotte Jarvis, performs "Starting from First Position" at the Edinburgh Festival (poetry and dancing).

2022 Publishes *The Last Gift of the Master Artists*, "The Secret Source" (short story, the *New Yorker*) and "To Katya, aged seven, in a

	bomb shelter in Kyiv" (poem, *The Guardian*). In November, gives a performance of T. S. Eliot's *The Waste Land* at the Marylebone Theatre in London to mark its one hundredth anniversary.
2023	Knighted for services to literature. Publishes "The Third Law of Magic" (short story, *The Atlantic*) and *Tiger Work: Stories, essays and poems about climate change*. His exhibition *Firedreams* in collaboration with Rosemary Clunie is shown at the Bomb Factory in London.

Conversations with
Ben Okri

Ben Okri

Jane Wilkinson / 1986 and 1990

From *Talking with African Writers* (London/Portsmouth: James Currey Ltd/Heinemann, 1992): 76–89. Reprinted by permission of Boydell and Brewer Limited through PLSclear.

The interview was held in London, July 1986, and completed on December 12, 1990.

Jane Wilkinson: Tell me about your beginnings, your childhood, where you grew up . . .

Ben Okri: I'd rather reserve that for the complex manipulations of memory that only fiction can provide. The writer's childhood is an important part of anything he writes. That's the only way you can explain why some writers seem to be secretive about aspects of their lives. It's an area that they want to keep inviolate for their writings. It's the only reservoir they've got and they want to keep that for themselves, for the benefit of those who are interested in reading them. I prefer to talk in terms of writing, of when I first started consciously writing.

Wilkinson: When was that?

Okri: 1976.

Wilkinson: And how did it come about?

Okri: My father returned from his law studies in London with a library of Western classics from Dickens to Mark Twain, the Greeks, the Romans, Austen, English essays, books he didn't actually have the time to read. Those books were my beginnings. While I read Aristotle he said "Look, Africa has got everything: it's got Aristotle, it's got Plato, it's got all these things and more." And it was from his library of undiscovered books, books that were just there, moldering away in this amazing landscape, eaten away by cockroaches and dust and heat, that I started to read and discover the extraordinary quality of the imagination, of fiction.

Wilkinson: And that inspired you to write, in your turn?

Okri: Not inspired, but gave me my beginnings. I began writing from my own failure, my failure to get a place at a university in Nigeria. I wrote while waiting, I wrote as a way of waiting: I wrote stories and poems. I wrote a play and a novel. I got a job in a paint company, and in 1976 I had my first article published, which was about the failure of rent tribunals in the ghetto, how landlords could charge you what they wanted, without anyone being able to control them. So from the beginning there was a dim awareness of social inequalities, of injustice. This is the thing: you cannot separate the environment from your conscience. Those were my beginnings, but I've not even begun to describe them.

Wilkinson: What literature did you do at school?

Okri: I didn't do literature at all. I was studying to be a scientist, a doctor, or an engineer. In fact I had very little interest in studying literature, as far as I remember. The books of literature that I read were my own secret pleasures. My earliest readings were of folktales and myths, Greek myths, German myths, Roman myths, African myths, African legends. And my mother always told me stories. All of them were intermingled. I didn't separate one thing from the other. Aladdin was as African to me as Ananse. Odysseus was just another variation of the tortoise myth. Literature depends first and foremost on the fact that one person can write something that another wants to read. How is it possible, if it weren't for the fact that essentially there's something that's shared? All this ghetto criticism ignores that essential point. You can't read a book, you can't absorb it, you can't appreciate an oral fable unless it speaks to you in some way. We are talking about the outer and inner dimensions of literature. As a kid you don't make these distinctions, you just read what enchants you and listen to what fascinates you. It's as simple as that.

Wilkinson: You were talking before about your writing while waiting. Did you actually consciously desire to become a writer, or was this a gradual development?

Okri: I had been writing for years actually, without knowing it. I'd been writing since I was twelve. All the essays and stories I wrote at secondary school were preparing me for it. The books that I'd read and that I enjoyed and the music that I loved were shaping my aesthetic frames. Reading prepares you for writing. It's an inseparable process. I'd always felt with the books I'd liked that they were written for me, that they were speaking to me. The readers select themselves in the process of reading. It is a secret aspect of writing. Writing begins in the secret recesses of the self, places that you don't know about, for reasons that you cannot find. I'd always enjoyed writing essays, but I'd never felt that I was actually writing till out of indignation and frustration I wrote about a social injustice. I had been affected by the high rents in the ghettos. Nobody could control the landlord. The rent edict was useless. So I wrote about it, collecting as much data as I could, and my essay was accepted. From that moment I understood something of the relation between what you *see* and what you have to *say*. The minute you see it, you have to say it. That's where responsibility begins.

When that article was published, I knew I was going to be a writer. I was seventeen.

Wilkinson: And how did you go on from there?

Okri: I just wrote, I just continued. I wrote many other articles, none of which were published. And when the articles were not published, I wrote short stories based on them. The stories were published. People read and liked them, not for the reasons that I wrote them, but for the fact that they could be read and enjoyed as fictions.

Wilkinson: Where were they published?

Okri: In women's journals in Nigeria and in the evening papers. I was surprised when they actually paid me: the joy of being able to write and of actually seeing my work published seemed enough at the time. I wrote about charlatans: our society lends greatly to writing about charlatans. And then I found that one of these stories in particular just kept on growing. It just grew and grew and all my friends thought I was mad because I spent so much time on it. That story became *Flowers and Shadows*.

Writers share the same thing that readers experience when they're reading something that interests them: curiosity. They're writing something and they think, my God, how did this person get here? What are they going to do next? How do I follow this sentence? That's what they mean when they say writing's connected with ability, it's connected with that irreducible, indefinable thing that they call talent. It's being able to just do it. The intuitive extraordinary ability to tell a story is a sign of talent. People who have talent think not of writing but of stories, moods, possibilities. They think in terms of narrative situations. You look at their work and somewhere in the first ten pages you see a set of predicaments, you hear someone speaking truly, you catch the music of a unique identity, you see the vague outlines of an individual, of human beings, caught in their peculiar fates, in their peculiar societies. It's very different from mathematics, but it shares the same thing in terms of logic, because good writing is impossible without logic. But good writing has got something else that's higher than logic.

Wilkinson: How long did it take you to write *Flowers and Shadows*? Did you take a long time going over it, revising it afterwards, when you'd got your main story out?

Okri: I didn't discover my main story till after I'd written it twice. I wrote it once and it was quite awful and then I started writing it again. You see I discovered what I was trying to say, the story I was trying to tell, while I was writing it. As I got deeper into it, I realized that what I was writing wasn't really what I should be writing. So I rewrote it and the story came out of the predicament that was most fictionable and most true. The set of opposites, youth and experience, that lent itself most to narrative. Because narrative essentially is tension, opposites, anything that pushes forward. Mathematics works itself backwards and forwards, but fiction, like music, presses in all directions.

Wilkinson: Was *Flowers and Shadows* autobiographical?

Okri: This is the astonishing thing. I'd written the thing so much that it had become autobiographical. And when it was published every reviewer, anyone who liked it, said it was an autobiographical novel. In fact nothing could be further from the truth! It was *not* autobiographical at all. My parents did *not* live in Ikoyi, my father was *not* a successful businessman who had reached his peak and was now being torn down by jealous relatives. If it's autobiographical, then it's autobiographical in terms of all the people who were young in Lagos at the time I was writing. By that I mean it shares the place, the mood of that time. But in terms of details of life it's an imagined piece of writing. You see it's when I realized this that I could begin to really accept the book, after it had been published. After I'd written *Landscapes*, I'd begun to want to distance myself from it. When I came to this book of stories, *Incidents*, I looked back and realized that *Flowers* is not about my life, it's not about the details of my life, which is the best place to start from for a writer. I'd actually invented a different set of propositions, a different basis. If there's any point in the book that's autobiographical, it's where it ends, in the ghetto. I'm only saying this because people had always thought that some of Henry Miller's books were autobiographical and had dismissed them for that reason, till they realized that in fact Henry Miller's life was the direct opposite. Then they appreciated the imaginative quality of it. Not only was it imagined, but to the reader it felt as if it must be autobiographical. That's an achievement you can't dismiss easily.

Wilkinson: What about *The Landscapes Within*, with the lonely artist figure?

Okri: That is more autobiographical in the landscape. I knew every detail of the terrain.

Wilkinson: When you talk about the terrain, are you talking about the landscape without or the landscape within?

Okri: The landscapes without. The landscape within is imagined, the external one is autobiographical. The details of his *condition* are not mine, the details of his *predicament*—to some extent—were.

Wilkinson: There are continual references to art in one form or another in the book. Are you reflecting consciously on the condition of the Nigerian artist?

Okri: The thing about *Landscapes* that has been misunderstood, and misunderstood for good reasons, is that it's often thought of as being about the possibilities of art in that particular environment, when in fact if you look at its center, my entire thesis was how to convey the *chaos* of life in Lagos, in Nigeria. And I thought that the best way to do it was to show it through the artist who was trying to organize it. So you got two kinds of realities. That was the tension, the internal tension, to show the life, the place, the environment, what it was doing to people, and then to show the artist, this young artist, who was not totally aware of the artist in him yet, organizing all of that. I mean it showed first of all the perniciousness of the environment and then the difficulty of art in that environment. It's a double mirror. It could reflect back and forth, for infinity.

Wilkinson: And I suppose all his "scumscapes" are expressing the same sort of thing; particularly the one he calls "Drifts," but perhaps even his painting of a Lagos traffic jam.

Okri: Exactly, exactly.

Wilkinson: But there were also references to art that seem to go beyond this, reflecting the young artist's relations to art in Africa. His visit to the Ebony gallery, for instance: "Photographed terracotta. Sculpted heads. African children. Negritude in ebony. They all glared reproachfully at him from the black walls. He looked at the crowding presences and the flimsy thought skimmed his mind: you are all dead."

Okri: Omovo, the main character, is at a very awkward point there, when the new is simply crowding out the old. The lucidity of that worldview expressed on the gallery walls spoke of a simpler universe, an older universe of nostalgias, untouched by everything I'd been describing. That kind of nostalgia will die because the environment will either render it impotent and useless, worthy only for tourists and devoid of power. That is why when he confronted his own painting, its rawness shocked *him*.

Wilkinson: Were you thinking of a possible way of writing?

Okri: I wasn't, no. But I've come to realize you can't write about Nigeria truthfully without a sense of violence. To be serene is to lie. Relations in Nigeria are violent relations. It's the way it is, for historical and all sorts of other reasons. In a way, for me, Omovo is an ideal artist. It's astonishing how people keep talking about him as the "young artist." When I think of Omovo it's not just as the young artist: he's what the artist in his progression through time, through age, through experience would end up as. So that's what you are when you're young, but that's what you *should* be, on a higher level, as you get older: seeing experience *pure*, seeing without preconceptions. The elucidation of what you see depends on how clearly you see it. People emphasized Omovo's youth, but they've completely ignored the fact that his innocence does not distort what he sees or what he paints. He's an ideal filter, a prism: in that sense he's an ideal artist. He's a complete contrast from the artists who have ideas, distort the world in terms of their ideas, and then reflect an idea-distorted universe. So it's not the world they're really writing about but something produced from a refusal to see.

You see, the subtext of all that is the American writer who said that art coming into this world does not disturb anything. But in an atmosphere of chaos art *has* to disturb something. For art to be distinctive it either has to be very cool, very clear—which, in relation to chaos, is a negative kind of disturbance—or it has to be more chaotic, more violent than the chaos around. Put that on one side. Now think of the fact that for anything new, for something good to come about, for it to reach a level of art, you have to liberate it from old kinds of perception, which is a kind of destruction. An old way of seeing things has to be destroyed for the new to be born.

Wilkinson: You say Omovo should be seen as the artist, not just as the young artist. But he is also a young man finding himself, isn't he? At the end of the novel he is learning about surviving, about becoming a "life artist" and "going through the familiar darkness, alone," which sounds like someone who is reaching maturity.

Okri: He's going through a passage. At the end of that passage it's impossible to say whether there's maturity or disintegration.

Wilkinson: I suppose I shall have to ask you the question that is always put to African writers in English: Who are you writing for?

Okri: Everything you write, the way you write, answers that question. In *Landscapes* I was obviously writing for those who are essentially interested in looking at the relationship between the environment and what it does to you inside. In *Landscapes* I was writing about something that hurts a lot of people.

Wilkinson: In *Landscapes* you write "Everything is alien and nauseating. The English language leaves him empty and deeply tainted: he cannot think freely. [. . .] The common language, in its profound betrayal, stings, coils, means nothing. Meaning and language clamor in the voids of several layers of alienation." What is your position on the language question?

Okri: To write in a language you have to be inhabited by it. That's basic. The thing about language is frames. You have feelings, mood—a way of life. A language inhabits you; if you know the language well enough and you know your feelings strongly enough and you're deeply rooted in your world and if you care enough about your art and about life you can get any language to say what you want to say. Even Shakespeare seemed to me to write from an invisible handicap. Where there isn't a handicap you have to invent one.

Wilkinson: How do you relate to the older generation, the "pioneers"?

Okri: I accept them.

Wilkinson: Do you disagree with the view that the new Nigerian poetry must do away with the external influences and quotations?

Okri: All I can say is that poetry should be luminous and should affect you by its mastery and its superior consciousness.

Wilkinson: From the novel to the short story. How did that come about?

Okri: Time, poverty, homelessness, desperation, hunger, fear. I had to go back to the basics. By the time I got around to putting this collection together I'd been so distanced from my two novels that I felt as if I was just learning to write, as if I was writing for the first time. My attitude to writing changed. My sense of an audience changed. My sense of words changed.

Wilkinson: Would you like to be more specific in your "sense of an audience" and your "sense of words," the way they've changed?

Okri: The short story form is one of the most neglected forms in fiction generally and African literature in particular. It's the most neglected and requires the most discipline. It is the closest to the essence of fiction; legends, myths, fables. The fact that I found myself writing short stories after the novels required a radical alteration of perception. It consisted of an atomization of the way I looked at craft. I had to look at words with new eyes. A novel is a river, but a short story is a glass of water. A novel is a forest, but the short story is a seed. It is more atomic. The atom may contain the secret structures of the universe.

Wilkinson: Why did you choose the title of "Incidents at the Shrine" as the title of your whole collection?

Okri: That's an interesting question. First of all, I think because the story itself is the most central. It refers to a new orientation, a return to origins, a different set of perceptions. The world is the shrine and the shrine is the world, as the imagemaker says: the way we worship is the way we live, the way we live is the way we worship. These short stories were pressured by the desire to catch as many layers of reality as I could. I wrote the stories the way poems are written.

Wilkinson: You move back and forward between Nigeria and England in these stories, which is something new for you, isn't it?

Okri: Yes, I suppose so. But I see that book of stories as being unified by the shrine.

Wilkinson: There are a lot of dreams in your work.

Okri: Dreams are part of reality. The best fiction has the effect on you that dreams do. The best fiction can become dreams which can influence reality. Dreams and fiction blur the boundaries. They become part of your experience, your life. That interests me. Dreams interest me. Writing is sometimes a continuation of dreaming. I enjoy inventing lives.

London, December 12, 1990

Wilkinson: The title of your new book, *The Famished Road*, raises memories in the reader's mind of Soyinka's *The Road*.

Okri: No, there's no connection. My road is quite different. My road is a way. It's a road that is meant to take you from one place to another, on a journey, towards a destination.

Wilkinson: It seems to me that there are two processes involved in your road. One is as you say a journey that may take you from one place to another. The other is a road that seems to be circling round itself as part of a kind of labyrinth.

Okri: Well, this really refers to the cycle of coming and going, the *abiku* cycle, the road of birth and death and life. I know people will see connections with Soyinka's road now, but perhaps in fifty years they won't.

Wilkinson: How about the structure of the book? It's very carefully structured, with its divisions into three sections, with each section divided into books, each book into chapters. But it also seems to connect up with the idea of divisions not really being divisions in the sense of separations, but suggesting a continuity. Could you talk to me about the divisions in your book?

Okri: The book is really intended to be a flow of life. So the divisions would be akin to moments in tidal waves, sea patterns, the way rollers race towards the shore, the way the water beats and then there are lappings and then it retreats. So that within each beginning is an ending, and within each ending is a beginning. It's like the process of birth and rebirth, and it's hard to say where it starts and where it stops. In some cases it's actually starting and stopping simultaneously, or it's being lived out simultaneously. So many things that will seem puzzling in the book are actually in the possibility of a life being lived simultaneously at different levels of consciousness and in different territories.

Wilkinson: You said "puzzling." "Puzzle," "enigma," "mystery," "riddle" are key words or leitmotifs running through the book. There are a series of variations on the theme of the riddle, for instance, that seem particularly significant. First you have "The world is full of riddles that only the dead can answer," then a reference to the "drama of the living that only the dead can understand," then about 150 pages on another [reference] to there being "many riddles of the dead that only the living can answer," till finally there is the assertion that "There are many riddles amongst us that neither the living nor the dead can answer," as if you are refusing any attempt to solve the mystery or enigma.

Okri: The novel moves towards infinity, basically. You're dealing with a consciousness, like the consciousness that emerges in the book—it's written in the first person, but the consciousness is not my consciousness—which is already aware of other lives behind and in front and also of people actually living their futures in the present. I suppose what I'm really trying to say is that the novel as a form, if it is not going to be artificial, can only move towards infinity.

Wilkinson: It must be a kind of open-ended process . . . .

Okri: It must open towards infinity. Otherwise it would have to end with a death, and this book cannot admit a death, because it began before death, outside the realm of birth and death.

Wilkinson: This openness seems to flow over into the characters themselves, not only Azaro, the *abiku* protagonist, who obviously contains within himself all his past and possibly future lives, but also some of the other characters, who also have something of the *abiku* multiplicity, I was thinking of Madame Koto, who seems to echo the figure of the goddess of the island who appeared at the beginning of the book.

Okri: This raises a question, from the main character's point of view. Isn't it just possible that we are all *abikus*? I don't say that of course, but why should there be some and not others? Why should the universe be distributed in that way? Essentially we're talking about reincarnation, though I don't want to use that word because it has metaphysical connotations. But it's impossible for a character like that, who sees that there are no divisions really in life, just a constant flow, forming and reforming, and who is looking at other characters, not to see that they themselves knowingly or unknowingly are flowing and reflowing, forming and reforming. That's why you have the three deaths of the father and the three births of the father. There are many, many ways in which the *abiku* set of variations takes place. It can take place on smaller, more visible levels and it can take place on larger levels, but it's all there.

Wilkinson: There seems to be a kind of opposition to this in the attempts that are made to appropriate the identity of the protagonist by characters who are trying to seize him and use him, reducing his identity potentials as it were. The island goddess, the police officer and his wife who try to make him assume the identity of the son they have lost, Madame Koto, the thugs, the spirits, the blind old man: they all seem to be trying to pin him down in one way or another.

Okri: I wouldn't say they were trying to pin him down. There is something unique about his destiny. One of the central oppositions in the book is the choice between living and dying. Remember there's a pact at the beginning with his spirit companions. This can be interpreted in many ways; I don't want to go into that now. What I'm trying to say is that because of the unique nature of his consciousness he is accompanied by certain forces. Madame Koto perceives him as a lucky child, as a magnet . . . . What seems like a constant attempt to pin down his identity is just that all of these different phenomena are different attempts to pull him one way or another: towards life or towards death. And it is part of his choice that he always has to move towards life.

Wilkinson: Life being a possibility of constant metamorphosis, change, growth . . .

Okri: Consciousness, and allowing infinity—and therefore possibilities— to grow in him. Because that's what infinity means when it's incarnated in the human consciousness. That's the opposition: infinity and human life.

Wilkinson: Can we go back a moment to the characters and their metamorphic capacities? You say for instance of the king of the spirit world that he has a hundred different names and faces and all sorts of incarnations: one can see him throughout the invisible book of world history. Mum, too, you see in all the different market women and all the things in the market. Both she and Dad, although they're very distinctive individuals, are also all people: all the people who are suffering, all the martyr figures . . . .

Okri: Well, that's the "famished" in the title, isn't it? For me one of the central themes in the book is suffering, probably the only paradoxically democratic thing about our condition: suffering on the one hand and joy on the other, but especially suffering. Suffering is one of the great characters of the book, the different ways people suffer. It defines the boundaries of self but also breaks down the boundaries of individual identifications. So when Azaro sees Mum in all the market women, they *are* Mum. Any one of their children telling their stories would be telling a story just like this one, but with its own particularity. There are hundreds of variations, but there is just one god there, and that god is suffering, pain. But he's not the supreme deity. The higher deity is joy. Again, that's just part of the paradox. Paradoxes keep running through the book, about what it is that redeems the suffering of that continent and what all the people go through. What is it that redeems it? How do people go on living?

One aspect of that is myth. Myth is important in the book too. I never state it particularly. We forget the value of myth, and we forget it more when we give the myth its name. When it's a living, sustaining thing, it's not myth. You give it that word—"myth"—when it has left that vital territory of living. But, when it is in that territory of life, myth is what makes it possible for those who suffer and struggle, whatever the suffering, to live and sleep and carry on. That's when it's most important. So the "famishment" has its shadow side in the book, which is joy, which is myth, which is the spirit. There are many mirrors in the book—if I start talking about one thing it leads me to talk about another.

Wilkinson: Of course, everything is connected. But going back to the subject of myth, the book itself has a mythic opening: "In the beginning...." And then we see myths as they form, events or people that are actually becoming myths: Madame Koto, the photographer, Black Tyger....

Okri: And Mum, underneath it all and surrounding it all.

Wilkinson: There is an oppositional relationship between Madame Koto and Dad at the end of the book, when she appears as a sucking, devouring incarnation of power and he is the desire for justice. But there is also a relationship between Madame Koto and Mum, between a devouring mother and a protecting, giving one, surely?

Okri: Yes, there is, of course. And it's Madame Koto who has the *abiku* trinity in her. But Madame Koto is actually an ambiguous figure. I feel a great compassion for her. But at the same time I think she's quite terrifying.

Wilkinson: A kind of fertility goddess, with an infinite capacity in her for both good and evil—and also suffering.

Okri: Yes, very much. That becomes visible when the boy goes into her room. But she's also connected to the *abiku* cycle in her own way. That's why the spirits are attracted to her. There is a great magnetic force in her. But it's difficult for me at this stage to say anything very coherent about this book, probably because it's not meant to be coherent. It's against the perception of the world as being coherent and therefore readable as a text. The world isn't really a text, contrary to what people like Borges say. It's more than a text. It's more akin to music.

Wilkinson: Or an infinity of texts, texts within texts within texts.

Okri: Texts without words. That's why I probably lean more towards dreams. The blurring of dreams and reality is also crucial. And that will have to take place if you're going to talk about the road in any meaningful sense. That's why there's so much about blurring of boundaries. The book does begin with "In the beginning," but it ends by saying that it's quite possible that there aren't any beginnings or any endings. So it does pull away from even the basis of its beginning. The way I read the world through it, it's just quite possible we're all living different phases and at different levels.

Wilkinson: This brings me to the time scheme of your novel. There are one or two references that give us some sort of clue as to how to place it, but even then one isn't quite sure. Past and future blend into each other and coexist. But there are two references to "our white rulers." This suggests a possible precolonial setting, but on the other hand not necessarily . . . .

Okri: It could be. That again depends on how you want to read the book. You could simply ask yourself: Yes, while it is true that everybody in a place like that could be affected by the colonial presence, isn't it just quite possible that within it there may be people who are living their lives almost completely unaware that it was happening? They were affected by it but they were almost completely unaware of it. Questions like that need to be asked, because there's been too much attribution of power to the effect of colonialism on our consciousness. Too much has been given to it. We've looked too much in that direction and have forgotten about our own aesthetic frames. Even though that was there and took place and invaded the social structure, it's quite possible that it didn't invade our spiritual and aesthetic and mythic internal structures, the way in which we perceive the world. Because if one were going to be investigative, one would probably say that a true invasion takes place not when a society has been taken over by another society in terms of its infrastructure, but in terms of its mind and its dreams and its myths, and its perception of reality. If the perception of reality has not been fundamentally, internally altered, then the experience itself is just transitional. There are certain areas of the African consciousness which will remain inviolate. Because it is their worldview that helps a people survive.

Wilkinson: Towards the end of the book there are more and more references to history. Earlier history is presented as a "weird delirium," but it is a delirium you are in no way seeking to escape from. The novel itself could be seen as an attempt to come to terms with history and to understand history, seen here as the "undiscovered continent deep in our souls." When Azaro's perception fuses with that of the duiker, in the last part of the book, he sees the whole of African history, its various phases; but it is also, as we see for example in the transcultural nature of the previous lives of the other explicit *abiku* character of the book, Ade, a universal history.

Okri: I am very interested in history and this book is also about history. It's one of the reasons why some of the spirit-children choose to—or not to—be born. If you know something about the life you are going to come to, the suffering or whatever, you may or may not choose to be born into all of this. History is actually in the book right from the beginning. But I prefer to say suffering rather than history. There's a great celebration of history, the great accomplishments of various kinds: space travel, moon travel, things like that. They are invisible histories and we have to change our perception of how we speak of people's accomplishments. Pyramids is one way, but there are pyramids of the spirit. And they can have their fruition in many, many different ways. One form of that could simply be the elasticity of a people's aesthetics, their survival. And Africa has an incredible capacity to not die and not be destroyed. Unlike China that was always unified and had this great wall to prevent invasion, Africa had no great wall, yet it manages to remain unique. It's things like that, the resilience of the spirit, the great dreaming capacities, the imaginative frames that are visible in the art, an art that has not remotely been understood. All these things are within the terrain of the book. But they're not different things. It's just one subject I'm addressing: the famished road.

Wilkinson: Then of course there is the story of the road—the unfinished road—that is told within the novel itself: the road that has been being built for two thousand years and that must not be finished in order that there may always be something to strive after. So that whenever the road is about to be completed catastrophes take place and a new generation comes along and begins again from the wreckage.

Okri: I think in our age you have to posit a different conception of history, because the facts of history alone are not enough to give an account of our consciousness and what we need to do with our age. We are in a very,

very interesting age: we could go either way. We could go towards destruction still and we could go towards the greatest stage of creativity yet, world creativity. But unless we change the way we perceive history, we're not going to be able to do this. This book is my modest effort to do that, just to alter the way in which we perceive what is valid and what is valuable, different measures and different values. Also, you can talk about small things in big ways and you can talk about big things in small ways. It's not the size of the subject that's important, it's what it leads to. As I said at the beginning of this interview, for me it has to lead to infinity, to endless possibilities within our limitations. I'm offering this to Africa and to the world. We can look at our condition in Africa in despair. On the other hand we can look at it and say "Well, we are some of the luckiest people at this time because we've got so much to invent and fight for." Time is actually a short thing and the future is all there to be created.

Wilkinson: To return more specifically to aesthetics and to different ways of seeing the African aesthetic, I would like you to talk about Dad and his developing interest in books—books of all kinds and origins—the books that he gets Azaro to read to him.

Okri: Well, first of all, the father can't read, so he goes to a bookshop and just picks up any old book: they're not books that he chose, they're just picked at random. That's why they involve everything from Chinese medicine to Homer's *Odyssey* and the tales of Sundjata and so on and so forth. But, if we're going to talk about affinities, the fact of having accidentally or by chance chosen those books could suggest that the African aesthetic could be found almost everywhere. I personally find the African aesthetic in Homer and in a lot of the Greeks, and that's not surprising because the Greeks got a lot of their aesthetics from Egypt, they got some of their gods from Egypt. So that's not surprising at all, that journey of worldviews through world history and world literature. Even the *Arabian Nights*, I find a lot of African aesthetics and African worldviews there.

Moving away from the book now, I'd like to propose that we stop making so narrow what constitutes the African aesthetic. It is not something that is bound only to place, it's bound to a way of looking at the world. It's bound to a way of looking at the world in more than three dimensions. It's the aesthetic of possibilities, of labyrinths, of riddles—we love riddles—of paradoxes. I think we miss this element when we try to fix it too much within national or tribal boundaries. I think it's more fluid and more interesting than that. When I read *Beowulf* I see Africa in that. A lot of the texts that

Okigbo bounces off in *Labyrinths* are texts that he found an Igbo affinity with, otherwise they wouldn't fit into textual manipulations. They are affinities along those lines. They're not just literary affinities, they're aesthetic affinities. I'm not saying that they're universal. I'm saying that they've been travelling through history and they still remain quite pure. They're very strong and they can be picked up two thousand miles away from where they originated. But who knows where they originated anyway?

Wilkinson: My personal experience of reading your book was in fact to recall Fagunwa, Tutuola, and Soyinka, but also the vast transnational literature of dream vision and vision generally; forests of the night together with forests of symbols, but also countless forests and labyrinths of literary modern cities.

Okri: I think when reading the novel one should just think of my primary sources as being the invisible books of the spirit. My primary sources are those invisible books. And I mean that very seriously.

Wilkinson: And your visible books?

Okri: Many of them I haven't read yet. And when I read them I'll feel I've always known them. But the great source finally has to be something that keeps flowing, not something that's fixed, and a book is fixed. This is why I tried to write an unfixed book, a river.

Wilkinson: Towards the beginning of your book you say something to the effect that life should be a movement towards vision, from blindness to vision, though very few people ever achieve it. And vision is constantly to the fore (as is blindness), even on the physical level of the references to eyes and to seeing and watching and of course photographing. The photographer, surely, is another mediator between what is seen . . . .

Okri: And what isn't, what is made visible that is not seen, like the ghosts. One of the things I wanted to do was just to make visible one of the stories of the river, that's all. Just one. Not even a life, or many years. Just one of the phases of consciousness. I'll go back to what I said earlier. It is consciousness, it is the way we perceive the world, it is our mythic frame that shapes the way we affect the world and the way the world affects us. It's these invisible things that shape the visible things. I'd like us to go back more often to our aesthetic and mythic frames, even while we're moving into the twenty-first century. For all our technology, we shouldn't abandon those invisible things in our world thinking; they're what shape us. In my last volume I wrote about visible things, visible history, objects, an assault of chaos. In this book I want to go to something more serene and therefore more hopeful. The unbreakable things in us. One shouldn't offer hope cheaply. One should be very, very serious when one is going to talk about hope. One has to know about the very hard facts of the world and one has to look at them and know how deadly and powerful they are before one can begin to think or dream oneself into positions out of which hope and then possibilities can come. It's one of the steps I try to take in this book.

An Interview with Ben Okri

Pietro Deandrea / 1990 and 1992

From *Africa America Asia Australia* 16 (1994): 55–82. Reprinted by permission of Pietro Deandrea.

The original interview was shortened and edited by Ben Okri in 2022, with Pietro Deandrea's permission.

London, December 17, 1990

Pietro Deandrea: I'd like to start with some biographical information.

Ben Okri: I was born in Minna, northern Nigeria; my father went to work there. He is an Urhobo lawyer, my mother is from Agbor, she's midwestern Igbo. She is a chef, in a restaurant in Lagos.

Deandrea: Did you grow up in a very large family?

Okri: It started small, then became big and complicated.

Deandrea: You said your father was a lawyer. Shall we say that the social environment you come from is quite middle bourgeois?

Okri: No, that's misleading. My father is a lawyer, but I spent my late adolescence in a ghetto of Lagos.

Deandrea: What kind of school did you attend?

Okri: I schooled here in England as a child. My dad came to study law. Then we went back to Nigeria and I went to different schools. Then studied at Urhobo College. I did my A levels at home. I wrote my first novel *Flowers and Shadows* around the age of seventeen and finished it a year later, and came to London at nineteen with the manuscript.

Deandrea: To find a publisher?

Okri: Yes, and to study and write.

Deandrea: Did you have financial problems during your first period here?

Okri: Oh yes. That's another story. I was for a time homeless.

Deandrea: Generally speaking, who are the authors that most influenced you and that you like best?

Okri: It's tricky to talk of influence. It leads to misunderstandings. You mention names and people then look for those writers in your work. But the best literary encounters help you liberate your own voice. In African literature, I like Achebe, Soyinka, Ngugi, Armah, Head, etc.

Deandrea: So now that you're living in London, what are your feelings toward your mothercountry and its political scene?

Okri: My attitude towards Nigeria is ambivalent, like any genuine attitude towards one's country. It can't be one thing. It's only a stupid writer who unreservedly loves their country. Otherwise you can't write about it. I have my quarrels with Nigeria.

Deandrea: Many of them?

Okri: Many.

Deandrea: So you are not willing to talk about its politics?

Okri: No. Yeats said somewhere that out of our quarrels with others comes rhetoric, and out of our quarrels with ourselves comes poetry. I feel the same with Nigeria. But my writing is not confined to my quarrels with Nigeria.

Deandrea: What do you think of the debate among African writers about the language that should be chosen? Some of them write in English or French, whereas others refuse the colonizers' languages.

Okri: That is an unhistorical perception. But the most important thing is the creation of a great literature.

Deandrea: Would you be able to write in Urhobo or Igbo or would you like to?

Okri: Those who can write in their language should do that. But that's not the point. You can write in your language and write very badly. The important thing is to create literature. It doesn't matter how you do it. That should be our chief interest: to create a great literature.

Deandrea: The characters of your works set in Lagos belong to various ethnic groups, but what's the actual ethnic composition of Lagos?

Okri: It's full of people from all over Nigeria and the rest of Africa. It's one of the most cosmopolitan cities in the world. It's where all the cultures meet. That's why it's so vibrant.

Deandrea: In *Flowers and Shadows* Jeffia, the main character, states that a writer should write about the ordinary. Does this reflect your point of view?

Okri: Not necessarily. The writer should write about what interests him. It depends on what the writer wants to accomplish. I found writing about ordinary people very interesting.

Deandrea: Like Emokhai and Marjomi....

Okri: Yes. I also write about the powerless, the voiceless, the silenced, who are unspoken for. I write about people who suffer and struggle.

Deandrea: How would you judge a writer who doesn't write about these people?

Okri: I don't judge them. It is just as important to write about the rich and powerful. It's not your subject that defines you. It is how you approach it, what you do with it. At this stage I'm writing about those who suffer. Later on I might write about the powerful and the rich. Even much later I might write about space. I might not write about human beings at all. That's my freedom as a human being and as a writer. I intend to claim this freedom to the fullest. I refuse to let anybody limit me or defining me as a human being or a writer.

Deandrea: Fredric Jameson has written that it's very difficult to draw a straight line between the public and the private dimension in African literature. Do you agree with that?

Okri: I don't like the notion of defining literature so easily. African literature is composed of a great number of people. Statements like this are only a façade. I refuse to accept that the literature of any people could be defined with a single sentence.

Deandrea: Could your short story "When the Lights Return" be interpreted as the crisis of an artist who almost refuses to get involved with the problems of his society?

Okri: No. I wouldn't say so at all. The point of the story is in the title... *Lights ... Return* .... On one level it may seem to be a story about electricity, the possibility of enlightenment. It is about transforming society. And by "light" I mean illumination, not just electricity. It's about darkness, a difficult period. It's about chaos. It's also a love story, and about the near impossibility of love in an atmosphere of chaos. It's also a story about art and redemption, and blindness.

Deandrea: Do you also mean metaphysical blindness, since when the electricity is on again the tragedy happens?

Okri: Exactly.

Deandrea: Does that mean that electric power and metaphysical blindness are on different sides?

Okri: "When the Lights Return" is when the tragedy occurs.

Deandrea: Does that also mean that the technological development doesn't reflect a real improvement of the people's conditions?

Okri: That's one way of seeing it. It depends on whether you think that Western capitalism represents light. In terms of what it does to the culture, it could also represent darkness. The point about light is simple: illumination is often preceded by crisis. The fact that you have light does not mean that everything is automatically right. It could be said that true illumination in society has to be a long process of nurturing. Otherwise the danger is that more chaos is created than before.

Deandrea: With respect to the word you said, "chaos," in your short story "In the City of Red Dust" you write that the Governor had created chaos "in order to rule." Do you think that this is the way postcolonial politicians behave? Do you think that chaos is expedient to this kind of society?

Okri: Though my stories are set in Nigeria, if they are good and true they are relevant everywhere. There is a relationship between chaos and power. The same thing can be said about Britain, about Andreotti in Italy . . . .

Deandrea: . . . the unsolved mystery of terrorism . . . .

Okri: Exactly. There is a relationship between chaos and power. It is difficult to maintain power if democracy is running exactly the way it should run. The suppression of democracy is always in the interest of those who are in power.

Deandrea: And so one becomes the "curfewmaker."

Okri: Yes, you become the manufacturer of curfews.

Deandrea: You've said that you don't try to offer any solutions with your writing, but you only want to describe things. How do you think literature can affect people? Could it console them?

Okri: I hope so. One of my aims is to affect the way people perceive reality. One of my dearest hopes, and one of the greatest things art can accomplish, is to help people see more clearly. This way people can solve their problems, because they can see what the real problem is. The hope is to make people aware of their possibilities. To help them realize that they are freer than they think. Society is subjugated by the mechanics of things that don't want us to be freer than we think we are. We can choose the nature of our society, the nature of our reality. But to do that, you have to understand how reality is manufactured and created. You have to know how these people in power, these ideologues, manipulate reality. To choose one's reality is one of the most important acts of the individual. The individual has to be able to decipher reality, to know what that political party is doing. The people should be able to understand that this politician is lying to them. This decoding of reality is very important. It is one of the great things that literature can do. Along with healing, consoling, creating new realities, opening our senses to the possibilities of the universe, widening our perception of reality, increasing the power of our dreams, reawakening towards the magnitude of myth, etc.

Deandrea: So the word "alienation" is not so misleading . . . .

Okri: It's a big word.

Deandrea: I use that word vis-à-vis a situation where people can't see reality as it is . . . .

Okri: So you use it to say blindness. I say blindness or refusal to see. Reality is very hard to see. T. S. Eliot said somewhere "Go go go, said the bird: humankind cannot bear very much reality." Most people actually don't want to know the truth, because it's very hard to take the truth. When you know truth, you've got to do something about it. That seems to be asking too much of people. So people would rather live with lies, which is what our politicians like. Literature explodes those lies and, without your being aware of it, tries to lead you into the labyrinth, the heart of reality. Then it leaves you there. This is why I'm interested in nightmares and dreams: because if you look carefully, reality is often worse than nightmares.

Deandrea: As in the ending of the short story "Stars of the New Curfew."

Okri: Yes.

Deandrea: The titles of your works are all symbolic. Is symbolism central to you?

Okri: I'm very conscious of my titles. It seems to me that everything is symbolic in this universe. That's the problem. What is real, and what is symbol? What is real, and what is dream? If you actually look at this life, it is hard to say what reality is.

Deandrea: But why are you using so many symbols?

Okri: They concentrate the mind. You can meditate on them. They can lead you into the heart of reality. People don't want to go there. They'll say "I want to dream, fantasy, happiness, illusion." But with symbols, with dreams, with narratives, with metaphors you can lead people right into the heart of reality, into the place they don't want to go. They can stay there and contemplate, or they can get away from it. But once you've got them there, they have got that place inside them.

Deandrea: You also seem to attach a great importance to painting in your works.

Okri: I wanted to be a painter when I was younger. The day I started writing very seriously it was raining; I was indoor, at home, in my Lagosian ghetto. That day I did two things: I took a blank piece of paper and drew what was on the mantelpiece. And then I wrote a poem. When I studied these two works,

I saw that the poem was better than the drawing. I might have been a mediocre painter. I painted for a while. Maybe later on I'll come back to it. But quite apart from that, painting relates to symbols, and to reality. The painter gets close to reality in a more immediate sense than the writer does. The painter is always working with metaphors and symbols and images, but they are instantaneous. The problem painters have with reality is a powerful way to deal with reality in writing. *The Landscapes Within* gave me the opportunity to write about that difficult chaos of Nigeria, by looking at this young painter trying to organize that chaos in his paintings. So in that novel you've got two things: the painter trying to organize chaos, and what the chaos is doing to the painter.

Deandrea: Would you say that at the end the painter wins?

Okri: There is no winning in reality.

Deandrea: Couldn't we consider his understanding of what the chaos is doing to him as a sort of victory?

Okri: Maybe his little victory is that, in spite of the chaos, he goes on creating. This means that the chaos has not defeated him. My hope is that this book has helped people be aware that as long as they go on thinking creatively about their environment they will always be able to transform it.

Deandrea: In *Flowers and Shadows* Jeffia manages to rescue a little puppy which is being tortured by some boys. In *The Landscapes Within* Omovo doesn't, with a goat which is experiencing the same cruelty. Does it mirror the artist's difficulty to play an active role in society without using his art?

Okri: Is he going to go round trying to prevent people from beating animals?

Deandrea: Actually I thought it was a symbolic event.

Okri: That's a moment. The novel is a series of such moments. If I remember well, that was the event preceding the moment in which it will start raining and he will have the idea for his painting. The book is full of epiphanies like that.

Deandrea: I thought that Omovo had shaved his head as an attempt to get closer to reality.

Okri: I'm ambiguous about that. As for the artist getting involved with reality, I've often wondered about that.

Deandrea: The death of Chris Okigbo is a significant example of that . . . .

Okri: He died in the war . . . .

Deandrea: So do you think his death was useless?

Okri: I'm not saying that. I'm just saying that I'd rather have him around today, writing poems. Go and ask what the war was really about. Most people won't be able to tell you. Imagine Soyinka and Achebe dying in that war. What a loss for our literature that would have been. The greatest opposition an artist can mount should always come from the art itself. The artist's job has not been understood. It is opposition to the establishment's reality, to orthodox reality. The writer is a questioner, an expander of consciousness, a widener of perception. That's a lifetime's work.

Deandrea: Because democracy can never be perfect....

Okri: Human beings are always asleep. We always need someone to wake us up. So the artist's job never stops.

Deandrea: At a point in *The Landscapes Within* you write of "a virgin" canvas that has to be "filled up": do you consider art something as lively as sex or nature?

Okri: Well, to tell you what I think about art would take me all the rest of my life. But I'll tell you one thing. After life, art. Life is life, but art is one of the highest acts of consciousness.

Deandrea: How much of your work could be defined as autobiographical? Speaking more specifically, I intended to ask you how much Okwe family is similar to yours...

Okri: Not similar at all.

Deandrea: ... or Jeffia and Omovo are similar to you.

Okri: Not similar at all. You've read the books, you see me now. Am I similar to them?

Deandrea: Well, maybe ten years ago ... how can I know?

Okri: But if that's true, like any good portrait that a painter paints, something of that must still be there, in the older person. My works are never autobiographical because I do not want to exhaust the source of my fiction, of my imagination. If I wrote about my life then I couldn't do it again. My books are works of my imagination. But they are often based on things that I know for sure. I never write about things I don't know, one way or another. Usually I have suffered those things.

Deandrea: Both your collections of short stories start with a story—"Laughter beneath the Bridge" and "In the Shadow of War"—whose narrator is a kid who is experiencing (or has experienced) the Biafran war. Does that mean that this event you lived through as a kid was the main factor in making you become an artist?

Okri: Yes, it's something autobiographical since it's something I went through.

Deandrea: But why did you put them both at the beginning of the two collections?

Okri: Not necessarily because of what you said. But I'll tell you one thing: I haven't started writing about the civil war yet. These were just short stories. I hope to do it in the future. It's a very difficult subject. Things like that take time.

Deandrea: Reading short stories like "A Hidden History," I would assume that one of the roles of the writer should be to salvage the history of his people, that colonialism has taken off, manipulated.

Okri: Yes, that is one of the roles. Another role of the artist is to redream our lives. I accept that role because it's an important aspect of African literature. Most of us are trying to redream what has been destroyed, distorted, lost or rigged out of existence.

Deandrea: But what about that particular short story?

Okri: It's set in England, in London.

Deandrea: Actually it's very ambiguous: it's not clear who the narrator is, what the listmaker should symbolize.

Okri: The last but one sentence is the key of that story: "Nothing can be pushed below the surface of memory." Power may think it will succeed in pushing things under, making people forget, destroying their history and memory. But that memory exists somewhere. The imagination and the dreams of people have access to it. Even objects remember. The manipulators of history don't actually win. They only think they win. Things they've been trying to suppress and push under become insurgent. They grow. But they grow underground. And when they start appearing in reality, they take very frightening forms. Nothing can be destroyed.

Deandrea: You seem reluctant to tell me about "A Hidden History."

Okri: I'll just tell you one thing. The narrator is a Black angel.

Deandrea: Besides, in its structure there is only one spacing. It would seem that, from this onwards, you move from a sort of realistic picture of the third world ghetto in London to an allegorical visual portrayal, which could be interpreted as a fresh start in time, with an ambiguous listmaker playing the colonialist role . . . .

Okri: That's one interpretation. I don't really think in terms of symbols, I just write. One of the most central aspects of the spirit of my writing is mood. This is almost musical. I am trying to catch in words something not so visible that flows in reality.

Deandrea: So you don't agree with my interpretation of that character . . . .

Okri: You have to find your own interpretation. Everything you need to know is in the story, in all of my stories. Everything is there. Let me tell you something about the way in which I write and the best way to read me. Earlier I said that the role of the writer is to decode reality better, which means that a human being has to be extremely vigilant and alive. You have to be alive and conscious. You have to have a very high consciousness. You have to be aware of that reality. When you read my texts, you have to read them in the same way. Nothing is accidental in my texts, especially in my short stories but even in my two earlier novels. You have to be conscious of everything. Nothing is accidental. Not a full stop, not a comma, not a dash. If you give your interpretation—but it won't be mine—you're free to do that. But I warn you: my texts will subvert you. If you try to impose something on my texts, sooner or later they will trip you.

Deandrea: Then I am always holding a question mark, many "perhaps."

Okri: Yes, many "perhaps."

Deandrea: In your two novels you act as an omniscient narrator, not only with Jeffia and Omovo but also with many other characters; you read the mind of several characters. Then, in the short stories, you change and experience various points of view, like the first person, and you seem to be more factual, as facts were considered more important than the characters' sensations or opinions. Why that?

Okri: That's not totally true. I mean, in *Flowers and Shadows* I move from the third to the first person at the end. In *The Landscapes Within* there's Omovo's diary, dreams, long dialogues . . .

Deandrea: Why do you like changing, anyway?

Okri: Because you cannot interpret reality in one way.

Deandrea: But do you think it's true that in your short stories you became more factual?

Okri: I became more compressed, gnomic, tighter. But *The Landscapes Within* is full of facts. I admit something changed. There's a four-year gap between that novel and *Incidents at the Shrine*, and my world view changed. My attitude, my perceptions, my thinking, my philosophy, a lot of things changed. I went through a revolution in my thinking. I'll accept that. But the same thing happened between *Flowers and Shadows* and *The Landscapes Within*.

Deandrea: In *Incidents at the Shrine* there seems to be a common "fil rouge," a linking thing, which is religion. Then, in *Stars of the New Curfew*, the linking thing seems to be the manufacturing of reality. Do you think it's true?

Okri: I think that imagination and powerlessness—which is the same thing as manufacturing reality—were the linking things.

Deandrea: Do you believe in using a linking thing when you write a collection of short stories?

Okri: Sometimes it happens that way. I don't throw texts together at random. I believe that if I start thinking about that ashtray or that lemon they could lead me to infinity, making me touch everything, leading me everywhere. They can tell you about capitalism and about the infinity of space, about relativity and chaos. In other words, everything is linked to everything else. It depends on the mind of the artist, but for me everything is connected.

Deandrea: Your short story called "Crooked Prayer" seems to be quite out of context, different: it's very light, very humorous. One is not confronted with human suffering, one does not meet the victims of society such as one does in the other short stories. What did you intend when writing it?

Okri: Are you saying you don't like it? That's a personal question....

Deandrea: Yes, a little bit.

Okri: I wanted to write a story in which, for a change, there was an absence of politics and all heavy things. I wanted to tell the story from a child's point of view, truthfully. That's why it's a first-person story. So I had to ruthlessly eliminate any complexity of thinking. I wanted it to be a clear story of a child, told by a child. So I had to get rid of anything that would show the adult mind.

Deandrea: Unlike "Laughter beneath the Bridge," where "the young shall grow."

Okri: Yes, in "Crooked Prayer" I just wanted to be very truthful, from a child's point of view.

Deandrea: So could we define it as a story of innocence?

Okri: Yes, but innocence amidst a complicated reality. You can read politics into it, if you want. It's all there. You can read many things into it.

Deandrea: Are you against abortion?

Okri: I'm not for or against it.

Deandrea: If you had to decide, would you grant people a free choice about that?

Okri: Yes, I would never impose my position on them.

Deandrea: I've asked you that because Jeffia seems to be quite against it, when his friend Dele wants his girlfriend to abort. I thought you could feel the same way.

Okri: You must not subscribe the motives of my characters to me. I'm different from them.

Deandrea: The English you employ is full of unusual adjectives and Latin-rooted words. How did you come to that kind of English?

Okri: I just look for the best possible words for what I'm trying to convey. It's very hard to convey reality. Sometimes the usual word won't do. But the usual word in an unusual way might work. It depends. I'm much more interested in conveying truth about sensations....

Deandrea: You know, some postcolonial writers think that the writer should be active in changing, in rethinking the colonizer's language. Do you think you're trying to do it, to reshape the language that your people were imposed on?

Okri: Yes, but that also seems like an exercise. I'm much more interested in transforming consciousness, which goes beyond colonialism.

Deandrea: You often employ repetition. I thought it could be an inheritance of your oral culture.

Okri: An important aspect of my creative thinking is music. In music, repetition of motifs is a primary activity. Take for instance a motif from Wagner, or a complex drum sequence. The first time you don't register it. When you repeat it on a higher key, then you register it. But the second one is different. What seems like repetition is actually making you go deeper into the atomic structure and the resonance of the phrase. One part of my writing is atomic in that sense. I move inwards as well as outwards. Taking you deeper into one atom, I'm also taking you further out into the universe. I like penetrating the structure of reality. Repetition is one way of doing that.

Deandrea: You don't seem to use much humor in your writing. Moreover, most of the laughter we find in your books is a sort of hysterical laughter prior to madness. Is that because of the fact that there is little to laugh about in contemporary Nigeria?

Okri: Humor is dangerous. Humor is more demonic than people realize. It belongs to the devil, rather than to the angel.

Deandrea: The evil character of Eco's *The Name of the Rose* says the same....

Okri: I've thought about humor a lot. Humor doesn't come out of serenity. It comes out of tension, conflict, disjuncture, out of strange angles on things. Humor comes out much more from the dark side of what it is to be human. The same thing about laughter. It is quite strange. It is not what we think. When you see people laughing, energy is pouring out of their mouths. I'd like scientists to study this someday.

Deandrea: What about satire? Don't you think it could be significant in the sense you were talking about, to make people more conscious?

Okri: Satire is useful. Humor is powerful. I use humor more than you think. Maybe you don't notice it. Sometimes my humor is in the tone of voice. Sometimes the idea is humorous.

Deandrea: Let's talk of the titles of your books. *Flowers and Shadows*, for instance: can we see it as good and evil, and do you think that shadows and darkness are always negative?

Okri: No, I don't. Shadow is natural. And darkness can be illumination as well as terror. In *The Landscapes Within* I frequently use darkness in relation to illumination.

Deandrea: It would seem, however, that one of the functions of shadows is to let the flowers grow stronger. Do you agree? Couldn't it be the answer to Achebe's quotation you appended to *The Landscapes Within*? Are shadows of any use when they are defeated?

Okri: You can't defeat shadows, why do you want to? You have to accept them, to come to terms with them. You can't speak of victory about things like these.

Deandrea: What about the structure of *The Landscapes Within*: "Losses," "Mazes," "Masks," and "Fragments"?

Okri: ... and the last part which has no name.

Deandrea: Yes?

Okri: People think it ends with "Fragments," but it doesn't. The book is about several things, but one thing is the journey through a soul.

Deandrea: But why "Masks"?

Okri: It refers to reality. The way you perceive it. The way reality changes our faces. It's not connected to anything traditional. Since I am from Nigeria the critics have always tried to read my books in relation to Nigeria. But if you look for ancestral masks in that section you won't find any. The critics forget that, apart from writing in an African context, I write in a universal one too. I'm an African writer, the rivers of Africa flow in my blood, but the rivers of the world also flow in my blood, the rivers of Mesopotamia, of . . . .

Deandrea: Po river, in Italy.

Okri: Yes. You've got to read me as an African, on one level, but also as a writer who is alive in the twentieth century. It makes a critic's job more difficult. I'm alive and conscious in the twentieth century.

Deandrea: To what degree does this stance apply to the short story called "Masquerades"?

Okri: Well, it could be ancestral on one hand. On the other hand it could just simply be that: masquerades. It could be "the masquerade in us," it could be "façade," "an image of your face." It could be all of these things at once.

Deandrea: What is exactly an Egungun?

Okri: It's simply an ancestral and ritual masquerade.

Deandrea: In *The Landscapes Within* there is a quotation from Joyce's *Portrait*. Have you been somehow influenced by Joyce? Did you write by using a Joycian method?

Okri: Well, in that novel I use certain metaphors that you might call "stream of consciousness," but I diverge with Joyce a little on the definition of "stream of consciousness."

Deandrea: So what is yours?

Okri: That's what I'm trying to show in *The Landscapes Within*. That's why the book is called that. We only live in reality, we internalize it as well. We have our history within us. We carry the twentieth century inside us.

Deandrea: In fact, unlike Joyce, you never seem to forget history.

Okri: I can't forget it. History is everywhere. Even objects remember. History is there in the flesh, in the memory, in your dreams. Joyce's perception of history and stream of consciousness are different from mine. His is aesthetic, mine is aesthetic and historical, realistic and fragmented, dreamlike and full of moments of clarity. It is hard and fluid. All of these things.

Deandrea: You know, when I say "Joycian method" I would define it like this: the artist lets reality get into himself, where it changes, and when the artist lets it out it is different. What I don't like of him is that he got rid of history: in his view the author should be passive vis-à-vis history.

Okri: Some people may disagree with your reading of Joyce. But even when artists seem passive they are creating reality. Whatever you do, you are creating reality and internalizing history. In *The Landscapes Within* reality is rough, hard, messy. It is not beautifully aesthetic. In the novel everything is there, from aesthetics to excrement.

Deandrea: The title of your short story "Disparities" seems to symbolize the different ways in which different social classes and ethnic groups are treated. Furthermore, it is strange that the two most intriguing short stories you have written, "Disparities" and "A Hidden History," are both set in England, the only two which are not occurring in Nigeria. How comes that?

Okri: England is part of my reality. Maybe the thing you've said is caused by the fact that there is more alienation for the characters here. Maybe because there's no cultural continuity, the tree has been planted in another soil . . .

Deandrea: . . . like the trees growing from the cement in "Disparities."

Okri: Yes. But I'm not sure that's the reason: I'm just proposing.

Deandrea: I keep wondering why you chose a title like "Converging City" for that short story.

Okri: In that story things converge. The man in the street, Agodi, does have something to do with the Head of the State, who is in the traffic jam and who gets shot. The purpose of the traffic jam was to stage a coup. There is a convergence in the streets of Lagos between a completely minor character and the Head of the State.

Deandrea: What image of the Head of the State did you intend to convey?

Okri: His image is in the story.

Deandrea: Occasionally he seems dull, but at the end he realizes two things: that he should hand the Government over to the civilians and that he's not controlling events, which go beyond his power. I could explain the latter, since it could be a natural consequence of a postcolonial politics, but not the former: is it an optimistic sanction of the Head of the State's train of thought?

Okri: I don't think it is optimistic. He has been defeated by chaos. He was creating chaos, like the Military Governor of "In the City of Red Dust," but he wasn't responsible for all of it.

Deandrea: Let's consider the lizard which turns into air at the end of the story. Is it a sort of magician's trick, a metaphysical truth, or what else? Did you have in mind something specific?

Okri: It's all there in the story. If you read that story enough times from a fresh point of view, the meaning will become clear. And it's not one meaning. He burns the lizard and it turns into air. Many things are happening there. It could be ancestral magic. It could be transformation. It could be that he too is defeated by a complex reality.

Deandrea: He comes back with a new faith, a new religion; in your books you often write about these new religions which come from the east. I would think of them as escapist ways out, as it was the case in the States of the sixties.

Okri: He underwent a transformation. He was overwhelmed by the chaos. He disappeared and returned with that new solution. Maybe it was an illusion, an escape, or a business. Maybe it was just another form of religious capitalism.

Deandrea: In short stories like "Incidents at the Shrine" and "Worlds that Flourish" we have a sort of journey back to the ancestral religion. Sometimes it seems to be positive, sometimes negative. What's your point of view?

Okri: I don't think of them in terms of positive and negative. I just think in terms of the things people do to escape chaos, to understand their lives, to live in that society. All these people are caught in desperate situations and chaotic places. They have to find a way to survive, a new way to live . . . .

Deandrea: . . . or something to believe in . . . .

Okri: Yes. It's the same thing.

Deandrea: But why does the main character of "Worlds that Flourish" frantically escape at the end?

Okri: Wouldn't you do the same if you were him? You would run. He escapes because the chaos becomes too much and because he's asked to see what is happening.

Deandrea: But he's refusing a discussion about life and death, a sort of final and metaphysical truth, because he's dead, and it's a temporary death....

Okri: Not refusing. Just dealing or not dealing with the terror he faces.

Deandrea: So he doesn't want to know the truth.

Okri: Would you?

Deandrea: Well, I would be curious about it.

Okri: For you as a reader comfortable in your reality, you might think you would be curious and would want to have a discussion about life and death, but if you are in his reality, with his history, in that time, with all that chaos, your reaction would be different from what you think. But if he had stayed there, he wouldn't face the old reality and doesn't fight it. This is a possibility. I'm only saying "what if." He's afraid, faced with that choice. You might be.

Deandrea: There is fear and there is curiosity, he should make up his mind on which of them is more important.

Okri: It depends: he was terrified, because he found the village very strange. In any case, he did make up his mind. The story came from that.

Deandrea: In two short stories of yours you employ the image of people living in trunks. I thought of it as a sort of metaphor of a journey back to nature, intending to give the natural environment its proper value.

Okri: Yes, it's that. It's an ancestral perception of the fact that trees have autonomous existences. Trees were spirits and houses of beings. They're living things. It's a possible interpretation....

Deandrea: Let's have a look at the short story called "The Dream-Vendor's August." Why did you choose that month?

Okri: In Nigeria, it's an interesting month. It's a richly symbolic month, a middle period between the two great seasons. It's a time when curious things happen. We don't have many seasons as you have here in the West, just the harmattan and the rainy seasons. In August we have a break. It's around that break that the story is set, between these two distinct seasons. It's a freak break. In my story there are no certainties. Things could be one thing or another.

Deandrea: What function did you have in mind for the midget? What was he to do?

Okri: But what does he do?

Deandrea: He gives Ajegunle Joe bad luck.

Okri: It may seem that way. Don't follow a rigorous logic so much, when thinking of this.

Deandrea: But do you think that the story's ending is a happy one?

Okri: What's the ending?

Deandrea: Well, he's fishing on a pond, with his best friend; everything is quiet, the weather is good and he is planning to write a book called *Turning Experience into Gold*. We'll find that very book in Marjomi's room, in the short story—of the next collection—called "In the City of Red Dust."

Okri: Yes, I'm glad you spotted it. You're the only one who has.

Deandrea: But I don't see that plan as a happy ending.

Okri: I don't think in terms of happy endings.

Deandrea: Well, let's put it like that: I don't think he has really changed something in his life.

Okri: He has. Something has changed.

Deandrea: But he's going to have the same kind of life.

Okri: No, he's going to write a book called *Turning Experience into Gold*, which is a very different pamphlet from all the other pamphlets he's been writing. It's a good idea. He makes his money from writing pamphlets that people want to buy. And you pointed out that you found it in Marjomi's house later, so obviously Marjomi has been reading it. His life has changed, that's why I gave the story that title. He knows a bit more who he is and what the world is like, just a little bit more. That's something.

Deandrea: So he's going to make money and to help people to make money through his experience.

Okri: *Turning Experience into Gold* does not mean making money. Gold can be an image, a symbol of wisdom, a symbol of joy.

Deandrea: But why did you choose that word? Money seems to affect the lives of many of your characters . . . .

Okri: You're damn right. "Life is a financial problem," as Ajegunle Joe says.

Deandrea: And I don't think that being so dependent on money seems a positive situation to you.

Okri: It's hellish, isn't it?

Deandrea: But the word "gold" can be immediately associated with "money."

Okri: I think you didn't follow the understructure of the words of the story. Ajegunle Joe is also interested in alchemy.

Deandrea: You often quote the Bible in your works. Has it been relevant to your cultural development?

Okri: Yes. The two big Cs came together, Christianity and colonialism.

Deandrea: Do you think that the former has been as negative as the latter?

Okri: Nigerians are very Christian, very religious. They're Muslim as well. Religion has been a mixed blessing.

Deandrea: And there are many Muslims in Nigeria.

Okri: Lots of Muslims. Probably more than Christians.

Deandrea: And what about the Jehovah's Witnesses?

Okri: They're quite a few.

Deandrea: In "Disparities" you write of a group of boys who are "Confemists." Who are they?

Okri: Oh, it's a combination of Communist and Feminist.

Deandrea: So it's a blend.

Okri: Yes, an invented word.

Deandrea: It would seem, anyway, that you consider Christianity as something negative, because of the very fact that it came with colonialism.

Okri: It was mixed. But at the same time a lot of Africans are Christian.

Deandrea: Are you a Christian?

Okri: I'm a spiritual person. Spiritual in terms of the universe. Christianity is a fact of our society. It's there.

Deandrea: I had come to that conclusion because, for instance, in *Flowers and Shadows* Jonan is compared to Samson, and at the end, when he has died, Jeffia thinks that the philistines have won. So you have turned the Bible's history the other way round. That's why I thought you consider Bible and Christianity as parallel to colonialist evil.

Okri: The worst things that Christianity did was that it destroyed people's connection with their past, made people despise their history and traditions, the philosophy of their ancestors and the ancient religions. Not the religions in themselves, but the philosophy and spirituality that went with those religions. Christianity nearly destroyed all of that. Although many of the Christian churches actually use African forms within their rituals, the spiritual continuity is nearly absent. The colonialists burnt the art of many tribes in the infamous auto-da-fé of 1857, in Benin. There was a bonfire in which sculptures and artefacts were destroyed. Think of that as the destruction of a great amount of religious works of art. It's as if a new religion were to come to Rome and burn Michelangelo's sculptures and all paintings by Leonardo da Vinci, Titian, Caravaggio, Giorgione, Raphael.

Imagine all the religious art of Renaissance Florence burnt in one big religious bonfire. That's an equivalent of what Christianity did.

Deandrea: But do you think that the Africans should try to get back to their ancestral religions?

Okri: No, all I'm saying is that we should carry our history with us, into our future. It's everybody's responsibility in contemporary Africa. You can't go back. What is bad and what is good: carry it, deal with it, make the best of it, learn from it and move into the future. Going back would mean being subverted by our past. That's a universal rule, true for everybody. Italy has to carry Fascism with it and deal with it, learn from the mistakes, just as Germany has to deal with, learn from, and transmute its Nazi past. You can't just say: "let's forget." That is part of what you are and you've got to deal with it courageously. None of us can afford to be blind to their history or to their past. That's why these things move in my work. We are forgetting. We are forgetting whole ways of thinking, forgetting rituals and wisdoms, the good things that came with history as well as the bad things.

Deandrea: What about the church that Omovo sees at a certain point in *The Landscapes Within*? It looks strange because it's surrounded by a fence. I had the impression that, according to you, Christianity is negative also because it is not available to everybody, to the people who are suffering, or it's only a facade, for them.

Okri: What is going on there is more complex than that. To talk about it would take a very long time. It is not necessarily a Christian church. It could be any number of things.

Deandrea: You sometimes write of gods or nature making tricks. That reminds me of *King Lear*, when men are seen as being the sport of gods. I thought you had used almost the same image because in both cases we see a world which is falling apart. As the medieval conception of society is falling apart, the same happens with the old African culture because of the coming of colonialists.

Okri: One of the themes of *The Landscapes Within* is seeing clearly. Seeing what is there clearly without judging it. Even, if possible, without naming it. My job there was to record the scene clearly. It is for the reader to interpret the book. They can make sense of all its different levels of reality.

Deandrea: Do the names of your characters have a meaning?

Okri: Some do, some don't. For instance Omovo means "out of egg."

Deandrea: A sort of birth.

Okri: If you like . . . it doesn't really matter. Look at the sounds, at those three Os. He's often called "egghead."

Deandrea: So the form parallels content.

Okri: It's all there in the book.

Deandrea: What about Blackie and the soldier Frank O'Nero? "Nero," as you probably know, means "black" in Italian. I thought their names could be a reflection of their being quite negative characters.

Okri: No. Why should black suggest negative? Anyway, Blackie is a fairly common working-class urban nickname. It means "dark-complexioned" and it's not meant to suggest anything negative. Frank O'Nero is a famous actor in the old westerns. In my story it is a nickname. Wasn't there a Frank O'Nero who married Vanessa Redgrave?

Deandrea: Oh, you mean Franco Nero the Italian actor . . . .

Okri: The actor of cowboy movies, yes.

Deandrea: Who is Ja-Ja Johnny?

Okri: You'll hear about him one day.

Deandrea: Has he got something to do with your new novel?

Okri: No.

Deandrea: Do you sometimes use minor characters as highly symbolic for something particular? For instance, Frank O'Nero seems to stand for the cruelty of Nigerian soldiers.

Okri: Remember I don't think in terms of symbols in that sense. My minor characters have a function, I don't just bring them in. They stand for something.

Deandrea: And why are your main characters always positive, at least to some degree? You never seem to choose negative protagonists.

Okri: I do. Omovo is an antihero.

Deandrea: I don't mean negative in that sense. You always manage to make the reader feel sympathetic to your main characters, even towards those like Emokhai, who is a thief, a snatcher.

Okri: I believe that if you look at anybody deeply enough you can find something to sympathize with in them.

Deandrea: But you don't seem to sympathize with Frank O'Nero, for instance.

Okri: I don't judge him. He's got a job to do. I never judge my characters.

Deandrea: Why have you created so few white characters?

Okri: I don't think I necessarily have to do that. I don't ask Calvino to create Black characters.

Deandrea: At the end of *The Landscapes Within* Omovo intends to name his drawing with a title which parallels *The Beautyful Ones Are Not Yet Born* by Armah, then he changes his mind. Why? Do you think they are born already?

Okri: Omovo wanted to name the painting and that title came to mind. Then he stopped, because he probably didn't agree with its implications.

Deandrea: But did you have that very title in mind?

Okri: I didn't. He did. *Related Losses* is bigger and more truthful. The first title didn't speak to the painter. If you look at all of my works, you'll come to the conclusion that not only are the beautiful ones, but they're here. They've always been here and will always be here.

Deandrea: When Omovo finishes painting something, he always feels detached from his work, as if he were not the author. Do you feel the same when writing?

Okri: The moment the artist finishes a work of art, it acquires an autonomous reality.

Deandrea: Is that the reason why you insist telling me "the meaning is there"?

Okri: It's all there. The work is an autonomous reality. It has its own life. It has gone, flown away, a stranger.

Deandrea: So can you accept possible interpretations of your books you never fancied?

Okri: Yes.

Deandrea: In your books there are some references to Western authors which convey a negative feeling. Taking into consideration the way they were used, do you think that European literature helped colonialism as the Bible did?

Okri: The colonialists imposed their own texts on colonized people. They used literature as an extension of the ideology of colonialism. I'm not sure all those texts were written for that purpose.

Deandrea: But you think they should be read, anyway.

Okri: Of course they should be read. But in the right context. The literature of the world should be read in Africa, alongside African works. And African works should be read in the world. There was a time in which Nigerians were reading only Western texts. It was the required reading if you wanted to get an education. It was imposed. But if the Western texts are read in their right context, that's different. They become a part of an education about the world. But when they are used as an extension of colonial and capitalist ideology, they become insidious.

Deandrea: In *The Landscapes Within* Omovo occasionally tries to read *The Interpreters* by Soyinka. I had the impression that Omovo didn't like that book. Didn't you like it yourself?

Okri: Omovo found it difficult to read. Soyinka's aesthetics doesn't touch his universe. He's living in a ghetto. Moreover, he's an artist and *The Landscapes Within* suggests a different way of presenting the consciousness of the artist. Soyinka's way is mythical; mine is ordinary, rough, awkward, with many dimensions in it, like life. The whole book is the story of one painting that travels through the consciousness of the character, from the first encounter in the park to the end of the narration. Sometimes I refer to the novel as "the *Pilgrim's Progress* of a painting," through Omovo's consciousness. One thing I wanted to convey is that the act of creation is a mysterious and arduous enterprise. I felt back then that Soyinka gives an easier impression of the artist's life in *The Interpreters*. I knew what it was like. I knew many artists in the ghetto. I knew just how difficult it is to be an artist, to carry the impossible notion of a painting in your head. A painting grows with your life. It suffers as you suffer. It's a living thing inside of you.

Deandrea: What kind of secondary school did you attend?

Okri: It was in Nigeria. Then I went to the university of Essex, studying comparative literature.

Deandrea: Some of your characters seem to get back to their ancestral roots only in order to exploit them for their westernized purposes. For instance, Jonan's juju.

Okri: Well, that's a belief system.

Deandrea: But used in the wrong way....

Okri: I don't know about the wrong way. Their worlds are crumbling. They need something to believe in. They need something to keep them going and they turn to that. Some of them turn to Christianity, some to Islam, some to juju. It's all part of an attempt to deal with reality.

Deandrea: You often write about sex and passions freely, with no restraint; there are moments when it comes out so irrepressibly to embarrass the character who experiences it.

Okri: Why should I censor the truth of the body? I am simply expressing the truth of the character. Desire is a human attribute.

Deandrea: Do you think that it could be seen as a part of that journey back to a more natural life? And to a better relationship with our mind, body and environment?

Okri: Yes, and also because it is true. The body has its desires, and these desires don't always make an announcement before they express themselves.

Deandrea: In the beginning of *Flowers and Shadows*, Jeffia mentions the "rats' escort." Would you elaborate on that point?

Okri: It's a story about two rats who are good friends. One visits the other and they have a good chat. The visitor says "I think I should be going home now." The other says "I'll see you off" but when he gets to his friend's house the friend offers to walk him back home. They keep going on like that, back and forth.

Deandrea: But is it an African tale?

Okri: Yes. It's a story about friendship and politeness.

Deandrea: You often write about rubbish, scums, bad smells, nausea. In your works the readers can find several images of that kind. Are they connected to moral dirtiness?

Okri: Possibly, possibly not.

Deandrea: In "Worlds That Flourish" the main character realizes that people in the town have handwriting on their faces. Is that image connected to the written culture brought by colonialism, opposed to the old oral culture?

Okri: No, no connection with that at all. But an intriguing interpretation.

Deandrea: Couldn't that be, anyway, the symbol of a people manipulated by the system?

Okri: There are many ways you can see it. If you choose those two, it's because of the frame you're using. Somebody else told me it reminds them of Revelations.

Deandrea: Do you mean "666"?

Okri: Not necessarily the number of the beast. Just people who have things written on them. Some say the damned. Others say those who are about to die. Then there are those who have mysterious words written on them that they cannot read. These are things that have been said to me. Then there are those who have their destinies written on them, their future histories. There have been many interpretations of this phenomenon.

Deandrea: Another consequence of postcolonial alienation I perceived in your works regards the choice, on the part of some characters, to make recourse to a "cool" accent, trying to sound English or American. I saw it as an unconscious consequence, on the linguistic level.

Okri: It's stranger and more tragic than that.

Deandrea: What about the several "been-to" feelings of some of your characters? Isn't it a consequence of that alienation?

Okri: Maybe. It's just that people are trying to move to places where they think life is easier. They want more opportunities. They want to escape from the chaos.

Deandrea: Another symbol of contemporary chaos seems to be embodied in cars and motors . . .

Okri: Lagos is a nightmare of cars. I'll tell you something that I find interesting. I hear people talking now about the horrible exhaust fumes from cars and lorries. But I wrote about that, then years ago, in *The Landscapes Within*. I wrote about the way the fumes hit the faces of commuters going to and coming back from work. It doesn't have to be a symbol. It is a reality.

Deandrea: In "In the City of Red Dust" dust is harassing people continuously. It could be seen as a biblical metaphor, but dust is actually raised by cars and tanks.

Okri: I didn't look at it as a symbol. It was something that was there. They make the best symbols.

Deandrea: But why is it red?

Okri: Because in that city the dust is red.

Deandrea: I have also thought of it as a symbol of the blood that Emokhai and Marjomi sell to the hospital.

Okri: If you choose that, then it is there. But dust is red in that city.

Deandrea: I really liked the ending of that short story. Emokhai and Marjomi end up smoking the marijuana raised in the Military Governor's farms. In other words, addiction is ruled by politicians who prefer dumb people rather than angry ones.

Okri: Yes. It's simple . . . and complicated.

Deandrea: Have you ever studied psychology?

Okri: Yes. Psychology interests me. Jung is interesting. He writes about archetypes, chance, structures, alchemy.

Deandrea: It would seem that you consider children as the main victims of your society: is there an implied indictment about the way they handle children?

Okri: Where there is chaos and corruption it's children that suffer the most. Chaos brutalizes everybody, and everybody takes out their brutalization on children, whether they know it or don't.

Deandrea: What about women? You've never used a woman as main character. What do you think are the causes of their plight?

Okri: All in good time. I'm aware of the subjugation of women in African culture. At the same time I'm aware of their great regenerative presence.

Deandrea: Is that the reason why you describe Monica in "Laughter beneath the Bridge" as a very aggressive character, or you write of the women's refusal to clean the compound in *The Landscapes Within*?

Okri: Yes. I don't think Monica is aggressive. She is the way she is because of the war. And with the women in *The Landscapes Within*, they are on strike.

Deandrea: Are those things realistic or simply part of your hopes?

Okri: They are realistic. These things are happening. The hope is in the choice to see and to show. Everyone sees but not everyone has chosen to show.

Deandrea: After *Flowers and Shadows*, it seemed to me that you grew more skeptical about the real possibility of living a love story in a society like yours.

Okri: Where there is chaos, love becomes more difficult.

Deandrea: But Jeffia and Cynthia are the only ones who manage.

Okri: That book was written in 1980, ten years ago. Things were a bit better then.

Deandrea: Were they?

Okri: A bit.

Deandrea: Let's get back for a moment to the several images of scum and rubbish. Were they conceived as a symbol of postcolonial Africa?

Okri: Omovo paints a scumscape called *Drift* and that painting is confiscated. Omovo doesn't judge. He just goes on painting. The people who see, they judge.

Deandrea: The nausea that some of your characters feel might be not only physical, but also metaphysical.

Okri: Too much reality, too much chaos.

Deandrea: Many of your characters get mad or risk getting mad. Is madness so widespread in contemporary Nigeria or is it a symbol of a society that could possibly bring to madness?

Okri: People are mad everywhere.

Deandrea: The best friends of both main characters in your first two novels have to do with journalism. Is there a specific reason for this?

Okri: Every work of mine is a set of mirrors that reflects things back and forth. In *The Landscapes Within* reality is painted by Omovo and written down by Keme, the journalist. Then you have me writing about these two people and their reality. With these mirrors and reflections you'll get the vision of the reality I'm trying to convey. There are different ways of conveying reality. Journalism is a good one.

Rome, October 1992

Deandrea: You said somewhere that African literature has been limited by too much politics.

Okri: Yes, but it has been necessarily attached to politics. The problems that affect Africa are largely political. African writers are very responsible. They feel the need to change society for the better. That is one of the strongest things about our literature. The writers feel an intense social responsibility.

The problem is that if you don't read it from a political point of view, if you want to read it from the point of view of pleasure or personal consolation, after a while it gets monotonous. I discovered that when I wanted to read just to take my mind off things. African literature is not something you can relax with. There's no space for that, because the writers are writing of difficult conditions. All African writers are weighted down with tremendous responsibility. And this is a great thing. But lightness and playfulness are not there so much. And that's a shame.

Deandrea: How do you feel when *The Famished Road* is being branded as an example of magic realism?

Okri: I get bored. I think critics are lazy when they do that.

Deandrea: It has been observed that *The Famished Road* breaks new grounds, going beyond the label of magic realism, producing a son of African postmodernism which stems from the oral tradition.

Okri: That's interesting. But it's more than just the African oral tradition. What I keep saying is that the world view of every people is intrinsically superstitious. According to Picasso, Spaniards cannot recognize people they know from their photographs. For them these are two different kinds of reality. Every world view is superstitious and unique, at the same time.

Deandrea: What about Italians?

Okri: They are superstitious about words. For them words are reality.

Deandrea: What about Kole Omotoso's theorization of the African "marvelous realism"?

Okri: In *The Famished Road* you have this spirit-child. One half of him is in the spirit world, the other is in the world of the real. Whenever he looks at reality, he does it through the eyes of a spirit as well as through those of a human being. So everything is both ordinary and transfigured, simultaneously. I'm not saying reality is fantastic as Márquez did. Azaro does not levitate. Because this boy is half spirit and half human, with the doors of death perpetually open inside him, therefore everything he sees is transfigured. Even time is different. What we perceive as future consequence for this child is the present. In *The Famished Road* there is this unique point of view because it's a first person narrative, if it were third person I wouldn't do that.

Deandrea: One would say that you managed to find a balance between these two worlds and between politics and aesthetics, through Azaro's point of view.

Okri: Yes. I needed this poetic point of view. Half here and half there, both one. Which will win, death or life, eternity or mortality. I don't do it by jumping from one to the other, but by developing both of them, simultaneously. It's all one at the same time, seen through the consciousness of this child who has chosen to live in this reality. It is a difficult point of view to write from. You have to inhabit it as well as be outside of it. I nearly went mad trying to keep that perspective all the time.

Deandrea: Why did you choose those beggars as the starting point for a new potential social change?

Okri: I think they came out of my consciousness as a fictional way of speaking of the insurgence of the suffering of the earth and the people. There's something very powerful about them. They will invade those who have power. Their weight will become so heavy that you will have to choose between killing them off in a sort of genocide—because you don't want to face that reality—or dealing with them as an unavoidable fact. I can't explain them, but the moment they entered my book I knew I had been blessed. They came into the book the same way they entered Azaro's house, sitting around as if they had always been there, with Helen stroking Azaro's father's leg.

Deandrea: Do you think the structure of *The Famished Road*, its ultimate concept of cyclical history and contemporaneity, can help your Nigerian readers to regain their lost cultural tradition without attempting a senseless escape from their present situation?

Okri: I think this is not only a Nigerian problem. We have become creatures who inhabit middle air, without any root connecting us with our past. The facts of history have no meaning anymore. Most Europeans have no consciousness of what imperialism has been and is at all. But basically I'm talking of certain old primeval values. The past must be always kept alive, carried with us, but kept new. I supposed I tried to do that in *The Famished Road*. I tried to do a lot of things. I was probably overambitious, but at least I tried to do them gently.

Deandrea: The figure of the artist in your works seems to be more a provocative witness than a committed artist marching in front of his people, in Achebe's words.

Okri: Why should artists lead revolts? It's absurd. Revolutionaries should be doing that. That's the problem with this romantic notion of the artist. The artist's role is very boring. They have to say "this happened," and that is a quality of our imagination. They are supposed to suffer and leave the greatest possible record of their consciousness and of the future possibilities of their people. Okigbo is an example of the artist who was torn between being a witness, the creative awakener of the people, and being a warrior. We lost a truly great poet. I am furious about it. The people who celebrate him for the fact that he got himself killed just have a sensational vision of the artist. Okigbo, today, might have reached the literary greatness of a Dante. At least he could have tried and striven. All the most important artists live long enough to build their work property, so that it can have an effect on people's consciousness for centuries. They create works that keep us awake and regenerate us.

That attitude you mentioned is just impatience. It's not effective in the long run. Staying at home to write is not a luxury. Subversive ideas can be very diverse. The amount of sufferance, pain, sacrifice and risk in being an artist is incredible. I find that view of the artist you spoke of to be very superficial. How many griots carried guns in the African tradition? The role of the artist is to plant delayed detonations. Something that detonates constantly for a hundred or thousands of years. Virgil's *Aeneid* is still detonating, still exploding.

Deandrea: Your poem "An African Elegy" was entirely taken from a prose passage of *The Famished Road*, simply putting it in verses. I think it gives evidence to the musical, lyrical qualities of your prose.

Okri: Yes, but it is a bit more complicated than it seems. It is a particular practice. Great choice is required. And then there has to be an understanding of how poetry works in a way different to prose. It is not as easy as just taking any old passage. Otherwise one will be doing it all the time. But one isn't. Please never assume that one simply does something. There is more rigour than meets the eye. And yes, a lot of *The Famished Road* was written as poetry.

Deandrea: In *The Famished Road* you develop the incident of the bad milk, already mentioned in *Stars of the New Curfew*. Did it really happen when you were in Nigeria?

Okri: Yes, it was a real event.

Deandrea: Two metaphors seem to dominate *The Famished Road*: the road and the abiku. The former is seen as a place of death and possibilities. Is it taken from ancestral culture? Soyinka employs it, too.

Okri: His road is very different from mine. In the long run people will see how different they are and similar. His is more ritualistic and metaphysical. Mine combines the metaphysical with the ordinary.

Deandrea: You said that all the world of the spirits in *The Famished Road* is just a way of looking deeper into this life.

Okri: It's true. One of the strongest impulses which made me write *The Famished Road* is that I got tired of the traditional artifices and realism of the novel. I wanted to cut all that. I wanted to get directly to the point in a different way, but still in the form of a novel.

Deandrea: You write that Nigeria is an abiku nation. Does that mean that you hope, as a Nigerian writer, to see your country making a choice like Azaro's one in the beginning of the book?

Okri: Yes, of course. But the whole nation has to want it. And want it passionately and intelligently and with tremendous persistence.

Deandrea: Some critics state that the novel, as a literary genre, has a greater import in Africa than in the rest of the world.

Okri: Maybe those who can read take novels more seriously, treating them like oracles or history. But in Nigeria there are still a lot of people who cannot read.

An Interview with Ben Okri

Carolyn Newton / 1992

From *Weekly Mail* (South Africa), republished in *South African Literary Review* 2, no. 3 (Sept. 1992): 5–6. Reprinted by permission of Carolyn Newton.

A big brouhaha over the increasingly controversial Booker Prize last year was punctuated by Nicolas Mosley's highly public resignation from the panel of judges. Among the six titles on the shortlist, there were, he said, no novels of ideas. Perhaps Mosley had not quite got round to reading the book that in the end took the prize; certainly he cannot have spoken to its author. Both are so full of ideas one feels giddy after prolonged exposure to either.

But it's a little unclear exactly what Mosley meant. Perhaps he thought none was intellectual, stretching the brain rather than hitting the heart. At best he was applying a narrow test to his definition, referring to the type of cerebral fiction that has a great tradition among writers in England. In that case, he may as well have brought out a bucket to bail out a flood. Last year's shortlist showed overwhelmingly the taste of England's readers for English-language fiction written by those born elsewhere. (The only exception was Martin Amis, with *Time's Arrow*—and it has been suggested that he tried to disguise the fact by writing backwards.) The trend has been growing for a time; past winners include Keri Hulme's *The Bone People* and J. M. Coetzee's *The Life & Times of Michael K*. The preference seems to be for fiction that crosses cultural boundaries and speaks in newer, more exotic voices.

Ben Okri is riding the crest of this wave. *The Famished Road* could not have been born of England's green and pleasant land; his is a heady cocktail of African legend and Western classicism, stream of consciousness and wry satire. Okri has created a style all his own and as long as one approaches the subject carefully, he is happy to admit it.

"I wanted to write a book that's a river, that keeps flowing and changing, so that each time you come back to read it, it's different. How do you do that when the words are fixed? By different waves, with different things going on beneath the surface of the text."

Okri calls it "mood-writing"; he sowed the seeds in his earlier short stories and brought it to flower in *The Famished Road*. He does not think it has been particularly understood. The spirits, for instance, which populate the novel: "People read them as specific things, when in fact they too are forms, they're moods, they're just the images of moods. We have no language to talk about our dreams. We have become too rational."

In finding this language, he was, he says, trying to create a different reality.

"When you begin to hint at other worlds, you expand the dimensions of this one. The ceiling gets higher, the walls further away, and suddenly there's more space in the world. This is very opposite from realist writing which tries to describe, or transcribe, the world as it is. It can make the world seem wonderful, or make you see it more clearly, but it's very different from creating spaces.

"When you do that," he says, with a long pause, "there's simply more space to occupy."

Probe further into the style and influences of his writing, and Okri fences. So anxious is he to avoid being labelled, he almost trips over his feet. His first two novels were published ten years ago by Longman Drumbeat, billed as "African Fiction." Today, those who refer to his work as African get short shrift. It's too limiting, he says; writers should be free. You should not be trapped inside the notion of "African" literature.

The central concept of *The Famished Road*, the spirit child or *abiku*, is straight out of Yoruba mythology; surely that's African? No, says Okri, it's there in Irish legends, in Germany, in Homer. It's always been there, and he's surprised nobody's taken the trouble to write about it before.

But call Okri's style (as it has been called) magic realism, and he is off in the opposite direction. His is an *African* world view, he says, in which myths are real, and when people sleep they go to other realms of existence. Westerners don't understand this way of life, they are too rational, they have lost their mysticism. The African's world is inhabited with spirits and beings, the spaces are filled with them. He talks about the influence of African storytelling on his writing. Had he spent all his life out of Africa, he would have written a very different book, he suggests. "I would have been more cerebral, more clever. I may not have had the peculiar, unique poetic atmosphere of the African world."

This frantic dodging of the nets is perhaps understandable in the light of his background. Ben Okri grew up in a dual world. Born in Minna, mid-Nigeria, he spent the first part of his childhood in England, where his father practiced law, and where the shelves of his house were lined with Virgil and Homer, Dante and Dickens. (One interview quaintly describes the pint-sized Okri given the job of dusting down the books, and one day opening the covers and starting to read them.) He was still quite small when he was whipped back to Nigeria, where he survived a double shock: the Biafran war, and a rough school for streetwise children.

He left school to return to England and Essex University. He wrote two novels in his first two years there, and they are filled with conflict between the pull of his roots and the draw of the West. His central characters are pro-African, anti-anyone with European pretensions. "I can't speak my language any more," bemoans Omovo in *The Landscapes Within*. "I speak a counterfeit. I will soon have to relearn it the way I once learned English. How did this happen to us? . . . We've been selling our souls without knowing it." In *Flowers and Shadows*, two friends argue about whether they should leave for England or America straight after school. Jeffiah thinks he should go to a local university; Ode says he'll be back in five years with an international education. "You'll be too westernized then," says Jeffiah. "I'll be a man of home, and we won't take back prodigal sons."

Has Okri sold his soul? Is he a prodigal son?

If he has misgivings, he won't admit them to me. He writes better away from home, he says; he needs the perspective. He has also said that there is no mental space to write in Nigeria. Life is too crowded, too much is happening. Nigeria suffers from so much reality, he told one interviewer, that it is impossible to "let a thought grow there."

One gets the impression that Ben Okri has spent most of his writing life sloughing off other people's expectations. He is often asked why his writing is not more overtly political. I bring up the subject tentatively; the man who five minutes previously said he disliked people who spoke before they thought, has a gut reaction: "I am sick of political novels." There was a time and place in Nigeria for political writing, he says; now it's time her children moved beyond that. He has described Africa's limitation by political writing as a one-color painting. In real life, he said, "politics take their place beside myth and facts, each one in turn has an ascendancy."

This healthy skepticism of the importance of politics filters through *The Famished Road*, with its Swiftian "Party of the Rich" and "Party of the Poor." Satire, yes; cynicism, no: "I will resist becoming cynical until my last breath—in fact after my last breath," he maintains, "because cynicism is the freezing of the blood and the nerves. Satire is just pointing out the bullshit."

Politics apart, Okri is constantly answering to other people's agendas. At a reading shortly after *The Famished Road* was published, someone from the floor asked Okri why he didn't write in Nigerian, for Nigerians. He refused to be limited, he said, by race and nationalism. "People can say this is a triumph for the African novel if it gives them comfort, but I say it is a triumph for the imagination, for what Baudelaire calls the texture of our sensuality."

Okri has a habit of dropping names from his highbrow background. Every interview is peppered with references to Homer and Defoe, Chinese philosophers and ancient mythology. Our occasion is not different. On the Booker Prize he opines: "There have been prizes throughout history. Sophocles walked away with the great prize virtually every year, he must have won it 123 times consecutively."

Not surprisingly, he thinks it's a good thing. "An award can stimulate excellence, raise standards, make people try a bit harder." On the other hand, he says his life has become much more difficult since the Booker, because he has to "fight the demon of arrogance. This is a time you can lose your head," he feels, "and I have to keep rooted to the earth; I have a responsibility to continue developing, to find more beauty, more life, more love."

He denies, though, any particular pressure to repeat his success. "There has always been pressure. I was always aware that if no one else was looking at my work, I certainly was. I don't want to be ashamed of it. The quality of your work eventually feeds the quality of your serenity; and that's important, something I'd like to reach, because you're a more powerful writer when you're serene."

This is heady stuff, and his voice almost carries it off, soft and floating, but careful where it lands.

We are sitting, as we talk, in his rooms at Trinity College, Cambridge. By the look of it, Ben Okri has assimilated completely. A small, neat man, nattily dressed, softly spoken, slow, almost dreamy. He directs our conversation at philosophical tangents. We talk about the death wish of the central character, Azaro, and half an hour later he has formulated a hypothesis of life: "The fact of death makes that part of the story which comes before it extraordinary. The moment we are born, immortality is out of the question. When we die, immortality becomes a possibility."

The single label Ben Okri will accept is one he has designed himself: "I see myself as a creative human being. I think we should all be creative human beings; that's our responsibility. Animals are creative too. If you present them with a problem, they solve it, sometimes more intelligently than we do. Even plants: you put human beings in a situation where there's light here, and dark there, half the time they go towards the darkness."

Immediately after winning the Booker Okri was prosaic about his success. The money would be very useful, he said; until then he had been playing the starving artist. When he arrived in England he slept in tube stations, or so the story goes, and he discontinued his studies after two years for lack of funds. Post-Booker, with £20,000 pile money and a two-year fellowship at Trinity College, Cambridge, he can afford to let the poetry of his situation take over. "Money is not the most important thing," he says now. "The most important thing is going further. Because you do your work and you die, and if you've done one or two good things from your spirit, you've made a gift to people who are left behind, and that's the best thing."

Whisperings of the Gods: An Interview with Ben Okri

Delia Falconer / 1996

From *Island Magazine* 71 (Winter 1997): 43–51. Reprinted by permission of Delia Falconer.

Delia Falconer: When you are interviewed about your work, you speak often of its "healing" function, and your "rage and desire" to "transform" the human condition. What drew you to the novel form as a vehicle for pursuing these interests?

Ben Okri: I don't just choose a novel form. In fact, I don't really consciously think of the choice of form—I think the impulse chooses the form; the mood and the material and the necessity itself choose a form. The possession chooses a form, if you like. Sudden things come to you and you think they're novels and after a while you realize actually, as it comes out of your fingers, actually it's a poem. And once it's come out as a poem, that's it, there's nothing that can be done about it, that's its true form, that's the only way it can be. And I follow that, I'm in many ways just a servant of these higher things that insist on coming through me. I'm not a professional writer.

Falconer: So, you don't feel that you have been influenced by any writers or canons or styles in particular? How would you react, for example, to *The Famished Road* being called a magic realist novel?

Okri: Strangely enough, it's not the subject or the history of the place or the personal philosophy or the culture that shapes the piece of work. It's something about the age which you live in, but it's something more to do with your secret true orientation to life that really does it. That's where writers have their true affinities. That's why I reject utterly the way in which my work is placed within the whole context of the margin, the periphery, postcolonial and stuff like that. I think those are very poor descriptions of the work that some of us are trying to do. Because it completely situates the work within a time/historical context and not within a context of self and inner necessity, which is bigger than that and beyond that. And there are affinities between writers that have more to do with that than they have to do with the fact that they both come from so-called ex-colonial nations. When people do that they're not seeing what I'm doing and they're completely missing the point and I feel sad about that.

Falconer: On the subject of having one's work placed on the margins, a lot of literature coming out of Africa tends to be placed by publishers into African writers' series (for example, the Heinemann African Writers series), which not only suggests it has an essential "Africanness" but sometimes also makes this writing quite difficult to access for an international audience. This has not been the case with your work. When you were first seeking publication, was this an issue for you, and did you come up with any strategies to avoid this categorization?

Okri: I don't have any strategies. I just have this stubborn relationship with my own truth. You're either a writer or you're not. You're either a dreamer or you're not. You're either at the service of this business of listening to the whisperings of the gods and the whisperings of nature and life and history and time, or you're not. If you are, you look for the best road by which this thing that you're mediating can be shared with all the peoples of this earth, because we're intimately connected with one another, our destinies are linked. It's important that what it is I'm trying to get across be got across and we should hear one another. It's our responsibility to not become little streams that don't get to the sea. We must get to the sea. It's the impulse of life; I follow that, I don't recognize any other. I really mean that.

Falconer: And yet, as an author, one is the product of the publishing industry, and its marketing strategies.

Okri: I don't think that you really do negotiate it; the work does it. I mean, my first novel was turned down by just about all the publishing houses that you're talking about. They turned it down. It's the way it goes in this world. If you're true enough, you would find that in relation to the structures of this world you seem to be quite awkward. So the wrong people will turn you down. And it will seem like bad luck at the time, it will seem like failure at the time; but many years later the right people in the right places, who are the best people to get that work to the widest number of people, they will somehow—I don't know, there's a mathematics of destiny involved in this—they will get it, and they will make the connection between the little stream and the great sea. I didn't make the strategy, I just got turned down. Fortunately. And I still depend on that; I still find a lot of my luck is related to the ways in which I am rejected.

Falconer: You said that the form of a novel almost chooses you. How do you account for the change of form between your earlier books like *The Famished Road* and *Songs of Enchantment*, large, chaotic, spilling novels, which have been acclaimed critically as interminglings of the classical Western novel form and the mythic narration of African folktales, and the more spare, contained form of your latest work, *Dangerous Love*?

Okri: I don't think I've moved, because then you're taking a lenient view of publishing; whereas in terms of consciousness and the work and the way the work comes about, there isn't a lenient view. That's why I have a shock when you say "your early books," and you say *The Famished Road*, and I say, is that an early book? It seems like my latest work, if you know what I mean. There are no time scales in there, in terms of the work. All that really sometimes tends to happen is that you get occupied by or haunted by a certain kind of necessity that insists that the form be burst open, because you're trying to say things that the form you've inherited seems too narrow to say. So, I suppose you have to blaspheme aesthetically, I suppose you have to risk being universally howled at and rejected and laughed at, which was what *The Famished Road* was for me. I thought to myself, well, if you're going to be seen as a fool, you may as well be your best fool, and just go for it, put it all there, say it, as truthfully and as best as you can. And if you're stoned out of town, well, you do it in good conscience. That was one kind of impulse out of this whole dimension of reality that I felt we've ignored in fiction. And it's not *magic*, it's just a dimension of the spiritual. It's a dimension of the self, a dimension that is transhistorical, that is beyond history. And when that, in many ways, was expressed, I got occupied by another kind of mood, which was *Songs of Enchantment*, which is very different from *The Famished Road*. People speak of it as a continuation and that's just laziness. It's very different, because there I was occupied by the need to express something of the spirit of change, the way in which change in history or in individual life is the modulation of several aspects of music at the same time. It's sort of several dreams dying and being born all into one another; it's that complete intermingling of the dying and the being born; the half-born, half-dead; prophetic hints of what's to come and what's dying and so on and so forth—very, very different mood and different necessity, completely. And when that was expressed—in a way—I found myself now being occupied by a mood to sing a purer song, a song of light, a light that comes out of the most intense suffering. And that's how it goes. And after that I wanted to face the real again, out of which all these things come, and out of which it must go, and sink into. I wanted to have that, not out of my own choice, but out of the something that I get occupied by, and that I do my best to realize. And that's passed, that season of mangoes or oranges or pineapples in me, is now passed, and that's taken out of me certain kinds of vitamins and certain kinds of nutrients and there are others left, which then need to be expressed and they may come out as guavas and . . . do you get what I'm saying? That's the way it is, these are not conscious choices I make, I simply can't make these choices. That's why I say I'm not a professional writer.

Falconer: Given that, I'm interested that, in *Dangerous Love*, you have returned to *The Landscapes Within*, an earlier work, and actually rewritten it. It seems like a very difficult thing to do, to reopen that finished text.

Okri: It's a horrible thing to do, it's the closest thing you can do to a complete public and private self-flagellation. It really is, it's quite a horrible thing to do. I think it's partly because, I realized, over the years, the way in which you pay, are punished, for an idea or a mood that's been given to you that you've not realized properly—if you've not actualized it properly—you suffer for it. It's almost like there's a deity of creativity that punishes artists if they badly actualize the ideas given to them. I can't speak for other writers, but I have suffered immensely because of that early book. I like to feel that at last I've done time and can be let out of prison now and be a free man.

Falconer: Perhaps that's the novelist's motivating fear, failing to live up to the potential of the idea of the novel.

Okri: It's not the case, really, of realizing all of its potential . . . it's not got to do with perfection, because perfection, that's not what art is about. Perfection is the enemy of art, perfection is the end; perfection kills art, it's not what it's about. You want to hear someone going on about perfection, believe me, they don't know what they're talking about, haven't thought about it, and don't know what it implies. Perfection kills dialogue; it brings it to an end. That's not what it's about. It's about continuing dialogue. It's whether you've shaped the work enough so that it can continue its dialogue and its song and its speech through each person, through time, through each generation, a new life form, that's what it's really about. To somehow have within it its own eternal self-regeneration. Damn fiendish thing, much more difficult than perfection, which is really just all angles and mathematics and geometry and phony framing and not taking risks.

Falconer: The ending of *Dangerous Love*, which speaks of intimations of the future and the difficult cycles ahead for Omovo, leaves the reader space to think about what might happen afterward; are you also leaving yourself space to take up Omovo's story again in another book?

Okri: No, it's exactly as I said to you, it's to create a space whereby the novel can continue in you, the reader; or, not the novel, but the life of it, can continue. For it to cast a shadow of life, that's what I wanted to do, or that's what I discovered that the book would have liked me to do. Whereas what I wanted to do when I was younger was something else. Strangely enough, the ambition was bigger, or, the ambition, being bigger, was smaller. It's one of those paradoxes.

Falconer: There is a moment, in *Dangerous Love*, where the artist Omovo admits to his friend Keme that he might have loved Ifeyiwa because she suffered and said that this is a "dangerous reason to love." Given that what he says is echoed by the title, I was wondering if you were suggesting that—in dealing with histories filled with suffering—the writer also had a duty to reflect a Utopian dimension in those lives he or she represents.

Okri: No, I don't know if it's our job to offer hope; we certainly don't want to be peddlers of hope. It's such a—in some ways—actually such a cheap and easy thing to do. A number of poems end with hope, hope, you must have hope and all of that—and you're bored to your eyeballs—you write this book and then you wheel out this cheap charlatan, this cheap . . . hope—and everyone breathes a sigh of relief and says, ah wonderful, yes, ha ha, yes. No, I don't think that's what we do at all. If hope turns up somewhere in the vision, it's from the least expected quarters, in the ways that you wouldn't have suspected or thought about, it really does turn up through the back door, through crevices in the ceiling, it leaks in. That's the way it ought to be, that's the way it does in life, it leaks in, you don't know how or where, out of the most improbable things, it leaks out of the most tragic depiction, painting, the bleakest possible picture. You think, yeah, I've got it, I'm going to tear their hearts to pieces, break their hearts, and make them face the fact that life is tough, awkward, difficult, unnegotiable, that destiny is sometimes implacable, blah blah blah, and so on and so forth, and you've put your pen down and you're delighted and pleased with yourself that you've really, really—and the years pass and you see in there this bright hidden light in the work, or readers come and they point it out to you, and you say, hang on a minute, I didn't put that there, it forced its way there out of the way the human spirit is. Hope is not something one should *put* in there; it's something that emerges out of the sheer necessity of its place in the pantheon of human survival and the human spirit. I think that's the way it should be. It's the counterpart to the unacceptable. It's the visible aspect in the work of the miraculous. My books that seem to be books of light are actually books of despair, and I always say that, with the passing of time, *Astonishing the Gods*, which is seen as the book of light, will grow darker, and a book like *Songs of Enchantment*, which is seen as a dark book, will grow lighter. It will just change over time.

Falconer: I know that your books have been on the British and Australian bestseller lists—I'm curious to know how available they are in Nigeria, where they are set. Do you write with a particular readership in mind?

Okri: These are questions I get asked a lot, and I always try to be very polite, but I think maybe a time comes when one shouldn't be so polite, and one really should say, it really is not my job, it's not my business; my business is to do the work, submit myself, do it as best I can, give in. And how it works out and so on, I can't kill myself over that, I mean I really can't, the book goes where it goes. The economic conditions in Nigeria are fiendish; I can't go back. My books are somehow able to—I really don't think it's anything I either have to justify myself about, or be proud about, crow about, celebrate, beat my breasts about, or anything like that. It really isn't. That's publishing, that's other dialectics, it's way out of my territory. I'm not an economist, I don't own publishing houses; living is difficult enough as it is, and then doing the work is difficult, and then making sure that the books get to Nigeria, and then making sure they get to the village; if one takes this question, I mean the next thing, I'm asked to publish the books and then go around to every single region, peddle the thing and then translate it into every language. The point comes when you say to folks, look, none of that is my business; my business is to sacrifice my heart, myself, my time, my suffering, my anguish, and my craft, to do that, to do it as best as I can. And after that, just try and regain my sanity, to stay sane and just live as long as I'm capable of living on this earth. The rest is not my business.

Falconer: Early in *Dangerous Love*, there is a scene, set in the Ebony art gallery, where Omovo's painting is hung. The artworks are "stuck side by side, unimaginatively" to affirm Africanness, national unity, tradition. They are praised and categorized by the critics there, whose "borrowed accents" and theories "sting" Omovo's ears. I was tempted to read this scene as, if not a rejection, at least, an expression about the critical placement of African art and literature.

Okri: Criticism is very important and is very old and goes back in the Western tradition to Aristotle and has been very influential and very powerful. Aristotle himself got Homer wrong, just like everybody else has; he initiated something that we do keep forgetting, which is that the function of the critic really should be to multiply the possibilities of interpretation of a work; to open up a work, to illuminate the world of a work; not to reduce it and to diminish it; to keep opening it up because that's what works do. And also mainly because reading is one of the most difficult things. People think that because they can read a sentence, follow a story, and follow a plot, that they've read a book. Actually, reading a book is living it, is suffering it, is reading it in your consciousness, is constantly having a dialogue with it. There are people who've read *Dangerous Love*, who *think* they've read it, and they say things like, oh, you give Ifeyiwa a bad time in the book, or they say, why did you make her die so early, and I say to them, you haven't begun to read this book yet. *I* didn't kill the poor girl, she partly killed herself; she made certain decisions, she didn't listen to certain advice, these things are there. I've taken great pains to point out the little hidden quiet things by which people create their destinies and what happens to them, side by side with the things that they can't control, the things that they do, that they don't deal with. I take great pains to do that and they don't see it. So that's one of the great functions of criticism; to draw slowly the reader's attention to the luminous hidden little scripts, and to say, that's important, that qualifies the bigger picture. It's helping the reader to see. It's not about opinions. Opinions? Go dump them somewhere. Illumination? Invaluable. Because they go back to why books and why literature are important. It's important because the best books, the good books, help us live better. And that's what criticism should do.

Falconer: Do you feel, then, that as a guest of a writers' festival you're being put in the position of "explaining" your books?

Okri: Yes, it's a pernicious position to be in—in some ways quite irritating and so on, but one should also be humble about the whole thing. For goodness' sake, it's a great development from the time when, you know, the great dreamers and the great bards had to sit down there with an instrument and sing their dreams to drunken and overfed kings. I'm thinking of people like Homer, who had to go from city to city, carrying these great big works in his head, having to perform them and render them to these rather bored people in their courts who had eaten too much beef and turkey, had far too much to drink, put their feet up and fallen asleep. It's a modest improvement from that. In some ways it does limit the text and so on and so forth, and one is put in positions that are sometimes really quite humiliating. Just in the sense that, you've tried to create a world that's autonomous, that's in some ways ashamed of you. The work really doesn't want you to be hanging around, the work wants to have a relationship with the reader quietly, it's between them. The work's its own soul and it just wants to have a dialogue with another soul in private. It really doesn't want you being around them, breathing down the reader's neck, spoiling the whole experience for them, guiding them to places where they're not supposed to be going. It's their own book; it's their own thing, you know. We're poor relations at the wedding of the book and the soul of the reader. And that's a shame. But, sometimes you do these things to help the books get to the sea, you know, to help the books make friends, and also, you must remember, we none of us are going to be here forever, one will pass away, and helping the book get out there might just help it make friends along the line, and if the books are good enough, they'll go on doing that. And if they're not, they'll be buried with you in some forgotten library. But hopefully, in sacrificing some of one's time, one helps them to find more life, more friends in the world. It's a difficult position, but one shouldn't be too arrogant about it, you know. A bit of humility, the fact of the people, is not such a bad thing.

I really don't believe so much that it's the gesture of the writer; the gesture of the writer can never be more important than the work itself. And so you have those writers who don't give interviews, don't do this, don't do that, don't drink water, they're vegetarians, don't eat fish; that's got nothing to do with it, it's just gestures. The only thing, the only gesture that counts and that lives, thankfully and wonderfully, is the work. Whether you dress completely in black, completely in white, wear a yellow hat, blue sunglasses, only talk with your head facing in one direction, are known for drunkenness, bad temper, whatever, it's all by the way: only the work, only the work.

An Interview with Ben Okri

Charles H. Rowell / 2005

From *Callaloo* 37, no. 2 (Spring 2014): 214–21. © 2014 Johns Hopkins University Press. Reprinted by permission of Johns Hopkins University Press.

Charles H. Rowell: This morning, as I opened the newspaper the *Daily Telegraph* in my hotel, I noticed that there was an article on an exhibition of European-American paintings, a small collection from New England. This exhibition is being mounted at the Dulwich Picture Gallery here in London. I love art in various forms. All of us as human beings love it, and some few of us create it. You are an artist, a maker, a creator. Your literary texts are art; your poetry is art; your fiction is art. What is this thing that you make? Will you talk about the fiction you make as art? Art is the essence of the narratives you create; the essence of your narratives is art. Will you talk about what you make as art? What is it, how it moves in the world, how you want it to exist in the world, and how you want us to respond to it or experience it?

Ben Okri: It is the most mysterious, and the most futuremaking, past-transforming, prophetic, death-consciousness-resonating, civilization-shaping, life-molding activity that we do. I see art as a bridge between the secular and spiritual aspects of humanity. In art I'm including everything from song, dance, architecture, painting, music, literature, conversation of a certain kind, even certain silences. Society is held together by laws, but is animated by art. When the art of a people dies, not long afterwards, the people die. It's the art that keeps the brightest and the most important aspects of a people, inwardly, alive. It keeps them alive to conscience, to their failings, to their missed roads, to their wrong turnings, to their great destination which keeps moving forward and taking us with it. Art connects the prophetic; aside from the spiritual, art is the next great realm of humanity. It is practically a continent just off paradise, within the spirit. That's how important it is. That's how important I see it. Therefore, it requires from us on the one hand the greatest consciousness in our execution of art, the greatest responsibility, the greatest freedom, the greatest wisdom, the greatest discipline. On the other hand, the greatest, the humblest, capacity of interpretation, because an art that is not originally an interpreter is like a sphinx that doesn't speak. Right now, we exist in a world where so many things in our art have been speaking to us and telling us all kinds of things we need to know about ourselves, the mistakes we've been making, the kind of human beings, the kind of society, the kind of families, the kind of people we can be; all of these works of art are speaking to us, but we're not hearing them because of poor interpretation. Interpretation is not something that should be left only to the cultural interpreters. It is the responsibility of every human being. The way we interpret art is a preparation for the way we interpret life, and vice versa. They are in a perpetual dialogue with one another. If you can't read a book, if you can't read a poem, you're not going to be able to read a situation that you find yourself in clearly; it's the same textual interpretation. We need the same moral intelligence, the same spiritual aliveness, the sense that everything is a text we can learn from. Whether it is literature, painting, music, dance, a building, it is always there speaking to us about our open possibilities. Interpretation should be an important part of the educational curriculum. This whole idea of interpretation has been too culturally isolated. Rap artists constantly are interpreting one another's performance. Interpretation is one of the most wonderful things we do; it's just that we separate it from critical interpretation. This broadened sense of art spreads that and becomes a life thing. Life and art complement one another, perpetually in dialogue, with our consciousness as the mediating place.

Rowell: I am convinced that art is necessary; it is a necessary thing for the human being as an individual, and it is necessary for societies.

Okri: If I can find a word that is a bit more than "necessary," I would say yes. People are really only as great as their art, and as their interpretation of art. You're not going to be greater than your art. Even your science is not going to be greater than your art. The science is only great in relation to the art, because art frees the human spirit, frees the place that talent and possibility pour out from. Art is closest to that place; everything else comes second, third, fourth, because an art thing is a life thing. It is not just that it is necessary: it is fundamental. This cannot be stressed strongly enough. People who do not respect art are in trouble. It will be pretty evident eventually. You can look at a people, and you will be able to tell just how much they value their art and how much they live, are lively, in relation to it.

Rowell: When you first started speaking you used the word "spiritual." I don't understand the word "spiritual" as you are using it, because I think you're saying something far beyond what I know or imagine, far from my own cultural background, my own historical background, of what "spiritual" means. It seems that your "spiritual" was beyond religion, but it had something to do with the soul; it had something to do with another world. And then there is the figuration you spoke of, the "spirit-child." Will you talk about that? Is it the same thing as the spirit, an embodiment of the spiritual?

Okri: Not really.

Rowell: What I'm trying to do is to get a landscape, to create a landscape that will aid us in reading your fiction. And I don't want to say "interpret" your work, but the way you were using the word "interpret," I would say "to interpret your work," but not the way I would use the word in a classroom of literature, for example.

Okri: I prefer "read" to "interpret." "Read" is more open. "Read" is great. For me the spiritual constitutes the central thing that makes us human. And you're right, I separate it from religion because religion tends to be, in one form or another, organized; whereas the spiritual is true for everybody. It is a domain that is in every human being, in our makeup. It is immeasurable, unisolatable. It can't be found in the DNA. It is what makes the whole self, the whole being. It is the first ground in humanity, the prime kingdom within the human spirit, within all of humanity. As for the way it relates to the idea of a creator, I think that's too contentious to go into here, except I'll say that the spiritual is what unites all of us. It is the most fundamental thing that unites all of us. When Shakespeare said, "If you prick me, do I not bleed?" talking about mercy, he really is invoking that oneness that all human beings share, regardless of where they're from. Without being able to invoke that oneness, we don't actually have a means of feeling for one another. The fact that we're just all human beings is not enough a basis for feeling this oneness that we mysteriously feel with one another. The spiritual *is* that oneness, is what connects us. Though you are sitting there and I'm sitting here, we are connected by this spiritual oneness. We are both animated by the spiritual, by this fourth-dimensional thing that makes us alive and makes us human. So, for me, that spiritual foundation that one assumes without even knowing that one assumes it is the basis for all the other resonances that take place in society: in art, in literature, in our dealings with one another, in our laws. Because we all assume that oneness. It is very strange that this universal quality that is invisible and cannot be shown or produced as evidence must be assumed in society, even in highly secular societies. It has to be assumed; otherwise, we are talking about societies being composed of millions of isolated and unconnected peoples, which we don't. We think of societies being one—many millions, but essentially one. We do that, and the intuition of doing that is this spiritual connection.

Rowell: Were you demonstrating the same in *In Arcadia*? Do you think the literary critics reviewing your novel fail to comprehend what you were demonstrating? Or were you—to put it another way—raising a question about that?

Okri: Yes, I was raising a question about that, because the very nature of the spiritual and the very nature of the presence of art in us also brings into view the very fact that a society has secret dreams as to where it wants to go. The more intelligent the society, the clearer those dreams are. There are many words in many languages, but only one word known for it in literature. That word is "Arcadia." Some would choose "utopia," some would say "Eden." In the Bible, in the past, and in the fall, too many things are associated with "Eden" and that is problematic. "Utopia" again is locked in this sense of an impossible dream, but "Arcadia" is sufficiently secular and unspoiled to allow this resonance, this influx of the idea of people's best dreams of where they want to go. This is true of the individual, as well as a people, as well as the human race. We are largely defined by the quality of our Arcadias. If you don't have an Arcadia, you are in trouble. We are only as rich or as alive as our dreams of who we want to be and where we want to go. It's that need to bring back into view the fact that deep down inside this unrest, this chaos, this suicidal, genocidal, serial-killing age that we're living in, inside it is still this hope, this desire for an Arcadia. That's what I was trying to bring out. Most of the critics didn't see it, but that's not so bad. The purpose of art is not to be seen immediately, but also to wait. Art is very patient.

Rowell: You have destroyed my next question. [*Laughter*] I realize that it is terrible to ask writers to respond to their critics. But I want to ask you your response to the blindness of your critics: that they were expecting you to do one thing while you were doing another, that they were expecting you to stick only with Nigerian culture rather than to use and critique European culture, and to show the oneness of all humanity in African culture, the oneness of humanity via European culture. I am suddenly reminded of the African American artist Romare Bearden in the United States, in his collages reinventing Odysseus, Bearden's rereading of the *Odyssey* using Black characters, and white critics were totally thrown off balance: "Why is he putting these Black people here?" So why were you tampering with their culture? That is, of course, I hope you get the sarcasm in my words.

Okri: Well, because it is not solely their culture; it belongs to the human race. To go back to our earlier conversation about the hidden assumption of the presence of the spiritual: this human oneness means that the great dreams that a people have don't belong only to them. We don't live in a world where peoples are isolated from one another. The dreams and the nightmares of one people definitely affect another. We know this in relation to all that has been going on over the past one hundred years in human history, whether it's communism, apartheid in South Africa, Tibet, and China, we're all impinged on by other people's dreams and ideas about how the world should be. Finally, once it enters into the realm of art, it has said goodbye to the people that it came from. If it is inside of people and not expressed, it belongs to the people. The minute it is expressed, it has said goodbye and made a journey into the world dream. In that sense, every important work of art is a world dream, a world contribution. It is the utmost in cultural selfishness for a people to think that their creation belongs to them alone. It is a startling and singular act of ungenerosity to say that an artist is going to dream for only this small bunch of people on this great globe. And yet, they put this dream-art into the world. If they are going to put the dream-art into the world, they should also put a sign with that dream saying "For English people only" or "For Black Americans only" or "For Nigerians only." It doesn't work like that. The minute an artistic dream leaves you it goes into the world in complete freedom. Just like we human beings go into the world, we go in complete freedom—but we forget it. And so, for me, all works of art are mine to enjoy and learn from and use; the whole history of art, the whole history of culture, is my personal possibility and history. And I expect everyone to think the same thing about everyone else's. What are we saying? Are we saying therefore that a work of art does not speak to another human being? The fundamental definition of a work of art, a true work of art, is that it speaks to anyone, it speaks to something in everyone. It is universal in that sense. How can you talk about the universality of art on the one hand and insist on its provinciality on the other? That is a kind of artistic apartheid. It is ultimately damaging. I think art wants to be part of the world family. And so when you say "Am I tampering with their Arcadia?" I say it never was theirs alone. The very fact of having this artistic dialogue continues the story of enrichment between us. Having said that, I also want to stress one fundamental thing about the nature of art, and that is its right to be misunderstood or to not be understood at the time. The definition of art is not that it is and should be immediately understood, or even that it is perfectly and completely understandable. Because it comes out of one person's consciousness and speaks to certain universal archetypes inside of all of us means, therefore, that art is both time contingent as well as perpetually mysterious: it cannot be ever completely unraveled. It is that perpetual question mark that relates art to Arcadia; for that reason it always takes us forward. Anything that can be completely understood fades. What keeps us interested in artistic creation is the fact that we think we've got it, we go to sleep, wake up, look at it, and we've lost it again. It has changed. It has become something else, because we are constantly becoming something else. Our relationship with the mysterious archetypes, the mysterious dreams within us, is itself evanescent and constantly changing. Change is the territory of our relationship with art and the universe. Because life itself is so fluid and the future is constantly defined and undefined. That's the magic of it. So I'm not overly concerned whether what one does is understood at the time. What is important is the quality of the dialogue. On the whole, my work has been generously received. But there have been here and there small-minded responses. I don't think it is because of the spiritual dimension. I think it is also what you are saying, the limiting rights that one should do only this, one should do only that, and one is going outside that territory—or reminding folks that there is no limited territory, there is just the human territory. One of the things that keeps me going is a belief in the fundamental freedom of the human imagination and of the artistic dream. We have a right to—we must—go everywhere. We're content to send astronauts to space and to distant planets, and we restrict our artists to their culture and their race and their tradition? That is madness. Freedom is universal; limiting the imagination doesn't make sense to me.

Rowell: I think also, for us in the West to begin closely reading your work, we need to know what you mean when you speak of "stories." I want to quote something where you used stories: "The greatest stories are those that resonate our beginnings and intuit our endings, our mysterious origins, and our destinies, and resolve them both into one." It's a very beautiful statement in form. Will you talk about that statement—especially as it relates to your own work?

Okri: You ask the most profound questions, and what is more deadly is that you ask them so beautifully and so nicely. You are a deadly man. I'm going to try and respond to the edge in that question. There is something that runs through the whole of creation the moment it becomes creation, and that is fundamental change, from a condition of changelessness. When you have the idea of creation, when you think "creation," you are already creating a break from a previous condition, which is, as it were, precreation. When you do that, you are setting into motion the grand theme, you are ringing the great bell of change. That great bell of change is the beginning of story.

Rowell: Those words have a greater rigor than the rigor of the statement I quoted. Will you give us a little more simplicity? Will you kindly explicate your explication? [*Laughter*]

Okri: My goodness, you sound like what someone said about Kant. [*Laughter*]

Rowell: Well, after all I am speaking with Ben Okri.

Okri: The fact of story sets into motion destinies; it sets into motion a world of cause and effect, action and reaction; it sets into motion a world of laws. It is a profound thing. It is hard to simplify. We think of story in these terms: this happened to this person, and then they did that, and then they got married and they were happy ever after. But that is talking about story in its smallest sense. In its largest sense, story begins a process of laws, destinies, responsibilities, chaos. Story is a primeval thing. A story is not something that just happens to us as human beings. When lightning strikes the side of a mountain, and a rock breaks off, that is story. There is story in the wind, there is story in the rocks, in continents, in continental shifts. We can speak of the story of the universe and its birth of stars. We can speak of collision and fusion. Story is something bigger than us. We are part of it, we tap into it. Story is cosmological force. Story is a god. Story is huge. We really have to transfigure our sense of what story is. We are narrow in our perception of story, and we have lost its secret magnitude. The very fact of story means that you are demarcating something. You have a sense of an ideal, you have a sense of the way you wish things could or should be. This carries already within it a moral universe, a world framed with all kinds of dimensions and boundaries. You shape a world when you begin a story. It's a significant thing. We are children in the realm and possibility of what story is and can be. It is not what E. M. Forster made it out to be. E. M. Forster made out story to be a rather primitive thing in the literary universe. "This happened and then that happened." You must excuse me; "this happened and then that happened"? "This happened" is the beginning of something awesome. Everything else follows from "this happened." A guy was going out one day, saw a coach, got into a fight with the guy who was in the coach, killed the guy, and then goes home, meets this woman, marries this woman, and lives happily ever after for about thirty years. And then one day, he is the king, and someone says, "Hey, the land is going to pieces." He says, "Well, what's that got to do with me?" "You're the king, do something about it." He tries to; things get worse. Then someone comes, "Well actually, you are connected to this problem. *You* are the problem." He says, "Me?" and then unravelling takes place and he finds that one day, when he set out and got into an argument with somebody, unbeknownst to him he had set into motion a whole universe that's going to affect his whole society and himself. Where does the story begin? We don't know its mysterious beginnings. Where does the story end? We don't know its mysterious resolution. Because it widens out, a pebble in an infinite lake with its circles, and touches all kinds of other lives and all kinds of other stories and gets involved in a grand complex mathematics of connections and interconnections. Excuse me: we're talking about something so awesome and mysterious here, so vast in its networks, that we are mere children in its possibilities. In the twenty-first century we'll be telling stories very differently.

Rowell: Were you describing *Starbook*?

Okri: [*Laughter*] This is not expected. Yes and no: let's just say that it is one thing to feel these things; it is another thing to find, or to be open to, the stories that enable one to touch the possibility of these larger stories. The implication of what you are saying, and of this conversation between us, is that a story is not a unitary thing: a story is a thing that cuts across time and dimensions and space. We need a new kind of storytelling. A story that began in Africa has its resonance and its worth in America, and all the way back again. And yet, this is a story of someone who woke up one morning. Do you get what I'm saying? The way in which we tell our stories therefore lies in direct relation to our acceptance, our perception, of the interconnection of things in life. If you think that we're living in a Copernican universe—not Copernican in terms of the stars, but Copernican in terms of one another, that is, I do something here, I get up, I shout, and the effect is just here—if you think that way, then your stories will have only this limited perception of effect or resonance. But you could have another perception, that when I get up and shout, stand up, get up, and SHOUT, that this shouting has a resonance outside this room—that it might affect my brothers, might affect folks in Nigeria, my relations, might affect folks in America, it might affect folks outside the wide rim of the world, not because of the shouting that I shouted here, but because of what the shouting did to me, what it did to you, and what it did to the dimensions in the air. Do you get what I'm saying? When we begin to think on a different level of resonance, we write differently. We have to. We cut across time and space. We become multilinear. We have to because we see destinies differently.

Rowell: I have no doubt that you are doing something very different from what we have seen in other West African writers—different it seems in the landscape from how you approach the world or how you invent a world. This is actually a comment, and yet I want to make it a question. How do you see yourself as a writer in relation to the traditions of West African writing? Where do you stand aesthetically and ideationally in relation to your literary precursors in Western Africa? What is the nature of your relationship to them? Or do you not view yourself as having a relationship to them at all? Or maybe what I am reading is an ethnic difference and the traditions of your ethnic group(s) as opposed to what I am used to seeing as Yoruba or Igbo. What is your relationship to West African literary traditions? To West African writers? I think that your answers to these questions will help us to read your work.

Okri: I think I'm best read freely.

Rowell: How do you mean?

Okri: One-to-one: me and you. Not me, you, and tradition, whatever that tradition is. What am I really saying? I am interested in the continents inside of the reader. I am interested in the freedom that dwells inside everybody, because without that freedom, I can't be free. This is a problem that folks . . . [*interruption by third party*] tell him to wait, tell him to wait for as long as it takes. What was the last thing I was talking about?

Rowell: To read freely. Yes, you want the reader to read freely. You want the reader to read one-on-one. You don't want the reader to read with you, the reader, the other traditions, but just the reader and the text, or the reader and you. And yet, if I were asking another question, that question would be this: isn't that reader going to bring to that text—you know that cliché of bringing all the world that he or she has experienced—what he/she knows to the text also?

Okri: Absolutely. But what they bring literally to the text depends on the relationship between their inner freedom, and what you talked about, the world they bring with them, the other texts, their readings, their ignorance. That relationship is the problem, the relationship between that freedom or lack of it and whatever it is you are. I begin with freedom. I really begin with freedom. I'm aware of boundaries, I'm aware of tradition, I'm aware of Achebe, Soyinka, I'm aware of all of that and I've read all of that. But to speak to another person in relation to what they already know, and to speak from myself, from what I already know, is not a true dialogue. But to go back to the beginning of our epic conversation—when we talked about art as containing in it the transformation of the past, some numinous destiny, some sense of where we are right now, some sense of our lost journey, some sense of where we could be going, some sense of our possibilities—when you go back to that original discussion we had about art, that for me is always a guiding intuition in the stories I tell. But to be able to do that, I have to begin in freedom. One starts at home, but when you take one step from home—which everybody does, that's part of being human—you take a step away from home, you leave the village: it's a story. You grow up, and you say one day, "Folks, there's a big world out there, and I'm going to go out there and be part of this story." You take a step out of that home one day. That is what the artist does. You take a step from out of home, whatever that tradition is, and you make your journey. And your journey is your contribution. You are either taking a step in freedom or in unfreedom. The step one takes is a step in freedom, which is to say, I'm not sure that one really knows consciously what it is that one is trying to do with each new story that one tells. I think something is being told through one, in relation to one's times and one's elective traditions. Truths can only come through you that can come through the holes in your spirit. In that sense, one's journey as an artist is mysterious. I wouldn't dare to define what I'm doing, because that wouldn't be evident for a long time afterwards. It took a hundred years for folks to be able to see what Melville was doing in *Moby-Dick*; I'm not so sure we see what Ellison was doing in *Invisible Man*. We have certain fixed perceptions of these things, but the truth is more mysterious than we sense it to be. What I'm really trying to say is this: I don't begin with definitions. I love tradition, but tradition is not destiny. Tradition is not the end of the journey. It is the place we set out from. Every new artist compels us to widen the perception of the tradition—to widen it and widen it until you simply don't have arms long enough to encompass it. That is one of the secret responsibilities of the artist. You've drawn the boundary of the world, you've drawn the map of the world and how it should be, and they come along and they make you have to redraw it. God knows, we are seriously ticked off that they make us do this, because we have invested a lot in this map: a lot of time, a lot of trouble. We've sat around, discussed it for a long time, we've come to an agreement, we've said, "This is the way that the world is. Folks, we can now go home and have some fun, drink, get on with our lives." Then someone comes along and says, "Excuse me. It's not quite like this." Then everyone has to go back around the table again and spend the next ten, twenty, thirty years redrawing it. This is seriously annoying, and society tends to punish the impudence of the little kid at the back of the class that says, "Excuse me, ma'am; excuse me, sir. That map doesn't have what Thomas Moore would call Utopia. That's a country too." That's what we do, because it is not healthy for us to have a fixed map of humanity, because humanity is not eternally fixed.

"The Book of Laughter and Forgetting": An Interview with Ben Okri

Nana Yaa Mensah / 2008

From *Wasafiri* 2, no. 2 (2008): 11–16. © Wasafiri. Reprinted by permission of Taylor & Francis Ltd. http://www.tandfonline.com, on behalf of *Wasafiri*.

The publication of a new work by Ben Okri is always an event of note; the appearance of his latest, *Starbook*, is especially so because this novel marks a departure by tackling themes that relate specifically to African slavery. The narrative consists of interlocking stories of a cast of characters, almost all of them unnamed, in an unspecified Arcadian idyll familiar from other novels by Okri such as *Astonishing the Gods* and *Dangerous Love*. However, despite the apparent placelessness, there can be no question from the outset that we are in Africa, probably on the Gulf of Guinea, and that we are witnessing life before colonization by the Europeans. Clearly, this is to be a big historical, and even political, novel and an act of imaginative reconstruction—but, as he points out when we meet in central London, the perspective is not quite so simple.

"The nature of what I wanted to do was so intangible that, with this one, there was nothing in my entire armory that could do it," he says. "I needed to go completely outside my range, my possibilities, myself."

The difficulty of the task he faced was how to layer a broad historical scope onto a love story that is also linked to a philosophical framework rooted in a tradition of early postindependence writing from Africa: an Achebe-like narrative, with a firm foundation in proverbial wisdom, but going well beyond the individual. There was also the challenge of how to do this in a way that, like *Things Fall Apart*, depicts the destructive encounter of African culture with "modern" ways of life and thinking without suggesting that the destruction is due entirely to that encounter. As the novel puts it early on: "How to tell the story of the tribe of artists that are my ancestors from the fragments that are gleaned from the sights seen in touching stones, or among the enigma of the stars . . ." (*Starbook* 142).

I wonder if he did not find even elements of inspiration in other writers' work. "No, nobody out there was any help to me," he says emphatically. "I think if there are two words that made this possible, the first one is humility." He is silent a long while, sipping coffee, and then continues: "The second is, I tapped into a huge sense of loss, because the book is primarily about loss and the transformation of loss. You know, we always talk and think about the slave trade and slavery as our people being taken from here to work over there and used to work to bring about conditions other people needed. We never think about it enough in terms of what was lost. When you take away hundreds of thousands of people, what has been lost here? What does it mean for the moral temperature of the world?"

A Wounded Psyche

"You know, in order to establish the true nature of the injustice involved in slavery, you first of all have to put back into the word 'slave' the complete dominion of humanity—of not just what it is to be human, but to have a home, a civilization, a life, a whole, rich world . . . . The other thing is just an outrage, an unrooted outrage, done to people. But when you see what the people were and what they could have been, it changes completely: it becomes more than outrage. That's what I wanted to do, to depict something of the dimensions of what we were.

"Why do that? Because I think, in a way, part of the problem of what we carry around today in Africa is not so much what was done to the people, as what was lost in the land. And we know that nothing is lost without there being fissures. You don't take away something without this emptiness collapsing on itself."

Would a fair comparison be with scar tissue pulling at a wound? "Exactly," he replies. "But this is more; this is like a hole that went right through the flesh and the body of Africa. And so there are ways in which Africa has been wandering around with holes in it—great big holes."

It is surprising to hear him sound quite so stridently political.

The novel itself shows how a nameless people suffer the erosion of their culture as they gradually become estranged from themselves. The alienation reaches its peak with the arrival of "the white wind," which literally and metaphorically blows through the continent, leading the people not only to question their way of life and to grow "sluggish in their reading of signs," but to lose everything they believe in. The loss takes the form of the erasure of a succession of gods—first of all the god of interpretation (the ability to delve beneath the surface), followed by the gods of harmony, memory, mysteries, love, thunder, and sacrifice, then all goddesses and, finally, the father god.

"We've focused on the slaves and the slave trading," Okri says, "but part of my focus on that and giving it its true perspective is this story about loss, the most profound kind of loss." He stops to think. "Is the loss permanent? Is it redeemable? To talk about these things we must first reconstitute something of the dimensions of what we were . . . . Then, maybe the gaps can be filled up, not with flesh, but with a higher psychic material."

Thus, *Starbook* reads in part rather like the ghost of a story, not just because it unfolds like film footage of the lives of people long dead and gone, but because it is a series of snapshots of absences—a negative image in which the spaces between people, or recurring "gaps in the forest," carry the most energy, the spectral presence of the characters coming a distant second.

The political frame makes an immediate impression. The nameless prince lives in an ordered kingdom with a modern system of democratic consultation, where his laughing father, the king, spends his time listening to his advisers and talking very little. The prince attempts to question his father, to talk directly to the people and to make proposals for more egalitarian ways of ordering affairs, inspired by the universal enthusiasm of youth. This is quite unlike the modern, corrupt politicians on the campaign trail in *Stars of the New Curfew*, for instance, and yet Okri makes no crude pretense of describing some paradise that is ruined only with the advent of a European political culture. Women play virtually no part in the political process: they are homemakers, and there is no queen to interfere by acting as counsel to her son, because the prince's mother died young. Equally, the king's trusted advisers are timeservers bent on hanging on to their sinecures and they later plot how to seize power for themselves. The most severe erosion of political trust starts to happen at the same time as young men and women begin to vanish mysteriously from the kingdom.

Okri describes the novel's structure as being starlike, narratives emerging from a center and radiating out in different directions. As his omniscient narrator plays trickster god with us, the story's dynamic grows ever more complex; correspondingly, the characters in this novel are not simplistically drawn. The roles they play are both very conventional, conforming to established hierarchies, and highly unusual, in the sense that every man has a right to have his opinions taken into account. The maiden with whom the prince falls in love lives in a parallel world occupied by the tribe of artists. Their art is not confined to aesthetic objects, but covers agriculture, war, literature, and sport. Their settlement is a space where people communicate publicly by leaving anonymous, gnomic works of art strategically positioned in unexpected places. It is a realm that seems much less hierarchical than the kingdom yet is organized according to a system of apprenticeships to master artists that requires total submission. This realm seems hermetically sealed, as does the kingdom, but there are repeated slippages, influences from foreign cultures cropping up in artwork, artists venturing abroad, or characters psychically undergoing a "through the looking-glass" experience that allows them to pass from one frame into the next, where time and space are both completely different and the same.

Perhaps this reflects Okri's own approach to entering the book's imaginative framework. He describes the process of writing the novel as "being like a serious fisherman": pulling it in after finding the central idea of the project—or rather, as he says, "letting it reel you in. It was very difficult. It's a book I had to listen for. I've never written anything in this way before."

Yet I wonder why it has been quite so long since his last novel, *In Arcadia*, which appeared in 2002. "[The difficulty] was partly the reason, and partly I just needed . . . ." His voice tails off, and then he confesses: "One can do one thing too much and lose one's way—or you can lose the taste or the feeling for it, all sorts of things. I wasn't losing it, but I was reaching a point where I thought, 'Ben Okri, I think you need to take a break. Just rest a bit, be human. Play, have fun. Read for pleasure, don't read for literature, don't read for writing. Just be.'"

He cleared his head by becoming a musician, entirely self-taught: "I took up the violin. So I'm playing the violin, badly! Not as good as Sherlock Holmes."

I profess astonishment. "I always throw myself in at the deep end," he says. "It's the only way I feel I can learn. Also, there's this thing I've always felt, which is that the quality of what you produce cannot be better than you. You are the measure of what comes out of you. If you want to transform your work, you have to first of all begin by transforming yourself."

Politics versus Art

We return to the question of restitution, perhaps unfairly, as the novel describes itself as "a magical tale of love and regeneration"—a story of regrowth, rather than repair. Does Okri not acknowledge that, although he knows of no previous attempts to address these matters in art, the very same thing has long been a political project for peoples of African descent, even if it has been pursued in a sporadic and inchoate way? Think of the Garveyite, the Rasta or the Black Power movements, or even today's middle-class African American migrants who move to Africa for the quality of life they can enjoy, or decide they would rather invest their skills and energy in the land of their forebears. Does he think that renegotiating what has been lost from Africa will also involve venturing out? Because, I remark, you could think of it as a process very much of looking inward.

"There are two processes that must be done. You must look inward, because if you don't, you don't know who you are inside the house . . . . All of this is part of what we are now, but what we've been has also got to be brought back into the spirit.

"That's why, in addition to what you were saying about the Garveyite movements and all the things that have been and are being done to recreate and enrich the African psyche, there has to be this cultural and artistic project of reclamation and transformation. Because the political project and the practical project need to be guided. Culture has always been one of the most evasive and powerful pillars of the African spirit. We're fundamentally a cultural people—which is to say that we're fundamentally a spiritual people. Is there anything that we do that is not touched with the resonance of art, one way or the other? Is there a justice or an interpretation that is made that is not in some way cultural? The organization of our homesteads is not done on an economic basis, it's done almost on a magical basis: the chief's hut in the center, the huts of the wives, all circular. The whole universe of the African spirit is one great, cultural matrix. What we're doing now is we're reversing it—we're starting with the politics first and forgetting the culture. And the culture we think of as additional accessories—bits of dances, bits of egungun. It's completely the wrong way round."

And he writes:

> [S]ometimes a people forget who they are, and lose their secret necessity, and start, slowly, to become strangers to themselves [. . .]. And then they dream up rituals, and fall into rites, and deeds, and enter into wars, and perform sundry

acts upon the stage of the earth to forget their forgetting, or to try to remember or redefine, or find who they were, and now should be. Such ventures are doomed. A skin shed is a skin shed. A loss is a loss. (*Starbook* 141)

Okri is adamant about the centrality of art to the regeneration of African lives. "Art is not a luxury. Art is a fundamental of culture, a fundamental part of humanity in society. Even before society, I think society came out of culture, rather than the other way round. Because first of all we have to . . . find a way to be comfortable with ourselves in this universe, and the act of doing that is culture. For us, culture, religion, spirituality, they're all intermingled. And part of the project of that is to say, 'Let's rediscover the inseparable aspects of all of the things that make us. Let's not compartmentalize them.' We never were separated. That's just one aspect of the project of *Starbook*. Maybe the other aspect is a deeply spiritual one."

Which brings us to the tricky question of religious belief. For all the oracular quality of his writing, his wandering ghosts and erring spirit children, despite his visionary tone, Okri has eluded categorization over what fuels the faith that runs like a clear thread through his novels. Given that spirituality is so tightly linked with the cultures in *Starbook*, you are tempted to hold it against him for not being more direct about the belief system that underpins the novel. It is almost as if he is proposing some sort of structure of a faith based on people's relationship with art and the natural environment and their relationship to other people. But he laughs off a question about religious submission, suggesting that I am trying to drive him to drink, and will only say, speaking broadly: "You've touched on something very deep and ambiguous and mysterious. Finally, the nature of art is to act as some sort of a bridge to the numinous. The purpose of art does not end in itself. I don't know any great work of art that says, 'End in me—stop there, just read the text . . . and that's it.' No. They're supposed to be things that throw us into the infinite."

So he will concede that his objective is transcendental.

"Yes. Great works of art don't begin and end in themselves. They are transparent to our yearning and enable us to grow through them into the infinity of ourselves. To ask questions about the mysteries that fringe human life. That's why they're endless. That's why we think about them for hundreds of years and can't get to the bottom of them. There is no bottom. It's like trying to get to the bottom of us. That's what they do: they throw the internal mirror back into the endlessness of us . . . .

"Your goal is understanding. First to understand is to fix it in this foursquare thing here." He points at the table. "In which case you've failed. The work has failed and you have failed. You have limited the work and yourself. That is why it must work by intuition, because understanding is a reduction of an infinite vibration into a finite form. That which goes beyond understanding is where our real quest begins. And whatever the quest is, where it starts is an incident. Where it takes you is its real purpose and point.

"So, the whole meditation on the majesty of the people before slavery and what happened as a result of that should start there, but where it should lead you is to a meditation about the perpetual loss and condition of slavery that exists as part of the human condition, every day and every year. It was done to a continent but we're still doing it. It hasn't stopped yet, because we've not examined what it means, we've not examined the abyss that we created as a result of it. Even though redemption is possible, to some degree, we still have to examine what was done and the nature of what was done, and what that relationship has with us as human beings, perpetually. So it's an ongoing parable of what we are. And slavery, as you know, is contemporary, still."

What It Is to Be Human

It would be too easy to typecast Okri as a humanist, but clearly one of his most urgent objectives is to restore humanity to the story of Africa.

"We've not given sufficient respect to what it is to be human," he says. "That is such a huge project. When we do that, I think that we simply wouldn't be able to do all of these things that we are doing to one another."

Starbook's faith in our ability to transcend life experience, coupled with an urge on Okri's part to immerse himself in the transformative powers of art and to show how culture is the motor of African societies, are what drive the novel. What has happened is important—which justifies the historical aspect of *Starbook*—but even more important is the endless destination, because there is always another destination beyond the one you think you have arrived at. On one level, it is a delightful story of love made good, but beyond that is the experience of the "white wind" sweeping through the land and snatching up the healthiest young men and women. And even beyond that, too, lies restitution. Yet this valuing of art's socially transformative powers above everything else is utterly at odds with the interpretation commonly imposed on African art, and particularly African fine art. The long-held critical assumption is that it is utilitarian, it serves a purpose, which may relate to faith or ritual, but the idea remains that African peoples create works of art for a specific purpose and that their culture is purely functional.

"It's completely wrong," he says bluntly. "That's part of the impulse of the book. It's impossible to create art only for a purpose. It's such a high impulse, and that impulse is the unavoidable basis of creativity, as part of what it is to be human. The minute that's there, it may seem to be that something is being created for a purpose, but the very act of what time does to that changes what the purpose is and what that work is.

"Look at many Greek vases—they're meant to contain wine. But you have these figures of Achilles, sometimes a nimbus, on the outside of them. After two thousand years, we've forgotten what their purpose is and they're still beautiful. The impulse is always bigger than what the purpose seemed to be at the time. That's what separates true works of art from artefacts. Critics tend to treat African art as artefacts, when in fact they are art in the highest sense of the word. The very proof of that is the way in which Western art was reinvigorated by its encounter with African art and its attempt to mimic its understanding of African art through Picasso, the cubists, the fauvists.

"That, if anything, shows something of the numinous power of art . . . . That was one of the most fruitful encounters that took place between the West and Africa, even though it didn't seem like it at the time. In that encounter, an alchemical change took place in the cultural condition of humanity. We both changed as a result of that, Africa and Europe.

"All of these things are looped in time. I have to deal in these big-time loops rather than the journalistic perception of things, because our phobias and art deal in a completely different time loop from economics and politics. It's the multiplicity that fascinates me," he enthuses, "the fact that finally, when it comes to the cultural matrix, is there really such a thing as African, European, Spanish? Isn't there one thing, really, which is the imagination, and beyond that the human spirit? Isn't it first of all from that place that we all really speak to one another? Rather than in conferences?" He corrects himself: "No, there's a higher place where it takes place, in dreams and sleep, in all of the things in which we are interpenetrated in being on this planet. That's highly contentious: it's only hinted at in the book. On a lower level, it's imagination and the human spirit, where it speaks in terms of culture. That kind of speaking is much better than the speaking we do with one another like this. But that precedes this. When that is done, this is easier. If you start with speaking first, it doesn't happen.

"So when you say faith . . . [i]t's because I've got enormous faith in the miracle of the human spirit. I see it all the time. One looks at history, one looks at how indestructible people are. Look at the slaves. They got taken over and what have they done? They have grown, in this barren condition in which they found themselves, and they're still growing. They've made themselves; they've not stopped being human. And all that is rich in them, broken and disguised here though it may be, is still being human and fertilizing the world. It's not stopped. We've not been destroyed by it. If that doesn't tell you about how extraordinary the human frame and the human spirit is, I don't know what does . . .

"I don't think we should be made despairing by the dreadful wars that rage across the continent, or by the famines that plague us. We should face those facts absolutely squarely, look at them but not be mesmerized by them or be rendered incapable of acting as a result of them. They're just facts. We've been there before. This is the meat and drink of our history."

Divide and Rule

It is his ability to telescope between the specific and the general that makes *Starbook* a more sober, but also more mature novel than some of Okri's earlier work, such as *The Famished Road*. Where the Booker-winning novel is a fast, swinging highlife number, *Starbook* is a moderately paced, mournful aria. And yet it is no tragedy. Humanity's strength may be epitomized in this narrative by the ability of the African spirit to transcend transatlantic enslavement—described obliquely, in the usual Okri style, in flashforwards and in an even earlier foreshadowing: the appearance of a strange statue of three men bound to a woman, heads bowed:

> It seemed like a suffering they bore as a sacrifice and purification for the continued history of humanity on earth. Only the abysmally great can bear such abhorrently great suffering. And the injustice of it, along with the hinted nobility of it, was what so broke the heart of the maiden who saw the work and was never the same again, as if she had been poisoned by a glimpse of her own destiny . . . . (*Starbook* 91)

"The business of slavery seems to be one of the endemic failings of humanity," he broods. "Why do we do it? Why don't we ask that question? What does it say about our perception of ourselves, and of one another? Finally, there are two things that strike me. One is that it comes from this sense that I am separate from you and that we're all divided on this planet. That dividedness is a fatal failure in human perception. That's what has given rise to most of our evils that we perpetrate on one another. But we're not divided; we're part of the same body, if only for the fact that we have the same sort of body . . . .

"I think the secret project of the book is to reawaken that sense of universal unity. Not divisiveness, not uniqueness—unity. Different, but united. If you go as far back as possible in the imagination and the history of all cultures, they all seem to have one thing in common: our creation myths, which all seem to suggest that we came from one place, or person, or group. I may say it's my place, you may say it's your place but . . . ."

"It's the same place?" I venture.

"Exactly. I think maybe that is it."

After such a positive interpretation of the book, I hesitate to revert to the question of tension, but how does he answer the putting down of African cultures by those who say they are out of time, backward and living in the Middle Ages? How does one even begin to address these disparities in senses of time?

"Well," he says philosophically, "there's something that the Vatican says: 'We think in terms of a hundred years.' Now, you journalists think in terms of one day. When I grew up, in my father's thinking and in the village, I had this feeling that Africa thought in terms of thousands of years. Time in Africa is very different from time everywhere else. Finally it's not really very relevant, the whole business of Western time and the way the West perceives Africa as being out of time. It's not going to change one thing. The transformation of things is going on at its own pace, in accordance with the way events unfold. Nothing can be done about that. Two thousand years ago the Romans came to Britain and thought they were ahead of the world in time. I mean, if you read commentaries of Caesar today, you have to smile. They're relevant in one sense: they're a record of what people felt, what people did. In another sense, they're not relevant . . . time gobbles that up."

As Okri writes:

> And many things were forgotten, even while they lived. The image of a dying prince was forgotten. The scandals were forgotten. The unease was forgotten, because it got worse, and therefore even more imperceptible. The tremors of art were forgotten. Rumours were forgotten. Suitors were forgotten. Purpose was forgotten. The way was forgotten . . . . And all this in the space of a dream, in no time at all, or all the time it takes for a people to be lost, to change, and then, one day, inexplicably, to vanish off the face of the earth, as if they never existed, or as if they had been taken away, as a whole, and repositioned in another place, another realm, another constellation in the universe. (*Starbook* 231)

"There is no final pause that stops," he says. "It's not possible. We're caught in a perpetual chain of cause and effect. No one is ever going to come along and say, this is how I want the whole world to be: stop, fix it in cement, no change ever again. It's not possible. Because the universe is outside the grasp of the whole of humanity put together. We're dealing in star time, star space, star dimensions. We're human beings in the body, a kind of minuscule thing amidst these great big causative powers that surround us and that we bring into motion with our dreams. I have to function on these two levels—on one that says this is what is happening to us, on another that looks and says, 'Oh well, this is just one of many histories.'"

Faith in Africa's Future

Okri's faith in things changing extends to what journalists love to refer to as "the problem of Africa."

"There's a wonderful thing Winston Churchill said," he recalls, "that some people stumble on a great discovery and they pick themselves up and carry on as if nothing had happened. It doesn't matter what's happened to you. All that counts is what you learn from it.

"We, as a people, have had a lot happen to us. I would say that we are hugely rich in what we're going to be able to do. I see our suffering as a great reservoir. It's already been manifest. In different parts of Africa we're slowly beginning to think, 'Okay, we did this. That was really stupid, wasn't it? Surely there's a better way of dealing with this? . . . Look, we did that when we were so stupid. It was a beacon of stupidity; there's no way we're going to make that mistake again. Enough is enough. From now on we're going to learn from this.' Europe had plenty of stupidities and mistakes that they learned from. Learned from. We're really, really rich in stupidities. Now is the harvest time, when we're going to reap from this great reservoir of our stupidities. The journalists are focusing still on the wars and the famines. I'm seeing the regeneration and the magic already happening. It's not dramatic, but it's happening."

He points to the examples of "our Mandelas," to South Africa shrugging off the legacy of apartheid, to Nigeria, "managing its imperfect form of democracy, the longest we've had since independence." Even of Zimbabwe, which he cites as an isolated case of dreadful misgovernance, he says confidently: "I see it as one of those great big beacons of stupidity that I talked about earlier—Mugabe and his cronies are not going to be there forever—inevitably it's going to change. And when it changes, that beacon of stupidity is going to be there, like the great Lighthouse of Pharos. That's how Europe changed. Bit by bit, by bit, by bit, slowly."

Doesn't he believe in the possibility of apocalypse?

"Africa is not going to wipe itself out. If anyone is going to wipe themselves out, it's other folks—they've got the means to do that. No, our condition is not as terminal as other people's. Our condition is messy, it's nasty, but it's not fatal. And behind all of this there is actually a greater wisdom at work in Africa. You don't see it, but it's there.... If there's one thing I could actually say is the most needed quality for looking at the way Africa is, I would say it's patience."

He points to Europe and remarks drily, "The Second World War is still within living memory. The beacon of stupidity can raise its head anytime, anywhere. We're not free from it. It's a never-ending story of the battle of human enlightenment against human stupidity ... As long as there are ten stupid people in a village, that village is in trouble. It takes one stupid person to get a machete, go to the next person's door and hack someone's head off. And for another stupid person to say, 'I want vengeance.'"

Grab before You're Grabbed

Although many of *Starbook*'s dramatic cruxes come from the clash of such binary oppositions, the author insists on going beyond these confrontations. I particularly wonder about the tension he presents between the prince and the Mamba, the master wrestler with whom he competes for the maiden's favor. The Mamba wants her largely because he values the importance that being attached to her will bring him. Is there a contradiction between Okri's idea about the supremacy of art and other ideas in the novel about the primacy of the collective? How does he reconcile his transcendental vision with economic facts? How do you transcend the greedy logic of individualism? Does it matter whether the greed comes from a sense of otherness ("us against them") or one of sameness ("let me grab before my brother next door does")?

"Yes, that is the beauty of our heritage—that we're both universal and specific. We're both individual and collective. We're both infinite and finite, big and small. We're both a people and a person."

He sighs. To him, he explains, the only outcome of individualism is "universal genocide." He expands: "I think that duality, for as long as we're alive, is unavoidable. But I think that duality still has to be guided by a sense of what we really are. There's no project complete without a proper consideration of the dimensions of what we are. We have to know what we are as individuals inside but also as a culture, as a people. Our destination is fatally connected with that. You put in a wonderful dynamic between the individual and the collective. The individual drives on the collective, but the collective also carries the individual. One does it and the whole does it. When the whole does it, today it's Europe, tomorrow it's Africa, the day after that it's the whole world. Don't you sense that this is happening already? That the West is burdened by its having successfully overarrogated the resources of the planet itself?"

For Okri, the process is cyclical and, indeed, cosmological. "There is an irresistible process of evolution," he says. "You would have to destroy everything on this planet and all of us completely for that to stop. It's an alchemical thing. We're all in this great big bowl called the earth. And we are fatally doomed, in the most beautiful way, to interact with one another, to fight, to hate, to love. Don't you see how history seems to be accelerating? That it's not possible any more to keep peoples so rigidly apart and to keep this homogeneity so completely intact? Every day, migration is changing all these hallowed corners, these places that wanted to keep themselves pure and on top. There's nothing you can do about it."

The specific thing that propels the intermingling of people's lives is neither globalization nor the simple ability to travel, but "some magical, indefinable thing in the human spirit. We're just immeasurably better than our condition. We just are. There's no other way to put it. If you want to know what the real impulse is, it's the human spirit. It's unstoppable. It's going up. It has to. Even when it does the most incredibly stupid things, what does time do to it? Time covers over those vast graves, all those places that blood was spilt on. Vegetables and plants and trees just grow there. You come back there one thousand years later and you would not believe that this is the place where ten thousand Greeks perished. Here is the land where more than one hundred thousand Trojans died. You wouldn't recognize it, because time has done its work. One cannot deny the realism of things, but I think that it's equally stupid to deny the magic of things."

Points of Enchantment

Sarah Fulford / 2008

From *Resurgence* 251 (Nov./Dec.) 2008: 48–50. All rights to this article are reserved to The Resurgence Trust. Reprinted by permission.

In 1991, the youngest writer to win the Booker Prize, for his epic novel *The Famished Road*, Ben Okri was heralded as the literary "spirit-child" of Nigeria. Born in 1959 in Minna, Northern Nigeria, he spent his early years in London, returning to Nigeria with his family in 1967.

Okri's early fiction is haunted by the political violence that he witnessed during the civil war in Nigeria. Returning to England to read literature at the University of Essex, he worked for the BBC World Service and subsequently published many novels. His poems are included in *Mental Fight*, the title of which is taken from William Blake's "Jerusalem," and his essays bearing an equally radical theme are found in *A Way of Being Free*.

Okri was a fellow in creative arts at Trinity College, Cambridge, and is a fellow of the Royal Society of Literature. Committed to freedom of speech, he is vice president of the English Centre of International PEN, was presented with the Crystal Award for outstanding contribution to the arts and to crosscultural understanding by the World Economic Forum, and received an OBE in 2001.

Recently awarded an honorary doctorate of literature at the University of Exeter, Okri confessed one of his reasons for attending was that he has always loved the Devon landscape. His forthcoming book is *Tales of Freedom*. He lives in London.

Sarah Fulford: Who or what inspires you and your writing?

Ben Okri: Not any one person, but rather music, Nature and paintings. These mediums provide me with spiritual sustenance. No writer can help me in the places I've got to go! If a work of art is truly good, it frees you. It's a matter of freedom. It's the freedom of the art and the artist—it's the courage of their spirit—it's the spirit behind their work—that's what is of value to me.

Picasso says of Cézanne, "Of course, what fascinates us about Cézanne is his anxiety: not the actual pictures, but Cézanne's anxiety." So you have to ask the question, not "What on Earth is Cézanne's anxiety?" but "What does Picasso see as Cézanne's anxiety?" Anxiety is a strange word to use. I sense what he's sensing and it's untranslatable. Is it an anxiety about painting? Is it an anxiety about being? Is it a particular kind of mood that he's trying to create? Is it his own temperamental anxiety about life in the face of the impossibility of creation? It's almost as though Picasso is saying, "If Cézanne is so anxious, what am I doing being so complacent?"

Fulford: You mention Nature as a major inspiration and you regard environmental destruction as a form of spiritual destruction. The physical world and the spiritual world are always linked in your work, and the way you celebrate nature and spiritual freedom makes me think of you as a twenty-first-century William Blake. Does his poetic and political philosophy inspire you?

Okri: Yes, there are places where Blake's circle and my circle interconnect. Blake interests me, but there are many ways of talking about life, history, time and the spirit of society. You can talk about society from the point of enchantment. But our way of *experiencing* these things has been handed down to us by tradition. We greatly diminish the dialogue between ourselves and the lives that we live when we limit the possibilities of these rings of experience. It's like being able to see twenty colors, but we've imposed upon ourselves and our children only three or four colors and banished the rest.

Fulford: Do you think that limiting our vision is just a way of coping with the multiple possibilities of life?

Okri: Nature has already sorted out the limits. Why do we have to impose more? It's as if we don't trust the process of our own evolution. We come along and narrow it all even more, when, in fact, everything in life and in nature is actually inclining towards evolution, more sensitivity, more possibility, more shades of things. That is evolution, not chaos. That's what I'm talking about—the richness of experience. So why do we crush our increasing sensitivity to the richness?

Fulford: In the past, you have questioned "realist fiction," which concerns itself with "ordinary life" and gives the impression that it faithfully reflects real life. In your view "realist fiction" tricks us into believing that what we read is real, and "realism" lures us into thinking that our view of the world is a fact that is entirely independent of our perception of it. In this way, "realist fiction" limits the multiple possibilities of storytelling, and a belief in "realism" imposes limits on the many different ways in which we can experience and understand the world.

Okri: We're going back to some primitive form of consciousness if we carry on insisting that realist fiction is anything like reality. I think our narratives have to evolve. We cannot be doing the same things for two or three hundred years. We have limited the possibilities of narrative. And that's because of the limitations of realism. But the possibilities of narrative are wide open. If you start a truly new novel you should have no idea where this is going to take you or what's going to unfold. I feel we've come to the end of the old mode of telling stories. If we carry on, we'll get to a point where we stop listening. The future of the novel is the end of realism as we have known it. We have to find a new kind of harmony along different narrative lines.

Fulford: You use the word "harmony." You often draw on musical metaphors.

Okri: Music has its own narrative. I see narrative as part of the condition of life. The rhythms of life are like a string of narratives. Imagine what jazz first sounded like to people trained only in classical music. Then translate that into the future of narrative. I'm not saying it's like jazz. I'm saying there is a loping beat, where the beat can be longer or shorter or combined in ways we do not expect, that does not follow a certain rhythm. There's a perfect rigor and beauty to it.

Fulford: So is it the difference between playing to the beat of a metronome or not?

Okri: Yes. Just like in a realist novel when a new character enters and you know exactly where they are going to fit into the beat of the narrative. But you never engage with that which you already expect. Pleasure is lost when you can anticipate the twist in the tale or when you anticipate how you are going to be surprised. It's bad for the wiring of the brain!

Fulford: So art must surprise and defamiliarize us. The writer must break away from his or her tradition.

Okri: Yes. Maybe we should just talk about undiscovered intentions in various writers and thinkers. We've not looked at what they themselves are saying specifically that is possibly quite counter to the age that we've put them in.

For example, take Manet and Cézanne. What is the similarity in their exploration? Cézanne is interested in Poussin, and Manet in Vermeer. And yet we group them together. And that grouping denies the revolution of each one's specific thought and rebellion. We have to declassify. Writers should stop thinking of themselves as British writers, German writers or French writers. That too destroys a tradition because they read their tradition for what they expect it to be and then they proceed to reproduce its features.

Categorization destroys writing. When you try to write creatively, the thing that gets in the way is that each time you write something you think to yourself, "Yes, that comes from so and so," or, "That comes from this tradition or this ideology," and this just destroys any attempt at originality. Maybe the writer has to get rid of that self-consciousness or the tendency to always anchor what is being done within a tradition.

Fulford: Yes, but we are taught to anchor, aren't we?

Okri: Well yes, it's certainly part and parcel of a Western education.

There are two things: one is that you react against something and in so doing you end up being part of what you're reacting against so you're still reproducing the limitations and caught within them. Then the other is to leave tradition alone and do your own thing and move and fly and travel and continue.... I'm inside and outside realism. I think the realist novel limits reality. Realism is less than reality.

Fulford: Where does your critique of realism come from?

Okri: As far back as I can remember. Since I was a child. I had an awareness that life is not what they told us that it is. From very early on I've been trying to find out the difference between the life we are told about and life as it really is. Something seemed wrong. Why are they making us see life like this when it is more? And if there really is more, then the possibilities are more. So why are they narrowing it?

It's as if we are birds and they're telling us to walk and I'm saying, "Hang on a minute—we're supposed to fly. Why are folks telling us not to fly? What does flight mean? What's the world like when you fly? Is it a different world?"

Everywhere this extra dimension of life has slowly been exterminated in the minds of people, in the minds of our children. Then they start to appear in different forms in science, but given different names. Then these extra dimensions don't have any relationship with our everyday living realities. But they're unavoidable. Light waves from stars are passing right through our bodies. If we acknowledge the fact that this place is not what we think it is and we say, "Well, we can't deal with this because it is too much, so let's agree not to," then that's fine. That would be a voluntary act. But that's not what we're doing. What we're saying is, "Nothing else is except this." Yet our lives are affected by those other dimensions, other realities. So how can we explain the way our lives go when we're affirming one thing and denying another, and the things that we're denying are affecting us? These are the things that have to be brought into our stories and into our poems.

Fulford: Art and the aesthetic can bring some of that back by questioning our habitual modes of understanding, questioning our beliefs.

Okri: Only a new aesthetic. Not the old. Only the new. I have not been read yet. The things going on in my work are not being seen.

Fulford: A new aesthetic demands a new form of criticism.

Okri: A new criticism has to have an acceptance of the fact that the old way can't serve the world anymore. Unfortunately we are still dealing with old maps. Outdated maps. These are maps where, if you travel over them, you come to an edge and fall over. These old maps just don't work anymore.

Fulford: You talk a lot about the freedom of the writer, but do you not think that there are some constraints on you as a writer from the publishing market, the whole culture industry? How can you possibly have any freedom as a writer?

Okri: Well, as to whether you can publish it the way you want, that's another thing: it depends on whether you want to publish it and have a huge big success and make lots of money and sell millions and millions of copies. It depends on what you want to accomplish. If it's the freedom you want then you can have that freedom and nobody can stop you having that freedom. All you need is paper, a pen and a door that you can lock, and you can have all the freedom you want. That's the last freedom left in the world. You don't have the same great freedom in the theatre anymore because of directors, staging and costs. Literature is the last true freedom that you have left in the world. The way the world is going right now we're dependent on those people who realize that freedom and use it with great responsibility.

Interview with Ben Okri

Rosemary Gray / 2011

From the *Journal of Literary Studies* 28, no. 4 (2012): 4–13. Reprinted by permission of Rosemary Gray, Professor Emerita, Department of English, University of Pretoria. Orcid: 0000-0002-6583-4319.

The interview was held in February 2011. The original version was shortened and edited by Ben Okri in 2022 with Rosemary Gray's permission.

Rosemary Gray: I'd like to begin by asking you to respond to my perception that throughout your oeuvre there seems to me to be a single guiding principle, a deeply embedded philosophical credo, if you like. Of course I could be mistaken, being driven in my reading of your work by my own horizons of expectation (to borrow a term from Robert Jauss). In other words, I may be being misled by my own reception aesthetics. The principle I refer to is, I believe, nowhere better expressed than towards the end of *Songs of Enchantment* when, from the silence of "unblindedness," Azaro's father, in conversation with his son, a "spirit-child," an *abiku*, is moved to muse that "[t]he light comes out of the darkness" (1993: 287). This is a catalyst for two other questions and for a request I should like to make, but perhaps you'd like to respond to my contention about your guiding principle before I pose the two questions that arise out of this one. Am I on the right track in attributing an innate optimism to you?

Ben Okri: I wouldn't call it optimism. It's more like realism. However, it is important how one defines realism. Realism takes in what is seen, felt, touched, tasted. But the primordial African spirit views reality from a wider spectrum. It is informed by the metaphysical sense embedded in all the great ancient traditions. This leads to a number of essential questions. What constitutes one's reality? Is one's reality true only for the individual? Is our reality limited to what we are taught to perceive?

A piano with five keys is a reality. But if we include all the keys, the white keys and the black keys, this is a different reality. It seems our sense of reality is based on our cultural perception of the keyboard of life. Using a fuller keyboard, Azaro reveals a new perception of what constitutes the nature of reality. Is reality outside oneself or fatally linked to human sensibilities? How does one construct reality? One cannot truthfully tell an African tale according to Jane Austen's reality or an early-nineteenth-century English tale according to an African reality. Dialogue with the West is somewhat complicated because perceptions of reality are not universal.

Gray: Is there an element of the Platonic notion of the "real" and the "really real" here?

Okri: Yes, but also the Scandinavian concept of reality. I can draw it for you. [This Okri did in my copy of *Starbook*.]

[...]

Gray: The bond between father and son is so tragically wanting in Achebe's seminal African text—*Things Fall Apart*. In your novels, especially in the *Famished Road* trilogy, this relationship is robust. I am wondering if this Telemachian aspect speaks of a healed or healing lineage in the postcolonial consciousness. Would you care to comment?

Okri: That is a difficult question. The father-son relationship is a mirror of the quality of freedom in society. Parental relationships mirror society. They are microcosms of the strategies of self-definition and emotional stability. In a brutalized society, the father-son relationship is distorted.

Gray: Yes, of course. Maya Angelou deals extensively with this aspect in her novels, doesn't she—especially in *I Know Why the Caged Bird Sings*? Damaged souls lead to a cyclic pattern of disaster.

Okri: Yes, the family is the intimate theatre of society. Novelists have sensed that this microtheatre reflects the larger social tensions. *The Famished Road* shows the extent to which a transition has taken place.

Gray: Also arising from my personal reception aesthetics is the question of an interrelationship between what the *abiku* child perceives as the wisdom emanating from the silence of his dad's regaining of his sight, his "unblindedness," and an Akashic still point. Is there a symbiosis between these two moments of enlightenment? Does such enlightenment spring from what Jung has termed the collective unconscious, or what Taoism calls the Akashic record, or am I yoking two disparate notions together by violence (to borrow loosely from Alexander Pope)?

Okri: A thread runs through all cultures. In ancient traditions certain individuals going through great suffering or intense revelation sometimes have experiences outside the common mode into something higher. Ancient Greek heroes visit the underworld. In Scandinavian sagas the indescribable experience happens outside the dome of the world. Most traditions have this. It is the breaking out that is the grandeur of tragedy.

Gray: Its cathartic potential?

Okri: In many cases suffering leads to enlightenment. They are connected. We are defined by the depths.

Gray: Staying with political issues, a prevalent argument (supported by historical evidence) holds that white colonial thieves stole African land by force; then imposed both Western civilization and the Christian religion upon the peoples. Works by several Black Africans (Achebe, Armah, Emechetta, Ngugi, Marachera, et al.) understandably write back to the imperial center. Your works and those of Wole Soyinka, in contradistinction, seem to go a step further in pushing aside any attempts to colonize either the mind or the heart of Africa. Would you like to comment on this "newer" creative approach?

Okri: The poetic axis is there. Chewing over the imperial or the colonial is well dealt with by others. Too much of this allows it to define our narrative. But there is a need to show aspects of the continuum. We are not defined by history. The human spirit is limitless and our job as writers is to unveil. It's not just the pistol shots in an opera, to adapt a phrase by Stendhal. Colonizing the mind is implied as a sort of backdrop, but this does not define the text. Soyinka and I are not sidestepping the issue. We have taken the punch and then carried on.

There is a profound responsibility of writer and readers. What you produce and what you interminably examine eventually becomes defining. The redemption of the human spirit occurs when we throw light on the ravages of history. When we illuminate, combat, and transcend.

[...]

Gray: In an extension of the previous question, Achebe's *Things Fall Apart*, Coetzee's *Waiting for the Barbarians*, and Conrad's *Heart of Darkness* seem to be three pillars of the stage on which the revelation of imperial/colonial savagery is based. Your work, however, appears to fly above these concerns while, at the same time, being predicated upon such truths. To what extent is this part of a conscious artistic strategy?

Okri: The music of an artistic tradition! The older artists start a phrase, and we coming behind take it in our own direction, responding to the necessities of our times. To use some other metaphors, our ancestors cut a path and we cut further paths. They carve out a foundation, and we build on it. We receive an energy from them and carry on. The process is both cyclical and vertical.

The duty of the artist is to extend the boundaries.

Gray: In his acceptance speech (December 7, 2010: 11), Mario Vargas Llosa points to the inherent paradox of storytelling. This most recent recipient of the Nobel Prize for Literature asserts that

> [l]iterature is a false representation of life that nevertheless helps us to understand life better, to orient ourselves in the labyrinth where we were born, pass by, and die. It compensates for the reverses and frustrations real life inflicts on us, and because of it we can decipher, at least partially, the hieroglyphic that existence tends to be for the great majority of human beings, principally those of us who generate more doubts than certainties and confess our perplexity before subjects like transcendence, individual and collective destiny, the soul, the sense or senselessness of history, the to and fro of rational knowledge.

Would you please respond to this view of fictionmaking?

Okri: I don't know about "false." Perhaps the word was lost in translation from the Spanish. It is not false. It is not the truth. There is a paradox. It is both. Art is a fiction that tells the truth. Life is imponderable so one cannot tell the whole truth. A reproduction on a stage, for instance, at once demarcates a new dimension. Literature is abstract and it is a guise. We bring it alive with the infinite permutation of our being. This is the magic of literature. How you perceive this magical transformation is central to writing. Literature creates a parallel reality, a magic mirror. We only see things when they are reflected. We perceive by translation. Literature is one further step in this translation.

[. . .]

Gray: Your writing celebrates the mythic and spiritual dimensions of the eternal African soul. Is this a reflection of an abiding interest in Taoist philosophy or is this attributable to your own Urhobo/Igbo consciousness or perhaps to perennial theology or to what Mircea Eliade calls "the myth of eternal return"? To what extent am I correct in the supposition that what you propound in your nonfictional writings and, essentially, in the novels *Astonishing the Gods* (1995) and *Starbook* (2007) is a freeing of the fetters of the past and a visualization of universal justice "through careful spiritual and social evolution" (*Astonishing the Gods* [1995] 1999: 72)? Is the frame of reference eclectic?

Okri: I am very crosscultural. This is not eclecticism. I am fascinated by similar threads that runs through the world's mythologies and philosophies. They appear to come from the primordial tradition. For example, visits to the underworld and trickster gods occur in literatures from very many parts of the world.

This is not only because human nature is one. It is more profound than that. These threads running through so many cultures give me a sense not of diversity, but of one source, a unity. Myths tell parallel stories. They enrich one another. The future of the race depends on paying more attention to these streams that fascinate us and enrich the quality of life.

[...]

Gray: The contest of the individual to gain and enjoy integrity is celebrated in a kaleidoscope of spiritual colors and forms in your work. At its first level, this contest seems to be the struggle to rise above the shadow of the governors general that tried to cow the bodies and minds of so many Africans. Higher up, this fight or flight for inner illumination takes us to a universal level of existential truth. How far would you agree with this estimation?

Okri: In many ways, this is a misperception. One book cannot define my work. I have journeyed through the reality of life in my early novels to a spiritual dimension. So this does not reflect the full dimension of my work. I would prefer to say that I fly with, not above. Life is a crucible. My quest is to attempt to touch all points: the human being in love, in crisis, in society, suffering, becoming, transforming, and so on. Sometimes I try to use the whole keyboard, to touch all dimensions in one novel. It is necessary to point to another aspect, to adopt a circular approach.

Gray: I have argued that your project is how to turn spiritual exhaustion into spiritual energy; how to distil human experience, how to "domesticate infinity" (to use your own words from *Mental Fight*) [see Rosemary Gray, 2007, "Domesticating Infinity in Ben Okri's *Mental Fight* and *Astonishing the Gods*," *English Academy Review* 24, no. 1, May 2007, 85–101]. The guiding spirit seems to be a universalist one in that you at once conflate the intellectual currents of German philosophy (with its will to transgress the boundary between the human and the divine) with the Judeo-Christian tendency to confront almost without mediation the problems of the absolute and its promises, and to move beyond this to a return to Arcadia, to a Blakean song of innocence. Please comment on this view.

Okri: African literature has a preponderance of the historical and the social because of its history. But it is also necessary to draw attention to something like *The Divine Comedy*. There should always be an attempt to tease out all dimensions. Writers ought to remind people of this—ought to enrich the interpretation of the hieroglyphics of life and history.

Gray: Many of your novels track self-development in the path of the traditional *Bildungsroman*, but straightaway one pulls back from that conclusion to consider whether you have not brought into being a unique genre of the novel—the *enlightenment novel*. Developing or becoming is not enough. "To be," we need light from within. We need, like your Azaro's dad and the classical Tiresius, to be blind in order to see! To what extent would you agree or disagree with this estimation, this attempt to pinpoint an emergent genre?

Okri: I like the term. It's interesting. *Astonishing the Gods* and *Starbook* are essentially books that aim at the enlightenment of the human spirit. It has been done in poetry—to ask questions in a nonreligious sense about the evolution of the human spirit. Is there something in all the myths? Myths and philosophy need to be part of the novel—not in a stream-of-consciousness sense but marrying the synchronic and the circular.

Gray: As well as the diachronic?

Okri: Yes, it has to do with ways of seeing. Is it possible that the human spirit can take a leap, become enriched? What will the implications for this be for the novel? If we strive for some transcendence would we not be better writers, better teachers?

Ben Okri: Interview

Saskia Vogel / 2011

From *Granta*, April 7, 2011. Reprinted by permission of Saskia Vogel.

Ben Okri grapples with deep, elemental issues in his latest book, *A Time for New Dreams*. With this series of "poetic essays," the Booker Prize–winner and one of *Granta*'s Best Young British Novelists employs a unique style to elucidate his ideas about the modern world. He illustrates how the economic meltdown and environmental catastrophes have brought us to a crossroads. *Granta*'s Saskia Vogel spoke with Ben about his new take on the essay form, his love of Montaigne and whether his new book represents a manifesto.

Saskia Vogel: The essays in your collection, *A Time for New Dreams*, are redolent with stirring observations on poetry, childhood and other themes. How did you come to write this new book? Were you writing for a specific reader?

Ben Okri: I tend to write books of essays with a theme running through them. It takes a while for the theme to coalesce for me. It can sometimes be years before I know that certain pieces of writing resonate and belong together. But I am always listening.

My first collection of essays, *A Way of Being Free*, coalesced around the idea of freedom, but it was more an attitude, an orientation even. It was generously received and it took me a while to think I could say something beyond that. *A Time for New Dreams* is not a collection of essays in a normal sense. Essays are usually a full exploration of an idea and they give evidence and quotations along the way. That was too laborious for what I was trying to do in this book. I felt a need to bring about a marriage of forms and was interested in finding the place where poetry and the essay meet, which is why *A Time for New Dreams* is subtitled "poetic essays." I sense that poetic essays, or what I tried to do in this book, should be an essay with the brevity and spring of poetry. The astonishing thing about poetry is that it leaps to place itself having already done all the thinking and imagining required and gives you the fruit of that meditation. That is what I wanted with this collection.

I imagine a reader who, like me, is a bit exasperated with the accumulation of the follies of our times, someone ready for a new way of looking, thinking and being; someone who combines youth and experience, idealism and realism. Someone who isn't afraid to dream but also is not afraid to roll up their sleeves and participate in the tough magic of life.

Vogel: In many of the essays—"The Romance of Difficult Times," for example—you number the paragraphs, some of which are as short as a single line. Other essays, such as "Photography and Immortality," take a more standard prose form. How do you decide on the structure of your texts?

Okri: I find that the structure emerges from the idea itself. Sometimes an idea can almost become too luxuriant in its expression and you need a structure, not to tame it, but to arrive at what, for me, is the ideal in the form of the compressed essay. This gives an idea of expressiveness combined with restraint, power held back by form, intensity that's not allowed to explode all over the place but to have a pouncing feel. And only the right form will do that.

Every piece ought to have something of the quality of a living thing—a slight quality of immeasurability—and only in its true form can it achieve this. Also, I like brevity of thought. There are few things more powerful in writing than a strong thought, whether a thesis or antithesis, expressed briefly. It is a paradox contained in a nutshell. I like powerful small units, so the aphorism threads its way through this volume.

There are these varied forms as the book is also structured round an idea of a suite, with a leading melody running through it—the melody of childhood. This is the foremost melody because, for most of us, childhood was a period of our most intense and furious dreaming. The title, *A Time for New Dreams*, is just a hint that it would be good to recover that dreaming in adulthood and to have that elasticity of imagination in our adult years. So the melody of childhood is the keynote, running against other melodies of politics and censorship.

Vogel: I felt an echo of Milan Kundera's *Art of the Novel* in your book. Do you feel *A Time for New Dreams* is in dialogue with certain other texts?

Okri: First of all, it is lovely that you felt Kundera's presence and at least some sort of dialogue with *The Art of the Novel*. Kundera is also inclined towards the aphoristic and the clearer, most direct statement—rather than endless exposition.

I have always loved the essay form and it is one of the forms I fell in love with very early on as I read my way through my father's library. I developed a real affection for great English essays of eighteenth century. But my chief affection has to be for the essays of Francis Bacon, which have an extraordinary combination of brevity and the highest thought. He is unmatched in the way in which he can say so much in such a short space. He boiled these essays down over years to such a point that people who read them at the time, his wife included, just couldn't make out what he was saying. They were so gnomic. This is the impact of the poetic on the essay form. It is the fruit, the distillation, not the whole journey.

The complete opposite of Bacon, I also love the essays of Montaigne—who is more expository and fluid, as he takes his time and wanders through classical antiquity. He loves his Greek and Roman authors, and quotes liberally—and he always expresses more uncertainty.

Between Bacon and Montaigne is something of where my feelings lie. Although I quoted from other writers in my early years, I am not a big fan of citing other people too much. I now think that if you have something you have thought about and want to share with folks, you need to say it yourself and find the best way to say it. People can always go back and read the old masters themselves.

Vogel: You write: "Beauty leads us all, finally, to the greatest questions of all, to the most significant quest of our lives." This transports me back to the first essay, "Poetry and Life." How do poetry and beauty mingle in their purposes, and in their effects on people?

Okri: Whenever we use the word beauty or we feel it, it comes from a sense of something indefinable. The mind can't quite pin down what it was that created that emotion or feeling. It is intangible; a poignant and haunting feeling that reaches places in you that you can't grasp or touch. It is as if some sleeping self wakes for a moment and expresses a note of wonder at something. It is that note of wonder that does it. Suddenly you become aware that you are more than what you thought you were. You feel a certain sweet inwardness, suddenly sense that the house has more rooms in it than you thought. That is what poetry does. That is what beauty does.

Vogel: You write poetry, essays, short stories, novels . . . . How do you choose how you will tell your stories?

Okri: Before a novel is born in the mind of the writer, it isn't a novel. Before a short story is conceived, it isn't a short story. A poem is often an incomplete swell of feeling, or maybe even just a beat that latches on to a wandering theme. The point I am trying to make is that, before they become what they are, all these forms are an insubstantial swirl of a mood inside us. How often has the mood or an idea of a short story become a novel?

Or the mood or idea of a novel become a short story? It is all in its original, precreative state. This becomes the germ of an idea, and depending on its inner potential for drawing all sorts of related elements in one consciousness, it will take a certain form. Which form this is depends on the inner magnetism of the idea itself. So I stress the idea of listening—you hear an idea, but what is it? The form of a thing doesn't reveal itself in the import of its creation, or even in the nature of its unfolding. Sometimes things are grown way beyond their destiny and sometimes things are undernurtured and abbreviated. So I think one of the most difficult things in a writer's life is knowing what a thing ought to be.

Vogel: To what extent do you feel *A Time for Dreams* is a manifesto?

Okri: I don't think it is. A manifesto is too definite, too deliberate. I am working with suggestiveness, with hints and orientations. In a way it is a cubist text because I am wandering round the different facets of this big subject—what it means to be where we are now, and how we are going to leap from this place to our new place with full consciousness and intelligence. It is more like a preparation for this new foundation—like cleaning our eyes so we can see clearly; like limbering up or toning the mind in preparation for the courage I feel we will need for these new times. We are at some kind of crossroads, and many, many of the old dreams are exhausted or are proving, one by one, to be moribund and severely limited in what they can give us. And we can't go on carrying those old dreams.

The Mysteries of the Word: A Conversation with Ben Okri

Anderson Tepper / 2011

From *Tin House* 49 (Fall 2011): 37–45. Reprinted by permission of Anderson Tepper.

"In the beginning there was a river. The river became a road and the road branched out to the whole world. And because the road was once a river it was always hungry." So begins Ben Okri's wondrous, sprawling 1991 Booker Prize–winning novel, *The Famished Road*, which follows Azaro, a "spirit-child," on his adventures through a violent, phantasmagorical African netherworld. It was a masterful achievement and went on to form a three-part cycle with *Songs of Enchantment* and *Infinite Riches*. Celebrating its twentieth anniversary this year, *The Famished Road* remains a critical bridge between the first wave of African writers—Chinua Achebe's *Things Fall Apart* marked its own fiftieth anniversary in 2008—and an astonishingly varied younger generation, from fellow Nigerians Chimamanda Ngozi Adichie, Helon Habila, and Chris Abani to the Kenyan Binyavanga Wainana, the Congolese Alain Mabanckou, and others. (Okri was also instrumental in founding the Caine Prize for African Writing in 2000, which helped launch many of these writers.)

But it would be misleading, and incomplete, to view Okri solely in relation to contemporary African writing. Okri is much more—he is a world writer, sure, but also something of a cosmic voice. His stories, poems, and novels in the years since *The Famished Road* trilogy have become increasingly spiritual and fablelike, dreamscapes stripped down to their essences. He has experimented with form, too, inventing such enigmatic hybrids as "stokus" and "poetic essays," and even dabbled in twitter poetry. In person, Okri exudes an unabashedly poetic approach to life, as well, as if the doors of perception were swung permanently open. We met at last May's PEN

World Voices Festival—it was the first visit to New York by the London-based author in nearly fifteen years—and began a free-flowing conversation that continued by phone over the next several months. It was a revelation to hear Okri dig for deeper meaning and connections in his long, winding journey as a writer; his belief in the magical power of words recalled for me those of a character from his early story collection *Incidents at the Shrine*: "I dreamed of several silk-yards of myths and realities and enchantments with which to remake the cracked music of all the wretched people."

I. The Road Less Traveled

Anderson Tepper: Tell me about your experience returning to New York last spring after such a long time. How did that come about?

Ben Okri: Well, for some years now, PEN had been trying to get me to come to New York for the festival, but the timing hadn't been right for me. Partly because of this whole aversion to flying that I have. (The last time I came, I sailed over on the *QE2*.) Suddenly, it just felt right—it was the right time, I was in the right place, I was ready to breathe the air again. Strangely enough, there wasn't any nervousness about the time that had elapsed. Actually, I found New York different from how I remembered it—I found it to be more open, there was a freer energy. Something had changed, though I can't quite put my finger on what it was. Maybe it was that New York had changed, maybe it was also that I had changed. I had come to a sort of new place in myself, a new tranquility, a new simplicity. I always associated New York with energy, but this time I felt things I hadn't noticed before. I noticed bits of Europe in New York. I noticed a certain kind of music—in the streets, in the architecture. It was a really liberating experience for me.

Tepper: Were you surprised by the warm response of the audiences here, especially to your new writing? Did you fear you had become out of touch with American readers?

Okri: Well, I did feel that fifteen years is a long time not to keep up a living, direct relationship with a place as important as America. But it's just the way things were, so I expected really to have to start the journey all over again. Almost like a complete reintroduction of my work from the beginning, which I didn't mind at all. I always like the idea of starting afresh. It's a humbling, strengthening experience to return to the A, B, C of things. But to my surprise, after the very first reading, there wasn't really a need to go back. It was almost as if some strand of a dialogue had continued. I read out my new poems, and I think they made an immediate connection. From then on, all I really had to do was follow the poetry.

Tepper: Your poetry collections haven't been published in the United States, so I suppose people weren't as familiar with your poetry as your novels.

Okri: Yes, that's true. I think even in England people know my novels more than my poetry. But the poetry is probably the most important part of my writing. It's the foundation; it's the source of everything else. When I first began to be a writer, consciously or unconsciously, it was poetry that I wrote. In Nigeria, in my teens, I used to write volumes of bad, youthful poetry—about rain, about the ghetto. I think the way that I knew that poetry was an important part of me was that my early poems were not about love, which is what it tends to be with most of us. It was literally about things I noticed every day—witchcraft, evil, suffering.

So poetry has always been a constant in my writing life, though it took me a long time to learn what my true way of writing poetry was. It's always been my parallel life—the most immediate mode in which I respond to life. Often, when I'm asked to write essays about things, I end up exasperating editors by writing poems instead, because it's the best way for me to express things.

Tepper: Is that how you came up with the concept of the "poetic essay," which you say you've been writing more of recently?

Okri: Well, the truth is that I really don't make that much of a distinction. I mean, there are differences in the line breaks and the formal techniques, but when I'm most thrilled by something I move into a poetic vein. And so I found that poetry and essay began to merge quite early for me. If you look at my first volume of essays, *A Way of Being Free*, you'd see that there is a flowing between one and the other. In the early short stories, I had to be very strict in keeping to the story form. I was trying to learn the mystery of fiction. And early on, I really felt the mystery of fiction was in the short story, its smallest unit, something that from its opening line enters you into a storytelling fictional universe.

Tepper: What was your experience like, then, as a young Nigerian writer in England?

Okri: Well, I arrived in the autumn of 1978, and it was quite traumatic and very, very difficult. I had never experienced that quality of failing light before. I think I was depressed, and the only thing that saved me was the draft of that first novel that I brought with me, which I spent the long winters rewriting. In a sense, it was writing that saved me. I was a bit of a down-and-out in London: I was broke; I didn't know anyone. Sometimes I found myself sleeping out on park benches. I went through some difficult times. It wasn't an easy journey.

Tepper: And all the while you were searching for your own voice and material?

Okri: Yes, but that came later. I really was struggling. It was around then that I learned there is a big difference between expression and true writing. Most of the stuff I wrote at that time was unfinished and didn't survive. It took a long time for me to make a connection between my personal heritage—my parents, my own life, what I'd experienced—and what I was doing as a writer. You'd think it was the most natural thing to do, but actually I had to discover that. I had to discover that by first of all being lost for a long time.

II. Finding the Center

Tepper: What compelled you to carry on writing during those struggling years? Were you committed to sticking it out and making it in London's literary world?

Okri: My thoughts were never as grand as that; I was just thinking of learning how to write. For me, that was the big adventure of my life, the big romance. I always felt, to be honest, there was something magical about literature and the art of writing. I always had a very awed feeling about words, about books, about great stories. I always felt that the true writer is a person who has written something which, purely by itself, charms its way through time. That, for me, was what the magic and adventure of writing was always about—joining that special tribe of magicians. And eventually I found that the magic itself had an art and a science behind it. I'd always seen the romance, but I was learning about the rigor, too.

But after I'd written my first two novels—especially after the second, *Landscapes Within*—I kind of came upon a crisis in my writing life. I was young and I kind of wrote myself out, in the sense that I wrote myself to the edge of what I was capable of doing at the time. So I stopped for a while and went to university. And while I was there, studying comparative literature, I found myself actually asking the question: What is the root of fictionality? What is it that makes a fictional universe live in words, on the page? That question really did excite me for many years, and I did a lot of going back to the basics of writing. I did a lot of beginnings work, origins work. And this led me to not just language but myths. And out of all that came a new book of stories, *Incidents at the Shrine*. If you look at those stories, you'll see that my tone changed. The person who had written those first two novels was not the person writing these stories. I'd actually become clearer in my spirit about something. I'd understood that there's an intrinsic relationship between life and myth. That's why the book is called *Incidents at the Shrine*. As a character says in one of the stories, "The world is the shrine and the shrine is the world. Everything must have a center."

So, for me, the turning point was not *The Famished Road*, which came later; the real breakthrough was the short stories of *Incidents at the Shrine*. It wasn't just new stories; it was a completely new orientation—a new tone, a new measure, a new way of trying to capture reality.

Tepper: And everything you've done since then has come from that discovery in your writing?

Okri: Oh, yes, everything has come out of that. *Incidents at the Shrine* was published in 1986, but I had been working on those stories, struggling with them, for many years. It was actually like finding a new vocabulary, a new tincture. Because the reality in literature is not really the story you're telling; it's the way in which it's told: the voice, the window, the perception. It comes down to almost a musical thing. It meant discovering not just a method but a mode.

Tepper: The earlier themes and ideas—the search for justice, the interest in the struggles of the Nigerian underclass, for example—were still there in the stories, though, right?

Okri: Yes, yes, the themes remained; they're part of my DNA as a writer. But they changed in this new laboratory I was working in. It was no longer just about the lower classes—that was still there, but something else had taken over, as well. And I think if I were to distill what it was, I would say I'd become fascinated by the question of how you convey a people's reality. How do you convey a reality—life in Lagos, say, or a Nigerian village—so that it has total integrity within itself so that, stripped of external clues, it still manages to tell readers all they need to know? This really takes you to a fundamental question of how reality is perceived in writing. It's a philosophical question—it comes down to the philosophy of reading.

Tepper: Interestingly, many Western reviewers and critics have resorted to a sort of shorthand label of "magic realism" to explain your work.

Okri: Much as I love the greatest works of magic realism, that's not what I do. What I am trying to do within the African tradition is tell stories about the world in which all the dimensions of reality, visible and invisible, have their natural places. I'm not doing this because of a poetic inflation, but because it's natural to people's way of seeing. I grew up with kids who would refer to an empty space and say, "Oh, my grandmother is here." If you tell a story like that in the Western naturalistic tradition, it's a ghost story. But if you tell it within the way it ought to be told, it's just part of the normal, natural way people see the world.

Tepper: And that worldview is rooted in uniquely African ideas of myth and reality?

Okri: Well, not rooted in African ideas. I'd say it's rooted in African reality itself. I'd go further and say it's rooted in all reality. But, you see, every people, every nation, has to come up with the intersection of myth and reality for themselves. You read Walt Whitman's *Leaves of Grass* and you see he's finding that connection at every point in each poem. And I think you can define literature, really, as the most expressive point of the revelation of a people's angle between their myth and reality. Take Mark Twain's *The Adventures of Huckleberry Finn*—he's uncovering a kind of hidden national myth. So is it an African thing? I'd say it's a world thing, but every people has to do their own mapping out of that particular revelation.

Tepper: And, for you, literature is a way to explore this?

Okri: Literature is the best way to express it, and to express it for all of us. It enables us to recognize that we are always walking in a living, mythic stream. And that suddenly allows individuals to feel that they are not merely individuals; they are touched with something special, something magical. That's what literature does. Literature puts wings on our backs.

Life and myth are big, resonating places of the early work. It began with *Incidents* and intensified in *Stars of the New Curfew*, where it became more of a trinity: life, myth, and politics. With *Stars*, I already had that new language and could now step out into the Technicolor of the richly created reality. So I could put more elements in it—bring in power and powerlessness, politics, history. So, you see, there's a long journey to get through before we get to where I am now. It's not a straight, simple arc from the early stories.

It's a very strange thing about the work we do, by the way. You would think that there is nothing more eloquent than words on a page. Actually, there is nothing more silent. You can have five words on a page that tell you nothing, but find someone who can give you a key and those five words sing aria. It's just a paradox of our trade how silent words are. They need to be helped, unlocked. I'm struck by the mystery of this. I think the whole key to a vast literature can be found in studying just a couple of words. I would like people to be more microscopic about literature and less telescopic. If it's really well done, a universe can be found in just a few words, even taken at random—whether it's Henry James, Shakespeare, Hemingway, Joyce, or Achebe.

III. Freedom Now

Tepper: Tell me more about how you came to write *The Famished Road*, which seems the culmination of much of your early work and creative energy.

Okri: With *The Famished Road*, I had been doing a lot of reading and thinking about contemporary Africa and the world in which I found myself, and the thing that was uppermost in my mind was the desire for renewal. I wanted to start afresh. I wanted to see the whole world afresh. For me, the really big thing at that point—and it was both personal as well political—was the question How do you renew the world? Given the kind of history, the *cycle* of history, that we've had in Africa and almost everywhere else, how do you begin again this narration of humanity? It seemed to me that the first thing you do is start with language, because the renewal of language helps the renewal of vision. But how do you start to see things as if for the very first time? It came to me very slowly that the only way to do that was, well, to begin again as a child. Slowly, the idea of Azaro, the "spirit-child," came to me. I grew up with "spirit-children," people who are half human, half dream or spirit, and who come and go in this world until things are right and they choose to stay. My sister was one. It was part of our upbringing; it is a profoundly West African phenomenon. As I followed my research, though, I realized this phenomenon exists in all traditions, just with different names.

When I came upon this idea, I realized this was one of those instances where the language, the vision, the necessity all come together. It was, in a way, the perfect vehicle to freight across the kinds of concerns I had about African history and the contemporary world. People think that in *The Famished Road* I'm talking only about Africa, but I'm not. If you look carefully, it's all there: "In the beginning there was a river. The river became a road and the road branched out to the whole world." That point between those two things—the river and the road—embodies all I'm trying to say about Africa and our modern condition. In that transformation is the conundrum, the enigma, of our life.

That is the opening vision of *The Famished Road*, the metaphor through which I'm trying to say all kinds of things about our world. But it's not the author saying this; it's a "spirit-child," who sees the world of our reality and the world of spiritual reality simultaneously. To describe the world from his point of view, you need a language that is elastic enough to convey the invisible things and tactile enough to convey the real things, and you need a philosophy behind it to unify the two.

Tepper: Why did you conceive of Azaro's story as a three-book cycle?

Okri: There is a kind of symbolic structure to the whole trilogy. It's meant to represent the three ages of man: youth, manhood, old age. *The Famished Road* represents Azaro's youth, hence the simplicity and wonder of the language. In *Songs of Enchantment*, that language gets richer and more complicated, and in *Infinite Riches* it's touched with tragedy. The books represent three stages in the development of a consciousness, but also three stages in the unfolding of the African spirit. There's also the idea of the nation—whether Nigeria or anywhere else—being something of a "spirit-child," in constant flux between coming into existence and dissolving. Another thread that runs through the books is the question of the road—if this road was once a river, there is a perpetual yearning to return to an original, freer condition. There are all these things, and then there's also a colonial aspect, which for me is both real and symbolic. It's not just the case that I wrote *The Famished Road* and then wrote sequels. They form complex structures together.

Tepper: Tell me about the non-Africa or "open" books that followed *The Famished Road* series.

Okri: It's not possible to ask really fundamental questions about language without asking questions about freedom. They're connected, and they've been an important part of my writing from the very beginning. Freedom, to me, has always been a big issue, because it has to do with how you define yourself and how others define you. There was a big debate among the writers of the Achebe/Soyinka generation as to what they were: were they African writers, Nigerian writers, Igbo writers, or what? The question was also very relevant to my generation. For me, it finally came down to the question of freedom. Partly as an answer to that question, I found myself writing from a place inside that I found to be the truest part of me. I call those works my "open" books, and they're very, very important to me.

Tepper: And these are the books you've been writing for the past decade or so?

Okri: Yes. The first of those was *Astonishing the Gods*, a small parable about visibility and invisibility. It's almost as if it was written with a different ink, and it has been much misunderstood, but it's one of my favorites. The next was *In Arcadia*, which ostensibly took the form of a train journey but actually is about freedom and art and the philosophical question of happiness in our lives. And the most recent book is *Tales of Freedom*, which is made up of a novella and thirteen "stokus."

Tepper: "Stokus" are an amalgam of short story and haiku that you've been experimenting with lately. As you write in *Tales of Freedom*, "Its origin is mysterious, its purpose is revelation, its form compact, its subject infinite."

Okri: Meditating on form, as I've said, has always been a very important part of my work. With "stokus," I'd become fascinated again by the question of the source of narration. One conclusion I came up with is that it comes from a dreamlike, subterranean place. It bubbles up and takes the form of structured narration. So I thought it would be interesting to go as close as possible to that bubbling place, before it bifurcates and becomes either poetry or story. The "stokus" come from that melding ground. And like haiku, they are meant to just brush against reality, not be a full exploration of it.

Tepper: Are you still working in traditional forms as well?

Okri: Yes, *Starbook* is my most recent novel. It goes back, *way back*, to precolonial Africa, to a cusp moment in our history . . . . As you know, it's been said that each writer has only one novel in him but writes many variations of it. I'd rephrase that and say each writer, if he's lucky, is born with one important question to ask about reality, about being alive, about being human. And to the degree that he asks that question under the right alignment of stars, at the right place in his life, that question will become as urgent for us as it is for him. It's a mysterious thing how this happens, how the writer's quest takes on such a tremendous resonance and importance for the rest of us as well.

Ben Okri in Conversation

Vanessa Guignery and Catherine Pesso-Miquel / 2012

From *The Famished Road: Ben Okri's Imaginary Homelands*, edited by Vanessa Guignery (Newcastle upon Tyne: Cambridge Scholars Publishing, 2013): 17–29. Reprinted by permission of Cambridge Scholars Publishing.

Ben Okri: Before we start this conversation, I want to say how much of a pleasure it is to be here. I've heard so much about this institution [the École Normale Supérieure de Lyon], its history, its place in French culture that it is a real thrill to be here. It's my first time in Lyon and I think it is beautiful. I went walking through the market today. When I go to a new place I tend to do two things: I go to its museums and its markets.

Question: We are very pleased and honored to welcome you today and are looking forward to hearing you talk about your art. My first question is related to your mode of writing. You once said "You can't write about Africa like Jane Austen,"[1] and therefore you needed to adapt your mode of writing to the place you were writing about. You needed to find a specific tone and narrative voice to write about that place. Would you mind defining that mode of writing?

BO: That comment has been interpreted as being an attack on Jane Austen, which it isn't, because I happen to love her writing enormously. All I was trying to express was that a piece of writing has an approximate or a resonating relationship with the place that's being written about. And every place has, as it were, a tone that helps it come into being. I'm not saying there's only one tone, but there are a family range of tones by which that place is brought into existence through words. Every place has a tonal equivalent in words. The variations can be vast: you can have a tone as different as Lewis Carroll, Henry Fielding, D. H. Lawrence, or Jane Austen. But in a sense they all fall within the tonal range of what brings alive Englishness and the mood of England on the page. You can't use a tone that best brings out one place to write about another place, partly because a place is not just the physical landscape. It is not just the trees and the buildings, it is not even the history of its civilization. Places are complex things: it is constituted of what has been done there, the quality and the nature of thought that has been had there, the way history has leaked into the landscape and the people. A place is a concentration of moods, histories, beliefs, superstitions. All of this is compacted into the tone that the best writers use to evoke a place.

To use the tone of a Jane Austen to try and evoke Africa is inappropriate. In Africa myth transfigures reality. By myth, I also mean the rituals and beliefs of a people. All worldviews are superstitious. The world is not as we see it. The world is as we perceive it. Our perception makes our world. And Africa has its unique perceptions. One of the things I struggled hardest with, when writing *The Famished Road*, was to find the musical tone to convey that universe. I spent ten years trying to find that tone. Without it, that world could not have been conveyed. It's not got to do with description. It's got to do with things not seen that are actually an essential part of that universe.

Q: You said several times that you consider yourself first and foremost as a poet, that "poetry is probably the most important part of [your] writing. It's the foundation: it's the source of everything else."[2] You also said that a "great deal of *The Famished Road* was actually written in poetry, metrically."[3] Could you share with us how you go about creating that rhythm, and could you also tell us whether or not the images come first and then the words later? How, in fact, can poetry be created within the prose?

BO: I think there are two kinds of writers. The one kind is, for want of a better word, the organic writer. The world they're trying to create, the book they're trying to write, has to have a completely self-generating source, out of which everything emerges. The integrity of the work comes from the inner growth of the idea. Then there's the other kind of writer, who, for want of a better phrase again, is an external, composite writer. They put the work together, they shape it, externally, like sculpture. *The Famished Road* is an integral work. Everything is contingent in the book. Its core is something impossible, the idea of the spirit-child. And the spirit-child is a poetic being. The core is poetry because of the consciousness of the narrator. The spirit-child is part here and part there, part in this world and part in the other world, part in the world of the real, and part in the world of dream. The poetry comes out of that. For me poetry is, of course, rhythm and meter, etc., but it is also a dual state of language, part here and part there, part dream and part reality, part intelligence and part intuition, part light and part shadow. The poetry of the book comes out of the fact that this character is constantly seeing the world with a dual consciousness. What appears not to be real to us is real to him, and what appears to be real to us is not real to him. The poetry is such that if you miss the beat, you are out of that world. The source is the open consciousness of the narrator.

Q: I must say I tend to read *The Famished Road* as poetic prose. Genre is of course a very arbitrary category but I tend to read your essays as poems, your poems as essays, your novels as poems, etc. . . . so that when I read your work I don't feel any boundaries between genres. Is this something you experience as well or do you establish clear generic differences between your works?

BO: I am a blender and a blurrer. I am fundamentally a poet, but primarily a novelist. This is another way of saying that for me everything comes out of the rich river. Why should an essay not partake of poetry, and why should poetry not partake of thought experiments that we associate with the essay? Demarcations are artificial things. Every genre is enriched by its boundlessness. Every genre for me always mutates into something else. The novel itself has never been fixed. Its boundaries have never really been defined. It's only recently that we've started to speak of one thing as being a novel and another thing as not being a novel. But actually the novel has always been a rather dangerous river that overflows its boundaries and invades the surrounding cities. That's the way it should be. It is a rich and fluid thing. Because we are talking finally, always, in the novel, about a rich and fluid condition, which is life. This doesn't mean I don't pay great attention to the perceived demarcations of genres. It's just that I am fascinated by the source, the origins. In the essay form my great favorites remain Plutarch, Montaigne, Camus. The Baconian essay is especially compressed. Poetry can learn from them. All the genres can learn from one another.

Q: You said at some point that, to you, the novel is a river.

BO: The novel is a river, the short story a glass of water.

Q: Talking about voice, Henry James explained in his preface to *What Maisy Knew* that he had wanted to restrict himself to the point of view of the child but had wondered whether he should adopt the vocabulary and language of a child. In the end he decided not to restrict himself to a limited vocabulary, but of course that novel has a third-person narrator. Since it is not always clear from which point in time Azaro (the narrator) is telling his story, I was wondering whether the fact that Azaro (the character) is a child had induced you to adapt the language in any way, or if that did not come into account. Did you need to make sure that the language would not be too complex, or was that never a question for you?

BO: It was an important question. From the great child narrators of *Huckleberry Finn* to modern times, there has always been an ambivalent relationship between vocabulary and the voice. In this particular instance it is complicated by the nature of his consciousness, by the fact that he is a spirit-child, and by the fact that this novel is retrospectively told. The point of view of the telling and the teller is ambiguous. It is not being told in the time of the person that you're reading about. That ambiguous distance complicates the vocabulary. The second thing is that some things are difficult to convey simply, certain states of mind, certain twilight conditions of perception. I agonized about the relationship between vocabulary and consciousness. I came to the conclusion that what is being felt, what is being sensed, are the most important things. Therefore I shouldn't worry too much about the register of vocabulary, so long as there's that transparency of the feeling and the perception coming through. Sometimes you can encounter a complex sentence in which a simple and pure emotion comes through. Sometimes you can encounter a simple sentence in which a complex and profound emotion comes through. The vocabulary is not really the primary means by which the emotion is expressed. It is sometimes the arrangement of words.

I've only spoken about what I'm about to say once. I'd like to express it again. It's about one of the ways in which *The Famished Road* was written. I used a technique which I now call "echo writing." We tend to think we read words on a page sequentially, going down the page. But that's not actually how we read. When you are reading a line of prose sequentially, your eye also sees one word here and sees another word there. You see contingent words. That was very much part of how the story was told— the way in which you read a sentence but pick up a word just diagonally below or above. This influences the way in which you actually read the sentence you're reading. In a sense it was written like painting. I frequently meet people who say: "When I reread *The Famished Road*, certain things that I thought I saw on certain pages, when I went back, were not there. What's happened to them?" We read contingently as well as sequentially. I was playing with this and other curious techniques a great deal in that text.

Q: I'm very interested in the voices in the novel that speak as indistinct and anonymous groups, as disembodied voices, commenting on what is going on (at the market for instance). It's not always clear whose voices these are as they're not identified individually. They might be said to symbolize public opinion sometimes, or they could be compared to a Greek chorus commenting on the situation. Can you tell us a bit more about the status of these voices?

BO: I don't want to overidentify them. That's the way it works in the novel. You know the famous line from *The Tempest* by Caliban who said the island was full of noises. When Gustav Jung came to Africa for the first time, that's what he said. He stood on the soil, and he said this place, its history, all of its hidden histories, just rise up at you. That's what Africa is like to anybody who is halfway sensitive. It is full of presences. It is full of all kinds of things that are ambiguous in the hierarchy of beings. Azaro hears them: nobody else does. When you're asking me for the exact identity of these voices you're asking me to break the seal of a mystery, which must remain that way. These voices are both in the text and in the world. They're dual. I'm trying to express the multifarious dimensions of textuality as well as of reality. There must be equivalents between these two things. The multidimensionality of reality must have its textual counterpart. Think of them as a rich opera of presences.

Q: I would like to talk about your depiction of poverty in *The Famished Road*. When I read the book I was struck by the character of Mum, the way you painted her, the courage, the quiet dignity, the resilience, in spite of not knowing what the next meal would be coming from and all that. Some critics tend to criticize writers for having a "voyeurism of the slums," the dregs, for trying to describe a lower social class. Could you elaborate on that and on your depiction of dire poverty?

BO: I didn't see it as dire poverty, because Azaro doesn't. Everything comes out of the integrity of a worldview. I'll keep coming back to this because until we get this straight, nothing else is really going to make sense. I'll be clear. He is a person with an ambiguous consciousness. Everything he sees is transfigured by knowledge of that which is beyond what he sees. He is a child born into the slums, into the ghettos of Lagos; incidentally, a place that I know well. I'm probably quite rare amongst African writers in that sense. I was fortunate enough to have spent a substantial part of my life amongst the poor. So I could write about it, not as if I were a traveler, but as if I were one of them. That has been the good fortune of my biography, as it were. I drew upon what I knew and what I had seen. In terms of the book this is significant, because Azaro's consciousness is elaborated by his condition. If Azaro had been born into a place like Ikoyi for instance, which is a rich part of Lagos, the orchestra of the story would have been diminished. The irony of having a consciousness of the infinite contained in the narrowness of poverty fascinated me a great deal. It allowed me to explore the irony of social conditions, because everything is modulated by consciousness.

The mother is for me a very tender creation, and Nigerian literature, African literature, is not very replete so far with mothers looked at in great depth from the first-person point of view. The qualities of her motherhood are strengthened and exacerbated by poverty. I was fascinated by the extremes. I was interested in putting this Azaro consciousness in an extreme condition, to see what happens when you do that. This part of our history has not been told very much in our fictions, and not told in this particular way. I'm not passing any judgment. It's not for me as a novelist to pass judgment on circumstances, but it is my responsibility to shed an unusual light on them, and that's what I wanted to do: to shed not the ordinary light of what the slums were like if you or I were living there, but what it is like seen through a vast consciousness. The mother for me represented a central aspect of the novel. She's the one who keeps Azaro here, who grounds him. She's the cause of his being here. She represents for me the bright side of the moon, the side that sheds light on what life means to a child.

Q: Another important, though very different, female figure is Madame Koto, a fascinating and ambivalent character. She moves from being a nurturer at the beginning, when she's actually supporting the poor population, to a representative of the new capitalistic elite at the end. Could you tell us more about this evolution of Madame Koto and about her character as a whole?

BO: As a writer, every now and again you are surprised by someone who turns up in a book you are writing. There are some people you invite, and others have a talent for inviting themselves. She came bursting through the door. I was surprised when she turned up, I must confess. I had made no plans for this lady. Now that I think about it across the space of the years, it seems the character of Madame Koto gave me an opportunity to look at one of the silent subjects of *The Famished Road*, which is the place of myth. There is in it a fictional meditation on the way in which the myths mutate or perish in their collision with history. There is in it an ambivalent attitude towards myth. Some people have felt that it is a novel primarily about myth. But I'm also looking at myth as an unintentional destroyer of a tradition. Myth is an ambivalent thing. It is the center and strength of a tradition, but it can also be that which prevents a tradition from growing and can actually choke and destroy it. Myth itself needs renewal, and reinvention.

Madame Koto was drawn from two sources. There's an aunt of mine who's a very powerful figure. She had a very big stall in a marketplace in Lagos and I used to visit her as a child, and then I didn't see her for a long time. Over the years, I kept asking myself, "Where did Madame Koto come from?" I think she owes a part of her to that aunt. But the other part is drawn perhaps from the myths and stories I grew up with. We have these powerful Isis figures in our mythology, and every community has a great woman like that. They are the invisible mountains that anchor a people. But their role changes with history. Colonialism altered their roles, from its clarity in ancestral times, to something more ambivalent with the changing necessities. It is not always the case of course, but she gave me an opportunity to examine that which changes in a people when their history has been affected so powerfully.

Q: Could you tell us more about your strategy of namelessness in a novel in which the words Lagos or Nigeria, for instance, are nowhere to be found? Is this related to your interest in the mythical dimension?

BO: Maybe things are truer when they are not named. Their essence is revealed. *We* are fascinated by naming because we have to demarcate the world, because for us the world is demarcated. This bottle exists in separation from those books over there, this table from that table. *We* see the world in demarcations. But Azaro as part spirit sees through the filter of a pure consciousness. There are very few characters who are named in the book. When they are named, it is an extreme act. Mum is not named and Dad is called Black Tyger in his fighting role. Madame Koto is unique, and Azaro's name has a defining history.

Q: *The Famished Road* is to me a synesthetic novel: I see with Azaro, I feel with him, I smell with him, I hear with him, and of course this made me think of what Joseph Conrad wanted to achieve, i.e., "to make you hear, to make you feel— [...] before all, to make you see." But I feel that you're going beyond that program precisely because of the nature of Azaro, because his vision is not only common vision, but a double vision, the vision of the third eye, a new seeing. Did you have in mind that program of a different type of seeing?

BO: The moment one stepped deeply into that subject, it was unavoidable. I believe that cultures have maybe one or two portals, perfect points of entry that go all the way to the heart of their mystery. In the African tradition the spirit-child is one of those. It goes right to the heart of what the people are, their beliefs, the implications of their beliefs, what will survive of it, the way in which it will affect time. As I thought about it, I realized just how central it was. It is a resonant entry into a whole tradition and a whole way of seeing. There were two ways of looking at this: you either look at it from the outside and say, "You have here a spirit-child," or you inhabit it fully. The moment you inhabit it, you have a completely different world, with altogether completely different implications. From the outside, it is merely a sociological phenomenon. But from the inside, it is philosophical, spiritual, metaphysical, metaphorical, allegorical. It contains so many levels inside it. When you attempt to make that real—which means a blurring of the spirit and the body, of the mind and the soul—all of the senses begin to flow into one another. That is because looking from out of that consciousness becomes a central question about the nature of reality itself. It makes you ask the question: what is reality? What does it mean to touch something? What is a sound? What does it mean to see something? For us it is demarcated, but for the spirit-child, it is not, because the world is a gradation of energies that are translated into one sense or the other. Reality is profoundly ambiguous. It really does depend on the consciousness perceiving it. The novel is therefore also a meditation on consciousness as it is modulated by tradition and history. This synesthesia, caused by a certain boundlessness, places enormous strain on the task of the writing. I had to dig really deep. For if that element were not there, you would not have the truth of the world as seen by him.

Q: Part of what we see and what the spirit-child sees are the photographer's images. I was very interested in this character who seems on the one hand to belong to the world of modernity because he is using modern technology and on the other hand has a certain magical aura as well as he is able to transform reality and manipulate it. Could you tell us more about this character?

BO: The photographer was a sort of counterpart to Azaro's consciousness. He is the representative of the real. He's a concretizer. He's also a social documenter and a representative of moments of history. He's the visualizer and the maker-realer. He gives the present where Azaro gives timelessness. He is also a representative of the changing consciousness of a people, the implication of technology, the dialogue between technology and tradition, the dialogue between technology and consciousness, the dialogue between technology and ancient ways of seeing. In the African worldview as I've seen it, there exist prototypes of technology. There is a metaphysical technology and there is also a physical technology. I was interested in these different dimensions. The photographer is an important character because he is the means by which history leaks into the community. He also leads the community out into contemporary history, along with Madame Koto. He is one of the two poles by which modernity has a dialogue with the people.

Q: One of your aphorisms in *A Time for New Dreams* is "To see, one must first be" (23), and then you write about becoming. I was wondering about these notions in relation to *The Famished Road* as one of the issues is whether the characters become something or are already themselves, in the way that Azaro is already himself or seems to be already himself, being a spirit-child, while Madame Koto or Dad seem to evolve. How do you deal with this notion of becoming and its relationship with being? I found quite puzzling this notion of becoming while already being oneself in a way.

BO: Yes, it is puzzling. I accept that. But the two things are constantly there. At every moment we are and yet we are not. These contradictions are the human condition. We are constantly moving towards being and yet we are constantly moving from a point of being. In terms of *The Famished Road* I've been accused by certain ruler-headed readers of repetition. I often wanted to sit them down with a nice glass of wine and say: "What you see as repetition is not really repetition. It's a spiral." It appears to go back to the same place but it doesn't. There's a constant micro transformation in perception at every point of that spiral. That's because I'm opposing two perceptions of time, which are the linear time of history and the cyclical time of myth. Then there's a third time that runs right through the center of that which is Azaro's time. It is neither cyclical nor linear. It is vertical. Time is one of the unmentioned characters of the book. Time affects the way in which the narration happens to you as a reader. Time affects the way in which certain scenes are contracted or expanded.

An example that comes to mind. There's a kiss that the mother gives Azaro on the forehead. The moment of that kiss is elongated. The kiss journeys from the head and goes all the way around and then comes back again. That moment is elongated because for Azaro, it is a moment outside of time, it's a vertical moment. There are many moments like that in the book. They are not, for Joyceans, epiphanies. They are vertical Azaro moments. In terms of seeing and being, in terms of the aphorisms you were referring to, I think the story of our lives is a constant journey towards being but being is never static. To arrive at a place is eventually to die. You arrive at a place and then you depart from it. There are constant arrivals and departures. It is the in-between state that is problematic and it is that in-between state that leads to a lot of fluidity in the reading of texts and of paintings. You stand before a painting and you look at it. The painting is interpreted exactly where you are in your consciousness at that particular time and what you see in it are crystallizations of your particular state of being at that moment. If you are in a state of becoming, you will see states of becoming in works of art. What we see is a constant reflection of moments between arrivals and departures. Keep that contradiction, that tension. Don't resolve it.

Q: You said that you opposed different perceptions of time and I feel that it's very much the same with place and the geography of the book. I feel that it is a book that you can just open wherever you wish and start reading, and I would like you to talk about that sense of disorientation. I wondered if you got lost writing it just as readers can get lost in it, not in a negative sense. In terms of the writing experience, did you look for that loss, for that disorientation or did you have a direction in mind?

BO: It's a complicated question. I didn't get lost while writing it, but that doesn't mean I knew what I was going to do next. I was following an absolute logic. It is a strange word to bring into this but unfortunately we have to. There was an inner logic that I was following at every point. A friend of mine was talking about the book on TV many years ago and said, "Oh Ben, it's a very wild book," and I said, "It may affect you as being wild—which is fine—but it is a deliberate book." That is because I was following this rigorous logic of consciousness which has an impact as much on time as it does on place. The truth is that place, like everything else, is perceived through consciousness. It is contingent on consciousness. Places can blur, depending on your state of mind. This is a pretty ordinary fact. If you're walking to go meet someone that you are in love with, the journey is much longer. You want to get there quicker, you want to obliterate distance, so it feels long. Whereas if you are walking to an exam that you don't want to take, you get there too quickly.

Everything is contingent. I am fascinated by contingency, by the way in which consciousness modulates, and transfigures, and distorts experience. You don't need to be in an extraordinary state of mind for this to happen. But in the case of Azaro we are dealing with an ambiguous consciousness. Everything is new to him: the forests, the streets, the faces. Everything is new in a way that is almost absolute. It is new to Azaro in a way that it was not new to me when I was walking down the streets. Everything has an unusual reality. We take reality for granted. I think Borges said that somewhere about this unforgivable aspect of the human mind. But we do. I was fascinated by this consciousness that cannot take reality for granted. The writer takes on something of the strength and the fluidity of fiction precisely because they don't take it for granted. Everything Azaro encounters on the one hand has the fixity of the human and on the other hand the fluidity of the eternal. Geography is as much subject to these morphological translations as anything else in the book, including time and myth.

Q: We've been imagining different interpretations for the title: metaphorical interpretations about the hunger being a will for change, the road standing for the people, the hunger of the people, and a mythical interpretation of the road as a mythical creature, a mythical appetite. But we're still famished for you to open more roads of interpretations about the title.

BO: Only three interpretations? Remember the first paragraph of the book: "In the beginning there was a river. The river became a road and the road branched out to the whole world. And because the road was once a river, it was always hungry." Everything is in the first paragraph. It's all there: "because the road was once a river, it was always hungry." Everything that flows out of the book flows out from that "because the road was once a river." On a simple level that which is defined was once free. There's a sense in which everything is hungry for its original condition. In terms of history, in terms of mythology, in terms of modern Africa, there's a sense in which something has been lost in going from the river to the road, something fundamental.

Q: I was wondering whether you thought of yourself as an African writer and whether you would agree to be called an African writer.

BO: What one does is primarily an act of refraction and creation. I am primarily a creative being. I feel Homer to be African. There are African writers who are German. There are English writers who are French and French writers who are English. Perhaps we should look for other ways of categorizing writers rather than their nations. I think their sympathies, their affinities, their literary families, their prophecies, their rebellions, their antipathies might be more fruitful. There are diagonal lines across literature. I dream of the day when literature will be talked about not only in terms of nations or periods but also in terms of magical affinities, contrasts and argument. Maybe in the twenty-second century, an academy like this will be talking about novels of the world that illuminate the great enigmas of life, novels that subvert reality in order to reveal it, or—and this happened with one of my readers—novels that make you miss your flight.

Notes

1. Davis Stenhouse, "It Came to Him Like a Dream," *Sunday Times* (Aug. 19, 2007): 7.
2. Anderson Tepper, "The Mysteries of the World: A Conversation with Ben Okri," *Tin House* 49 (Fall 2011): 39.
3. Pietro Deandrea, "An Interview with Ben Okri," *Africa America Asia Australia* 16 (1994): 82.

Painter of Secrets

Anupama Raju / 2012

From *Frontline* (India), Nov. 30, 2012: 105–8. Reprinted by permission of Anupama Raju.

A writer is a like a magician, says Ben Okri, keeping you enchanted with his craft. And in the process, he gives you new ways of seeing the world.

What does it mean to be Ben Okri? A Booker Prize winning writer who rises above stereotypes? A truth seeker? A student of reality? It may not be possible to answer the question fully. But perhaps, one of the best ways of knowing a writer is through his own writing and the way he approaches writing. In Okri's own words, a writer's personality shines through his or her work.

Born in Nigeria and based in London, Okri started receiving international acclaim early in his life. A prolific writer who has written novels, short story collections, essays, and poetry, he won the Booker Prize in 1991 for *The Famished Road* when he was just thirty-two.

He had become a fellow of the Royal Society of Literature when he was much younger. This year, he was chosen to give the prestigious Steve Biko Memorial Lecture. Yet, Okri wears fame very lightly. There is an almost spiritual quality about his humility.

In Thiruvananthapuram, Kerala, for the World Malayalam Festival (October 31–November 1), Okri spoke, in an interview, about writing as an act of meditation, offering glimpses into his personality. Excerpts from the interview.

Anupama Raju: What does writing mean to you?

Ben Okri: Writing has become, in a personal sense, a form of meditation. It wasn't, to begin with. That's because in the early years I had more anxiety about writing. I so much wanted to do certain things. Whereas now, I let it do what it can do. So, writing has meant different things to me over the years. At first, maybe it was a way of bearing witness to the world and its injustices. Then it became a way of trying to understand the mysterious nature of reality and trying to reveal some of the hidden forces, hidden motivations, behind life. Then it became an art, and art is something you do to communicate, of course; art is something that you do more for itself, because of the possibility of what you can do with it.

At some point it became, and it still remains for me, an act of magic but it has always been, more now than ever, a high act of consciousness. Because the extraordinary thing about writing, of any art form, is that it's a chemical operation that takes place inside the consciousness. With music, you hear the sounds complete, so there's no translation happening inside you. With painting you see it complete and take it in complete. With writing you take in these abstract symbols and you convert them into things in your mind. So one becomes a machine for the conversion of abstract notions into ideas, feelings, thoughts, philosophies, and so on. So we are, really, a laboratory in which writing takes place and activates. So, writing places an enormous responsibility and power, and it is very much an operation of tremendous inwardness. And that's why I find it so fascinating.

Raju: So, who runs this machine?

Okri: The self. If you are spiritually inclined, you would say the soul. If you are a psychologist, you would say the mind. We human beings are extremely rich and complex. We have many great centers inside us: emotions, mind, spirit, memory, imagination, so many powerful forces. I think the thing about writing is that it makes you aware of the question, while reading, of the unified eye. The consciousness of the self while reading is a very fascinating one, which is why the act of reading is such a great pleasure when you're reading a good book because it's not just the pleasure of reading, but it's also the pleasure of your awareness of your own consciousness in the state of reading. It's very, very close to unconscious meditation. Very, very, close. Not quite, but close.

Raju: You talk elsewhere about the difficulty of seeing things. Does this machine see things?

Okri: Let's call it a sublime machine, shall we? Seeing is a very complex operation. It really is. Really good writing challenges the quality of our seeing. Because you can only get from a piece of writing what you see in it. It can only awaken in you what you see in the world. So everything you do with a piece of reading is qualified by the quality of your seeing. So yes, this sublime machine sees but we have unconscious seeing as well as conscious seeing. And I think that we are quite lazy seers.

Raju: Or is it that we choose to see something and we choose not to see something?

Okri: I think we choose more to see than choose not to see. I think when we choose not to see, it is an unconscious choosing and of course it tends to be true that we see only what we want to see. Which is quite extraordinary actually. I'm frequently fascinated by what people don't see, what is right in front of them; what people don't notice. There is a wonderful line in J. D. Salinger's *The Catcher in the Rye* where he says about adults that they don't notice anything. It's true.

Raju: This thing about what we do not see and what remains invisible is something you often talk about. You also said once that you wanted your readers to finish your book and at the same time, not finish it. What did you mean by that and why?

Okri: Because, on the whole, people read with the purpose of finishing. You get a book and your sole purpose is to get to the end of it. It's ironic that you buy something for pleasure and your whole *raison d'être* is to get rid of it, finish it, get over it as quickly as possible. I don't know if all writers write to be read, to be finished. I think most writers encourage you by the pace, to finish it very quickly, but I don't. The way I write, the effect of what I'm trying to do to you is at its most powerful when you're actually in the midst of reading. So the longer you can stay there, the longer you can stay in this world of enchantment that I'm trying to create. And I'm constantly trying to create a rich level of realities and enchantments, suggestions, hints; I'm like a painter that's got so many hidden secrets, details many of which you are not going to see the first three times you read it. But even when you're not seeing, it gives you a subliminal effect. And so, I want my readers to actually want to stay inside that world. I don't want them to get out of there quickly. Because if they are out of there quickly, they are out of the magic space that I'm creating.

Raju: This magic space that you create in your own writing, to what extent does it connect you to the world around you? Or to your inner world?

Okri: I don't know if there's such a great degree of separation between the two things. Because if you didn't have an inner world, even if you were sitting in the midst of a revolution, you wouldn't notice it. We only notice things because we have an inner world through which we feel about them. So really, the greatest place of feeling or sensibility and appreciation about the world is inward. The richer that inner world is, the richer you would feel about the world around you. It's not the other way around. I believe that consciousness, and expanded consciousness, is what enriches reality because we perceive it more. Not less. So yes, it's a way of profoundly helping, contributing to, our engagement with the world through our engagement with ourselves.

Raju: You have a preoccupation with the concept of reality. How would you define reality, if it were possible to define it?

Okri: That's what we're constantly trying to do. Besides, everyone's reality is different. Reality is how we perceive the world. That's all it is. Your question really is not "What is reality?" but "Is there an absolute reality?" Because we each have an individual reality. Your perception is unique to you because of your history, your tradition, education, your superstitions, your beliefs. So, we only see reality through the filter of the mind. What the best writers do is to induce you out of your own way of seeing the world for a moment and give you another set of lenses through which to see the world. So you start to say, Oh my God! Someone else sees the world like this? I thought the world was like this. Is it possible that it can also be like this? How shocking. You put the book down and go back to that. But for a long time after that, you're haunted that you have seen the world slightly differently. In a sense your perception of the world has been widened a little bit. That's what all writing really is trying to do. It's to get us to make a connection with the infinite plasma of reality.

When you ask me "What is reality?," I would say that it is the single greatest mystery of our lives. If you could find someone who could answer that question or who could answer that question for you through your unconsciousness, I think most of life's solutions would be found. The question of reality is very fundamental to every single aspect of society. Whether its politics, history, psychology, whatever it is, our perception of reality is absolutely central to it. So when writers wrestle with the question of reality, they are wrestling with the greatest question that we have to deal with, as human beings.

Raju: Has your own sense of reality changed over the years as a writer?

Okri: Absolutely. It has been changed by books I've read, by the fine minds I've come into contact with, by friendship, by opposition, by the act of writing itself. The act of writing itself is a continual adjustment of our sensibility to the difficult task of representing the world.

The art of writing is not just to do with the organization of words and making words more beautiful. Actually, it's trying to get words to be more reflective of how we see the world. It's a very mysterious activity and the more you do it, in a sense, the more refined the machinery of perception becomes.

Raju: In your recent book, *A Time for New Dreams*, you describe poetry as a river of soul murmurings. What made you describe poetry as a river? Why not an ocean or a lake or a pond?

Okri: [*Laughs*] Because poetry is not just what poets write. Poetry is not just what readers read. I think poetry is a condition of consciousness, which we all share to some degree or the other. The poetry on the page is just one small part of the poetry of being. Because being is primarily poetic and it's unavoidably so. Here in Kerala, a lady was telling me about her daughter or her son aged nine months old, who would just sit up and stare out of the window when it's raining, just watching the rain falling down, [in] absolute astonishment. And I said to her: Poetry is falling into your son's mind.

Being alive is a poetic condition because everything is not quite what it seems. Everything is tinged with the mysterious. A table: How did it come to be? A plank of wood with four legs does not stand for a table. Why not three? Why not one? A table is something you just put something on [but] it's more than just its function. It is also a metaphor for many other things which poetry discovers for us. So if poetry discovers all of these different possibilities for a container, for a spoon, or for a knife, does it not mean that all of these possibilities are already latent in a spoon, in a knife or in a table? It's all in there. It's just that the poetic mind keeps discovering new metaphoric uses for things. As if it's the elasticity of the mind that does it when, in fact, it is actually the elasticity of reality itself. That is what is poetic. And that's the river that runs through all of us.

Raju: So do you see any differences between yourself as a poet and as a novelist?

Okri: They're just different forms. The form has its own organic nature. You can't take a poem by Yeats like "Leda and the Swan" and turn it into a short story. You can't take a short story by Somerset Maugham and somehow compress it into a poem. Because, if it's good in what it is, it is natural to its own form. And that's really all it is. The idea for a novel comes with all of the things that will make it a novel. So you have an inspiration to write a novel about a woman who is sitting by herself in a railway carriage and you say: Wow, I just have this idea for a novel. And for some reason it's all in that image.

The minute you start writing about this woman sitting in this railway carriage, before you know it, you give her a history and when you give her a history, people will mysteriously appear in this history. The reason why she is waiting will slowly, incredibly, become apparent. Her story would just, as it were, emerge completely, fully formed, as it were, from this one image that you began with. As if all of that was folded inside the image.

That's what it really all is. Each form, if were true to an idea, yields all that it needs to realize its fullness. The writer just has to be particularly attentive.

Raju: Talking of your own poetry, your latest book of poetry, *Wild* (2012), comes after a gap of thirteen years. The last one was *Mental Fight* (1999).

What happened in these thirteen years? Has there been any transformation in your own poetic vision?

Okri: Yes, actually. That's a very good question. It's not that I wasn't writing poetry during that time. It's just that I wasn't publishing very much. I write poetry all the time. It's almost second nature with me. And in my first volume of poems, I really believed poetry to be richness and even to some degree, a thing of complexity. When I began publishing poetry, I actually perceived of poetry as being gifted with a particular kind of obscurity. And I liked poems that you bite into and probably break a tooth.

But, over the years, as I listened to other people's poems and read poems, I came to the conclusion—the tentative conclusion—that the difficulty of poetry should not be on the outside but on the inside. So, I began to think that maybe poetry should be like life. Life does not appear to hide any mystery. A tree just grows. Inside it, very complex processes are taking place. Cell reproduction, photosynthesis and the sap running up. It does all of it quietly. You don't notice it. All you see is, one day a leaf comes out and another day a branch comes out. And what it does on the outside gives no sign of the complex activity going on inside. And I slowly began to think to myself that poetry ought to be like that. It ought to be apparently transparent like nature but when you look into it, it's actually much more complex than it appears to be.

And so, I strove for a new kind of simplicity. I worked very, very hard at doing that. While doing that, I was aware of people who didn't read what I was writing carefully, who just thought it was simple. So I had to live with the possibility that people would just think it is simple and not understand that there are more complex things going on. But I didn't mind that.

You know, apparent simplicity is one of the most deceptive ways by which things enter into us. So I've been working with that surface. *Wild* is in a way a fruit of that. I strove very hard to make everything clear and yet when you look at it, it's not quite as clear as it seems.

Raju: Whose poetry do you read?

Okri: I tend to read the people that I have liked in the past. I am a returner. I tend to go back to old loves. It's not that I don't make new loves. I am very slow to do that. Also, it takes time to adapt to the poet's voice. Or even the personality of the poet.

I think more than the language of poetry, what we respond to most is the soul of the poet, the personality of the poet. And I suppose that is what defines great poetry. It's not just that it is great language. But then, somehow the greatness of the soul shines through the verse. And you're magnetized by this soul, by this personality, by this spirit that is sort of hiding behind all this. Then you've kind of found people that you're good with and you tend to stick with them. So I tend to go back to Rilke, Neruda, you know, people like that. I'm a revisitor.

Raju: Does your poetry influence your prose? Your new collection of essays, *A Time for New Dreams*, is said to be poetic.

Okri: It's nice people feel that way, but I've been interested in boundaries and I've never been entirely sure that we would be able to make such a strong demarcation between essay and poetry. And besides, the idea of the essay, as we have inherited it, does not appeal to me.

I don't like spending long pages trying to persuade you of something and bringing in endless quotations. And make it longer than it needs to be. Too many essays I read are just too long for their own good. I like the essay to get to its point quickly but mysteriously.

The thing about the poetic; it introduces a penumbra about everything it touches. I like that quality a lot. I like that way in which a simple thing like a spoon gets charged with the poetic way of looking at it.

I thought: Why shouldn't we borrow that for the essay? To combine brevity and this penumbra, this charged atmosphere, I thought would be a great thing to do, to make it as short as possible and yet [*gestures with hands, to indicate something enchanting*].

Lookin Back: James Ogude in Conversation with Ben Okri

James Ogude / 2014

From the *Journal of Literary Studies/Tydskrif vir Literatuurwetenskap* 36, no. 3 (Sept. 2020): 26–35. Reprinted by permission of James Ogude and the *Journal of Literary Studies*.

James Ogude: Thanks, Ben, for giving me a chance to interview you. I want to start with this honor that you have received, the honorary doctorate from the University of Pretoria. Our understanding is that the University of Pretoria is the first university in Africa to bestow an honorary doctorate upon you. How significant is this honor to you?

Ben Okri: Every recognition received for work done out of love and out of passion is significant. In this particular instance, it is very moving. African universities have been slow to appreciate the work that I have been doing. It is fitting that South Africa is the first from the continent. It says something beautiful about where South Africa is right now. It says something about its spirit, the way it perceives itself and the world. It speaks well for South African intellectual society. I am aware that when Chinua Achebe was here many years ago to give the Steve Biko lecture that South Africa also took the opportunity to recognize the immense contribution he has made. This shows that South Africa has a long and profound relationship with the continent's writers. I am thrilled to be appreciated in this way. But the feeling is reciprocal, because I have a soft spot for South Africa too and consider myself an adopted son of the land. My writing seems to strike a chord with South African people. Perhaps it's because of the theme of freedom that informs my work, the need to go beyond boundaries in exploring the wider possibilities of our art and our humanity.

Ogude: Thank you. You will probably be happy to know that last year we also honored Professor Njabulo Ndebele, whom you must know very well.

Okri: Yes. A wonderful writer.

Ogude: I know you have talked about the significance of South Africa to you. Is it important to you that this honor is happening in South Africa? This year South Africa is celebrating twenty years into democracy which will be on the twenty-seventh of April.

Okri: That adds layers of significance to the honor. It is worth contemplating what it means that South Africa is enjoying twenty years of its independence, that it continues the extraordinary journey it has made since freeing itself from apartheid, under the interested gaze of the world, and that it remains a largely peaceful society, an important presence on the world stage. To those of us who are South African watchers across the world it has been a source of satisfaction that it has managed these last twenty years without much acrimony. It has its problems but then which postindependence nation doesn't? The first two or three decades after independence are bound to be difficult ones, bound to be transitional. It takes a while for nations to acquire the right balance, to begin to realize their possibilities. Twenty years is a milestone and South Africa has done a lot better than many other African countries in their postcolonial story. It hasn't succumbed to the dangerous temptations of civil war and revenge. It continues its journey of democracy. And there is still much to be done. You are no longer a minor at twenty. You are now a grown up among the nations of the world. Congratulations in getting here.

Ogude: You make a very important point that the project of nation formation or building is never a very simple one and that brings me to how people tend to be very pessimistic about the destiny of the continent and the sentiments that we get here are very similar: "you are all heading the same way." But you seem to have a very strong sense of optimism and this is something I also pick up from your own writing, not just about the whole continent, but humanity in general. What do you say about that in relation to Africa's future?

Okri: There are people who have made a career out of predicting doomsday scenarios for Africa. If you read these people you would get the impression that Africa should long have disappeared under the weight of its inefficiency and corruption. By now Africa would have ceased to exist. But all you have to do is speak to the economists. Some of the largest growing economies in the world right now are African nations. The world is turning to Africa as the scene of the next great economic expansion.

My optimism about Africa is well founded. I know the inner matrix of the African spirit. I also grasp what appears to have been the causes for the perception of despair. It could be put down to two or three factors. One is the adjustment of one mode of being to another. From the African past to the African future a journey is being made. All nations go through periods in which they appear to falter. If you look at the long-complicated histories of America, England, France, or Russia, any of the so-called great nations of the world, you'll see that they all went through these great challenges of poverty, chaos, corruption, justice, etc. They are still going through them, in their advanced stages. It is part of the growth of nations. And the growth of nations has to do with the ethical and cultural education of its people. This cannot be done by force. When it is done by force it often leads to an inward collapse of a system in the end. It has to happen organically. The African spirit is communal and family oriented, with a sense of shared responsibility, shared progress. In the dialogue between Africa and the rest of the world that has been taking place over the last fifty years there has been a slow but significant transformation in the African ethos. The next hundred years will be important for Africa. This depends on two factors. One is how it deals with the problem of disguised neocolonial threats. A degree of responsibility about how we handle our resources, how we handle our land (there is too much selling off of our land), and how we handle the perception of our future will be very important. I don't need to name what I am talking about. People will understand what I am saying. We are going through a second phase of a quiet new colonial threat. The whole continent needs to be vigilant right now. The other thing is a greater sense of social justice. This is paramount in Africa. We have too many slums, too much poverty, too much inequality. There are too many loopholes for siphoning money from our national coffers, for the nonpayment of taxes by those who should pay them as a fair contribution to their societies. These are things that politicians, as they gain strength and confidence in their responsibilities, will hopefully eventually deal with. The African spirit is essentially progressive. All you have to do is look at its art, its rituals, its literature, listen to its songs, study its dances. The African spirit is very quick. It learns fast. We are a very adaptive people.

Ogude: So would you say that it is in the terrain of culture where this spirit, what you call the African spirit or the African inner matrix, is sustained?

Okri: Culture is at the core of the African spirit. It is where our ability to survive and our sense of humor comes from, our inner strengths and creativity. It is the source of our resilience in the face of innumerable attacks on our identity. I am talking about culture in all its aspects, literature, music, art, dance, rituals, traditional modes of being. Africa has to deal with the world on its own terms. But this takes time.

To go back to your original question about pessimism and the African condition. I heard two people wondering about the progress that has been made in the last twenty years. But on a different scale twenty years is quite short in the lives of nations. It took many nations two hundred years to achieve the possibility of democracy. We are having to accomplish the many things older nations accomplished, in a short time. That is a great deal of expectation. But having said this, look around. The terrain has changed. The trouble is that because we are living through these changes we don't notice them. There is still much for Africa to do, and there are still some invisible shackles to throw off, but Africa's potential is huge. It is tremendous. If we are wise enough, if we are hardworking enough, the future is African. But only if we have vision, rigor, and hard work.

Ogude: I will come back to that later but I want to take you back to this honor. As a writer do you think the academy, especially in Africa, has a role in affirming our men and women of letters? In other words is legitimation important for a sustained career in writing?

Okri: Something happened in the late sixties in many independent African nations. The universities decided to teach the people their own literature. When I was growing up most people read trashy American and English novels. Many of them still do. I could give you names but I don't want to make more famous people who are already bad enough as writers. It was only by the corrective teaching of the best of our literature that the continent began to have an important dialogue with itself. This is crucial. People need to read the world's writers. But they really need to read their own writers. They need to read their best writers. They need to expect from their writers the highest standards. They need to expect their writers to be as good as, if not better than, writers anywhere in the world. There should not be a selective appreciation of our writers just because they are our writers. We should demand from them the highest standards. We should demand them to extend the possibilities of their art, their novels, their stories, their poems, their dances, their paintings. They should push the possibilities forward so that the achievement of our writers should also be the achievement of the human race. I take the view that writers write both for their people and the world. It is a dual thing. In the past writers have been made to feel that they should write only for their people, their people being defined in national terms and, in some cases, tribal terms. That is regressive. Our writers should write for us but they should also write for the world. Because we should all read the best writers in the world. We read Shakespeare not because he wrote for us, but because we limit our humanity by not reading him. The same should be true of our best writers. The world should be diminished by not reading us. We must write so well, and so truthfully, that to not read us would limit your humanity wherever in the world you come from.

The academy should appreciate, but only with the highest standards. It should never be a validation of mediocrity. It should be a validation of excellence. For that reason it is not too bad to be a little bit slow in the appreciation of writers. I think that sometimes a too quick appreciation of writers can as it were . . .

Ogude: Get to their head?

Okri: . . . or encourage them in what could actually be a lazy stage in their development. Writers are very strange creatures. Some writers do their best work very early and do nothing worthwhile afterwards. Some get better as they get older, as they understand the complexity and the depth of their art, and the complexity and the depth of the human spirit. It is not easy creating an art commensurate to what you have experienced or what your people have suffered or what you perceive of the world about you. It takes time to achieve the synthesis of self and world, to find a unique tone for expressing the complexity of your experiences and perceptions. When writers are appreciated too early, there is a danger we might deprive them of the deeper gifts of their artistic discoveries. But what does too early mean? It is a relative thing. I incline towards slowness. I'm just entering the deep strange territory of my art.

Ogude: Would you say that the best of the arts should necessarily aspire towards the universal?

Okri: Achebe believed that the writer should be local first, that they could only be universal by being local. He is a wonderful example of that. Except that he breaks his own rule. He is universal as well as being local. The same is true with Soyinka. But if you are local and do not achieve universality then all is lost. The great writers in the world understand that it is not just a Russian, German, French or English condition, but that it is primarily a human condition. It may have the reality of a particular place, but its grasp must touch in a deep way the human in all of us. It is in the human that the universal lies. You cannot really touch the local if you do not touch the universal.

Ogude: Is this about our human connectedness?

Okri: About the human connectedness but mainly about the human condition. When you pick up a book or when you go to watch a play, and the curtain opens you are not watching as a Xhosa person or a Luo person or an Urhobo person. You are in there as a human being affected by your particular experience and history. But first of all, your heart, your spirit, your compassion, your sense of outrage, needs to be engaged. It is you as a human being that must be touched. That is the only way in which works can speak to us. African literature is at its best when it is also universal. I remember a conversation with Achebe many years ago. He spoke about his meeting with James Baldwin. When James Baldwin read *Things Fall Apart* the first thing he said was, "Okonkwo, that's my father." The novel made a connection to Baldwin in a personal way. It spoke to Baldwin across tribe and continents. That's what literature does.

Ogude: Let me take you back a little bit, when did you realize if ever, that you have some creative talent—that you can write?

Okri: I didn't realize it suddenly to be honest with you. At school I was going to be scientist. My dream was to be an inventor.

Ogude: That is what you share with Achebe.

Okri: Was he going to be a scientist too?

Ogude: He was going to be a medical doctor.

Okri: He was going to be a doctor, so he was going into the healing side. Mine was invention. I wanted to be an inventor. I wanted to make things. I wanted to create things. One of my dreams was a jacket that could also be a radio. Invention was my thing, along with physics and mathematics. Then something strange happened around the age of fourteen. I had finished school. There was a year in which I was not doing anything. I was waiting for my results. I began reading the books in my father's library. They were books I was forbidden to read. I began my reading with the great classics, the Greeks, the Russians, the *Arabian Nights*, Shakespeare, Dickens. My first conscious reading was Plato, the *Symposium*, then *Timaeus*, then *Critias*. That started something. It started a set of questions. By the time that summer was over, and I had worked my way through one shelf of my father's books, my destiny had changed.

I read myself from one kind of destiny to another. The other factor was the discussions I used to have with my father about Greek philosophy, ethics, and African philosophy. I used to argue with him about African philosophy. Did it exist? My father would say yes, there is African philosophy, very great African philosophy. I used to ask him where these books were so I could read them. He would say the books were there but much more significantly—and then he would make a gesture that included the world about me. I did not understand what he meant till many years later during times of poverty and nostalgia in England. I started thinking about the implication of my father's gesture. Those thoughts lead to the mode of writing that became *Incidents at the Shrine* and eventually *The Famished Road*. The third factor is the stories my mother told me. She told me oblique stories. They all had odd angles. My form of storytelling is oblique, with odd angles. I got it from my mother. When she wanted to tell me something, she didn't say it straight away. She never said, "Ben don't do this, Ben don't do that." She would tell me a story instead. The story was always oblique. I could never quite work out what she was trying to tell me. That made me think. It made me question. Years later I came to realize that the best African storytelling is also oblique. African art at its best is oblique. That is our mode. There is a whole philosophy in this.

Ogude: From what you are telling your models were fairly complex. You have got your African, your classical European sources.

Okri: And then African literature itself which I came to rather late. You were taught Achebe and Soyinka and other Nigerian writers in school alongside the classics of the world. But I discovered African literature in my late teens. I had already started writing by the time I discovered it. I really discovered it when I was away from Africa. It was so much fresher for that reason, so much purer. It came to me as itself. You read African literature in Africa as part of your growing up and you don't see it quite so clearly, because the text is within the text of the world it is situated in. But you read it away from home and you just have the text, and the text is a world. For me it was fuller, richer. Just having the text and not having the text of its world complicated my reality. It gave me a great excuse to study over an intense period, the heart, the core and the edges of what we consider African literature. That came quite late but it was fortunate because it meant I already had an open vision of literature before I came to our own.

Ogude: Any particular writer that stands out for you in this period?

Okri: The names are endless. I wouldn't do them justice. Here are some: Alex La Guma, Bessie Head, Peter Abrahams, Es'kia Mphahlele, Aidoo, Ngugi, Achebe, Coetzee, Soyinka, Okigbo, Peters, Okot p'Bitek, Gordimer. I read widely and intensely and continue to do so.

Ogude: You are, or at least are seen as, part of the Black diaspora in the West. Has this shaped your writing in any significant way and is location important when it comes to writing—at least for you?

Okri: It has shaped my understanding of craft. This is the unspoken subject in modern African criticism—the subject of craft. I do not know if I am a diasporic African writer or not. I think that the writer writes. If the work is any good it is a contribution to where you are and where you are from.

Being in England has compelled me to write with not only a profound sense of Africa at the tip of my pen but also with a sense of the contemporary and historical challenge that it is important for us to meet. Which is to say, we are not only writing in the context of Africa, we are also writing in the context of Tolstoy, Shakespeare, Austen, Joyce, Camus; it is not only Achebe, Bessie Head, Soyinka, Okot p'Bitek. It is also Walcott, Toni Morrison, Dostoyevsky; it is a world context. You suddenly realize that your responsibility to your literature is also responsibility to the literature of the world. Being in the West compelled me realize the worldwide context of writing.

Ogude: You are steeped in a fairly complex world of writers and you are emphasizing the idea of craft. Is this the art of doing it?

Okri: It is the art of doing it to the best of your ability, doing it well. Craft is one of the invisible elements which contributes to a work's endurance. It is the means by which a character presented is clear in your mind, the means by which a story moves, the means by which a story enters your subconscious, goes deep into you and becomes part of you. The craft is the means by which the complex nature of what you are saying is freighted in the most permanent way to present and future generations. It is the unspoken subject in African criticism. By that I mean African criticism tends to look at the functionality of the literature: themes, ideology, schools, and so on. But the element of craft, which has had a huge impact on twentieth-century writing across the world, especially the period of modernism and afterwards, is not much addressed. In African criticism you will get studies of the postcolonial, the postmodern, the application of theory, but you will rarely get an analysis of sentences or a study of how a paragraph gets its effect.

Because of the legacy of Flaubert, Camus cannot write an innocent sentence. He knows he is writing under the rigorous shadow of the master. In craft you inherit a great fire of difficulty. You don't just write any old sentence. You are aware. All the time.

Ogude: You are carrying a complex tradition with you.

Okri: A complex and difficult tradition. A tradition that has been pushed forward so far that to write in complete innocence, without being aware of what has been done in the tradition of your art, is to write yourself into oblivion. That is where we are right now. It can no longer be denied.

Ogude: Does it matter which language you are using?

Okri: It does not matter what language you are writing in. You still have to deal with the achievements that have been wrought in your field. You still have to deal with the great discoveries that have altered the history of your art. You can write innocently in Urhobo or Ibo or Yoruba but sooner or later it will be seen in terms of the greater achievement of the novel, the poem, the short story everywhere. It will be read in relation to *Ulysses*, *Death of the King's Horseman*, *Don Quixote*, *Beloved*, *The Sound and the Fury*, Ralph Ellison's *Invisible Man*, the short stories of Chekhov, *War and Peace*, Achebe's African trilogy, *Crime and Punishment*, the poems of Emily Dickinson, and so on. In that sense the world of literature has shrunken, not expanded. When you ask me what the implication has been of writing in London, I would say it has made the pen more ambiguous, more difficult to wield, heavier with responsibility, and yet more joyful.

Ogude: I know writers don't like labels—being confined to philosophical categories—but many would insist you are Africa's foremost magical realist and after the release of *The Famished Road*, Anthony Appiah made a very important point that, although you are writing through the mode of magical realism, there is a sense in which your kind of magical realism is very different from that of Latin American writers. His argument was that while the spirit is not metaphorical or imaginary for you it is more real than the world of the everyday—what do you say to that? Do you make a distinction between the real and the spirit world, the secular and the spiritual?

Okri: Appiah's comment was very prescient. He subsequently made other comments about my work which will be found to be incorrect. However, he is a philosopher whom I respect. I have no quarrels with the label magical realism, but when it is applied to my work it shows that people are not seeing what I am doing at the level of sentences. Nor do they see the deeper themes and intentions and techniques. The phrase magical realism has people imagining that in every sentence something fantastical, illogical, and wonderful is happening without any basis in reality or in the text. It gives an impression of flightiness, wonder and fabulous poetry that doesn't grapple with real things. That is not applicable in my case. Having said that magical realism—though a very broad church—has few genuine masterpieces. A distinction needs to be made between the many texts of magical realism and the few that give that label its distinction and power. When critics label my work as magic realism they are not aware of what I am doing at the level of sentences, and sometimes in the space between sentences, or in the architecture. It is important to go back and look at what I am doing. Looking at the short story collections *Incidents at the Shrine* and *Stars of the New Curfew* and the novels *Dangerous Love* and *The Famished Road* sentence by sentence brings one to a different and a much more complicated conclusion. One of the things that becomes apparent is that I am working with reality. Reality is wider than realism. Reality includes the visible and the invisible and is the perfect synthesis of both. Reality includes consciousness. Our consciousness is part of our reality. The way a people see the world is their reality. Otherwise you are privileging the philosophy that has pervasively determined what our perception of the real world is and should be. The color yellow means different things to the Chinese than to the African. A tree has a different resonance for the Japanese than it does for the Nigerian. Consciousness is part of this. Myth, perception, and belief are implicated in consciousness. But all this is nothing without a craft that creates a new synthesis, an art that creates a new reality, an imaginative and a spiritual one, an enrichment of worlds. Philosophy is not enough. The inclusion of myth and beliefs are not enough in themselves. There must be a commensurate form and a consummate technique to embody it all, and there must be something to say. This is the most difficult thing. This is the holy grail of literature and art. It is why certain works stand out above all the others, why they endure, why they appear endless in possibility and interpretation. The writers have made something new and made them permanent.

An Interview with Ben Okri

Vanessa Guignery / 2015

From *Callaloo* 38, no. 5, "Ben Okri: A Special Issue" (Fall 2015): 1053–63. Copyright © 2015 Johns Hopkins University Press. Reprinted by permission of Johns Hopkins University Press.

Vanessa Guignery: Your most recent novel, *The Age of Magic*, appeared in 2014, seven years after your previous novel *Starbook*, and it appears as a follow-up to *In Arcadia*, published twelve years before in 2002. In the meantime, you published stokus, essays, and poems. Had you been writing the novel during all these years when you were working in other forms? And why did you choose to set the novel in Switzerland?

Ben Okri: The novel existed, in one form or another, all these years, and was influenced by the different forms that I was working on at the time. I do and I do not think of it as a continuation of *In Arcadia*. It looks at the Arcadian idea from the aspect of magic, for want of a better word. *In Arcadia* has to do with initiation and with the energy of beginnings. That is why it is written in that particular way. *The Age of Magic* is quieter, the technique cubistic. It explores the relationship between Faust and Arcadia, and the chaos unleashed in quests for Arcadia. It is about internal Arcadias. Switzerland was an excuse, an alchemical bowl in which many secret preoccupations would come to the surface. It is about the town itself. It is about the relationship between what you are, what you seek, and the place in which you seek it. There has to be extraordinary resonance between the three things for the true narrative to emerge.

Guignery: *The Age of Magic* is a journey just as *In Arcadia* was a journey. Would you say that all your books are journeys to a certain extent—literal, metaphorical, imaginary, or spiritual journeys?

Okri: In *The Age of Magic* the journey is vertical. The real journey takes place into stratas of consciousness, into Arcadias and anti-Arcadias. Journeys interest me. All my books are not about journeys. I wouldn't say *The Famished Road* is about journeys.

Guignery: And yet *The Famished Road* puts forward the road, and the evolution of Azaro is a form of journey, isn't it?

Okri: It is not a physical journey. Now that you mention roads, the journey comes into mind. I can see the paradox of what I am saying. The journey is a great archetype. There aren't that many archetypes in literature. If you examine any writer's work deeply enough, you'll find they tend to gravitate around a few great archetypes that enable them to best express the complex ideas. If there's anything I like about the journey, it is its revelatory quality. It carries within it the reality of change. The person who leaves is not the same as the person who arrives. By its very nature journey lends itself to narrative, to analysis, and to revelation. A journey can be a physical vehicle for something more mysterious. Maybe the greatest problem with the novel is finding the right vehicle for the inner narrative to emerge. The inner narrative is what interests me. The outer form is an excuse.

Guignery: An important book about a journey—which I know is very dear to you—is the *Odyssey*, and one aspect that particularly interests you about the *Odyssey* is that it's a book about homecoming (Ismail). The first book of *The Age of Magic* is entitled "The Journey as Home" and the Quylph tells Lao that the luckiest place to be is "to be at home everywhere." Later on, a character called Emily says home is "the place for feelings of peace." Why is homecoming so appealing to you? And what is home to you?

Okri: Maybe homecoming is the central theme of all literature. All the stories we tell are about human beings in exile, in one form or another. Being alive is, in itself, a state of exile. Homecoming combines all our journeys, our spiritual, physical, and intellectual journeys. But homecoming is maybe the most difficult thing that we embark on. It is easier to leave home, harder to return. This is because of the ambiguity of what home really means and what home really is. Our idea of home changes by the time we return. Home is a complex idea. Novalis said that philosophy is homesickness. When you contemplate that idea of homesickness, while you are alive, what does it mean? It carries the notion that it is almost impossible to be totally at home in the world, in life. Some people will say that death is homecoming. For some, however, death is a continuation of the journey. Homecoming is mysterious. One could speak of homecoming as enlightenment. Intellectually, homecoming is the complete circularity of your life's thoughts and your life's work. For some, home is in the body of work they have spent their life shaping, the recipient of their life's finest energies, their life's finest thoughts. For me, home is also connected to the imagination. I am most at home when writing and not aware that I am writing. I am also at home when reading, or in the company of people whose spirit I find delightful. Home for me is a thing of the spirit, where one can grow and transform.

Guignery: When you went to India (which you visited several times), you said that you felt at home there, maybe more than in England.

Okri: Yes, I do.

Guignery: Why is that? You referred to your interest in Indian myths, in the Mahabharata. Is it a mythical, a literary connection?

Okri: It is more mysterious than that. It is not uncommon to feel more at home in places other than where you were born. It is hard to explain why. I have been to some lands and thought, "I know this place. My spirit knows this land." Yet I've never been there before. I feel it with some people that I've known them before. With India, I feel I've been there before, I've lived there. I know the place in me, in some really strange way. There are a few other places I've felt that about as well, but rarely as strongly as with India. The idea of home, for me, is definitely transterrestrial.

Guignery: When we talked about *The Age of Magic* at the beginning, I mentioned the fact that it's a follow-up to *In Arcadia*, which you tended to disagree with, and yet I feel that there is a continuum between your books. *The Famished Road* (1991) is the first volume of a trilogy, together with *Songs of Enchantment* (1993) and *Infinite Riches* (1998); *Dangerous Love* (1996) is the rewriting of your second novel *The Landscapes Within* (1981). Some writers insist on thinking of each book as separate from all the others and once one is over, it is finished and they want to forget about it. Your conception seems to be very different. When you wrote *Dangerous Love*, you said it was because *The Landscapes Within* was haunting you. Do you feel haunted by your books and that is why I feel a continuum that maybe you don't feel yourself so much?

Okri: You've put your finger on something. You've caught a restlessness among my books. The idea of a book being finished is a bit strange to me. Books continue to clamor. Books continue to ask questions. They are restless. The questions that have been awoken go on resonating. I am not sure it is possible to answer all the questions that a true novel awakens. It wouldn't be a good novel if it did. The sense of unfinished questions, but also of unfinished quests continually drives me. Not just in terms of theme or philosophy. It is also sometimes questions about form. Sometimes I cannot answer it in that book. It gets answered in another book in a completely different way. The relationship between books would be something like this: *The Age of Magic* is related to *Astonishing the Gods* as well as to *In Arcadia*. And *The Age of Magic* is also related to *The Famished Road*. Maybe there is just one coin. But there are two sides to the questions. With one side I ask a question about suffering and history and myth and so on. The other side of that coin is happiness, Arcadia. That is what *The Age of Magic* represents, the other side of the coin. Something that transcends history. Something simpler than history.

Camus said that maybe the greatest motivation for his work was happiness. I am paraphrasing, of course. He talks about happiness, but his work rarely has it. It is almost as if he didn't live long enough to get round to that great preoccupation. It is a difficult preoccupation. Maybe one of the most difficult to write about. It is so undynamic. It is almost against the idea of narrative. Happiness is a vertical thing. It lends itself more to poetry than it does to the novel. Writers are preoccupied with the dramatic side of human existence, but rarely with the still side, the nondramatic side. But the nondramatic side is an important part of what we are. This need to complete both sides of the human picture explains this swing that you experience in my work. It took me a long time to earn the freedom. This is one of the weaknesses of the literary ethos we have inherited.

Guignery: You have used the word "myth," a word I always find difficult to understand and to define. You once wrote: "What is most missing in the landscape of our times is the sustaining power of myths that we can live by" (Okri 30). What is missing is our understanding of myth, our connection with myth. How do you define "myth"?

Okri: We are talking about Myth with a capital M. Let's make that clear. Myth is the long and tremendous wisdom of the human race, whereby we have, over the course of our suffering, our laughter, our history, our experiences, distilled certain stories and archetypes that hold in perfect resonance the biggest questions that we ask about life and contain in them the greatest solutions. Myth is the most concentrated wisdom of the race. Myth is not something than can be done overnight. You can't sit down and write a Myth. It is an alchemical distillate, in narrative terms. All of our follies, our wisdom, our mistakes, our profound understanding are distilled in great concentration into these narratives. That is what Myth is. This is why Myth has to be symbolic. You cannot get the greatest concentration without symbolism. A normal, unfolding narration won't do it. It is only into symbol and metaphor that you can pack in, fold in, so much. One tincture of Myth unfolded in time and meaning and resonance is the equivalent of a hundred years of history. When I say that we have lost a sense of Myth, and the resonance of Myth, and the underlying ways in which Myth is constantly working itself out in our lives, it is a way of saying that we have lost touch with the great wisdom of the race, the great wisdom of time and timelessness.

Myth is not something in the past. It is a living river. A living under-river that touches every single person's life. It is not possible to live without mythic resonance working itself through one's life in some way. It is like gravity. It is like a centrifugal force. All those great natural forces. Myth is one of the great forces of the spiritual, psychic, and emotional realms in which we live. It is completely unavoidable. It contains archetypes, but it is bigger than archetypes. We pass it on casually, without knowing it, to each succeeding generation in those stories we tell that have a resonance. In every culture in the world, it is passed on in one form or another. And it is not because one influential group of people—like they say the Greeks did—went around and spread their myths everywhere. It is not that. It is an emotional and psychic archeology that every tribe, every race, has engaged in. They have lived, they have made mistakes, and they have discovered these things. They have found these myths running through their lives. It is the same myths clothed in different forms because we are all subject to the same great underlaws of our lives. These are the laws that have not yet found their great science. Maybe the true scientists of these great laws are the novelists, the storytellers.

Guignery: Another revered word or practice or concept in your vocabulary is "dreaming," or "redreaming." In your work, you seem to take dreaming to a different level from what we usually assume dreaming to be.

Okri: We don't really understand the nature of dreams, or what the dreaming universe is. Even with Jung's and Freud's great works, we are only at the tip of the Everest of what dreaming implies, what it really is in relation to human life.

Guignery: And for you, dreaming is not just dreaming at night.

Okri: It is not just dreaming at night, although that is the Rosetta Stone. It is the thing that we touch when we think about it. But that is not all that it is. We cannot understand what it is without having a proper understanding of what it is to dream at night. The science of dreaming is still young. When we fall asleep at night, or in the afternoon, we experience a complete universe, different from this but made up of its elements. It has its own logic. It is as real as anything that we experience here. The air we breathe, the things that we do, have their consequences. It is a world in which you live and you have your being. We assume that the brain has made up this world. That is a poor understanding of what dreaming is. If the brain has made up *that* world, then it already says something about *this* world. If the brain has made up *that* world, then it already puts a question mark over *this* world. Then we can't know for sure if the brain isn't making up *this* world as well.

In this way, the foundation of reality is automatically called into question. What is the foundation of reality? What does it mean when we talk about the real world? When we talk about reality and the things that we see and hear and touch? Are we creating the world that we experience? Does the world exist utterly, separate from us? Is the world indeed as we perceive it to be? Or is it quite different? Is there any way of seeing the world as it really is, given the fact that we only experience it through our senses, and with the intermediary of our brains? All of these are crucial questions about the nature of reality. And the nature of reality is central to the nature of literature, to the nature of fiction. These are the root areas in which I operate. If to dream is to inhabit a world with its own logic, a world as apparently real as the one we are living in, to redream is to take that capacity to a more conscious level. It implies that some aspect of us has a link to the core of reality itself. It is more than knowledge. It is related to the foundation of the making of the world itself. It is a creation thing. These things are related to creation myths and creation realities.

Guignery: In several of your texts, you write that "we" can or must redream the world and what I would call a specific Okrian stylistic feature is your frequent use of the pronoun "we" in your essays, poems, and novels (more than "I" or "they"), maybe a humanistic type of "we." Where does that "we" come from?

Okri: We have talked about dreams and the foundation of reality. We are not entirely sure whether we are making up the world, or whether it is our consciousness that's doing it. This immediately calls into question the individual's place in the scheme of things. If we are making up the world individually, then we must be making up the world together in order to live in it. There is a sense in which we are all cocreating the world. An aspect of this is fed from what can only be called the communal. It is like the communal perception of the African consciousness, which is different from the individual perception of the European consciousness. It is informed by the communal perception I got from my forefathers and foremothers, and enriched by the sense of cocreating the world that we are constantly engaged in. That might be where that "we" comes from. It is humanistic, but there are real roots to it.

Guignery: You said in an interview that you value the discipline in Maupassant and Chekhov (Kapur). What is discipline for you? Is it the action of looking for the right word, *le mot juste* as Gustave Flaubert would say?

Okri: Every serious writer has to incarnate the highest discipline of their art. I think that's *de rigueur*. You cannot be any less disciplined than your masters. But we interpret that discipline in accordance with our philosophical pursuits. That discipline is difficult and has a philosophical basis. It goes back to everything we were saying earlier. The philosophy of everything I write is of a whole. It runs through everything. It has infinite ramifications. We talked about the nature of reality, and how tricky the nature of this reality is. We cannot completely pin it down, because we don't know its cause. The world that we see is not necessarily the world that is there. It is constantly being refracted through our eyes, our ears, our education, our culture. Anything that we are looking at is already qualified by these factors, including the state of our health, the development of our spirit and judgment, and so on and so forth.

Thus the world becomes problematic for narration. Problematic because to tell stories through time is to ignore the fact that reality itself transcends time. You already have a time problem with the telling of stories. The sequential way in which things appear to happen in reality might not be the way in which they actually do happen. This affects the way in which one tells stories. The other thing is that, since the world that we look at is not necessarily the world that is there, the words that we choose to resonate the things that we see already themselves become problematic. We now have a real difficulty of bridging the world as we perceive it and the words by which we resonate it. That's where the discipline of the craft is central.

It is not just about finding the right word. It is not just about Flaubert's *mot juste*. That is assuming that there is one word for a fixed and unalterable reality. But the minute your sense of that reality is affected by the influence of Myth, by the transcendence of time, you have a different kind of *mot juste*, probably. It is no longer just a word. It is *a* word in a continuum of words that is capable of catching, reflecting, hinting at, refracting this multi-layered reality that one is trying to elucidate. It goes beyond a word and now becomes a body of fluid constructions. That explains the dream logic in my work. It is the word in its right place, but it is the word amongst others. The world is as fluid as our perception is, and the words by which we try and catch that have to have something of that fluidity as well as the rigor of precision. It is a double problem.

So it is a different kind of discipline and a different kind of rigor. One aspect of that is related to the nature of form. Everything I have said also has its impact on form. In the pre-Copernican universe as applied to things, a tree is exactly as it appears to be. But in the postimpressionist, poststructuralist universe, the tree that we are looking at is most certainly not the tree that is there. The form of things has to undergo alterations. Form affects not just the form of the story, the way in which it is told, but the form of paragraphs, the form of words within a sentence. It is difficult, in short . . . You can't imagine the number of times I have to rewrite and reshape because of this. That is why the stoku is important to me. It gives me the smallest form in which to work out these difficulties.

Guignery: One of the specificities of your style is parataxis (the deliberate erasure of connecting words between sentences). Would you say this feature has intimate links with West African orature?

Okri: There is an element of that. At an important stage between *The Landscapes Within* and *Incidents at the Shrine*, I went through a bit of a crisis. It was a crisis that had to do with the axis of the world as I perceived it. I realized that the naturalistic form of narration does not work in relation to reality as I've known it. I began this long research into the African way of seeing, its presence and storytelling in riddles, in paintings and sculpture, the way in which we use angles to qualify, to layer, to dimensionalize. The whole way in which context itself is a powerful source for creating disjunction and therefore freedom in the mind. There was a big research. Everything that I write has been affected by the fruits of that research. The fruits are a definite part of the way I see the world and the way I write about the world. Even if I were to write about this table here in Little Venice. There is an element of that. But only an element. In the sense of a tincture. In the sense of something that I've distilled. I would say it is certain moments in orature. It is not all moments in orature. A large percentage of aspects of orature are normal narrative strategies. There are moments in orature, in traditional storytelling, that have these leaps and disjunctions, these ways in which a space is suggested between two statements so as to create the possibility of a third and a fourth and a fifth. But then I have found that it exists not just in Africa.

Guignery: In March 2012 you posted the title poem of *Wild*, line by line, on Twitter. What attracted you to Twitter at that time?

Okri: It was the possibility of the form. It was attractive. There are two movements to my work and to my thought. One movement is towards smaller and smaller things. I go microscopic, to the source of things, to the heart of things, to how things are made, to the building blocks of things. The other movement is out, bigger and bigger towards Myth and the cosmos and worlds. I go through phases when I go in small, and other phases when I go out big. That time coincided with a going-in-small phase. I was working on stokus, and the stoku is the smallest unit of fictionality. With those poems I was interested in the smallest units of poetry, in how many syllables it takes for the beginnings of the fragrance of a poem to be possible. Twitter was this public form that gave one an opportunity to look at that.

Guignery: Poems and stokus partake indeed of the same tendency towards what you've called an "atomization" (Wilkinson 82). The third literary genre involved in this process may be the essays in *A Time for New Dreams*. The collection is subtitled *Poetic Essays*, which you define as "an essay with the brevity and spring of poetry" (Vogel). Some of these essays are aphorisms and thus very small units. Why is brevity of expression so appealing to you?

Okri: When you work on different forms over the same period of time they begin to connect. It is like cooking. Whatever you're cooking, whatever else you're cooking at that time works its way into the flavor of your central dish. I discovered the essay early through philosophy and through Montaigne, found in my father's library. Units of the expression of thought have long interested me. I like Bacon and Camus for that reason. I like essays to be short. It has got to do with what I said about Myth. We are best when we compress a lot of experience into the smallest space. Portability is the secret of nature itself. Nature experiments. It does things small first, before it does them big. We human beings do that too. We pass on to the next generation a history of forebears in little stories that we tell. My family's history came to me as little stories that Mum would tell me, casually, while eating, or when I was about to go on a journey. I'd say: "Mum, I've been here all this time, you could have taken more time with the stories. Why are you giving me this compressed version now that I'm about to leave?" And she'd say: "So you can carry it with you."

Guignery: There is one dimension which is not often discussed in analyses of your work, and that is humor. Readers and critics don't seem to perceive it.

Okri: No, they don't get it.

Guignery: And yet there are many instances of humor in your work, in the stokus for instance or in the description of the crew at the beginning of *In Arcadia*. But humor is sometimes conveyed in such an oblique way that some readers might not see it at first hand. Is humor important to you?

Okri: You've shown your usual unerring instincts. You are absolutely right. Humor is central. It has its roots in a disjunction between us and our reality. The human condition is fundamentally a humorous one. We live with complete certainty in the world. We are not what we think we are. The world is not what we think it is. We do not have the kind of effect on the world that we think we do. Novalis said that humanity is a humorous role, and he's right. We are in a comic position. We are living, not with a sense of absurdity, but with a sense of disjunction. There is a disjunction between us and our reality. If someone were to look at us from a fifth dimensional point of view, they would not be able to stop laughing. Humor is already implied in what it is to be human. We live in constant misunderstanding with everything around us, with ourselves and with one another and with nature. When *The Famished Road* first came out, I said: "It's a humorous book. You are also meant to be laughing." But people read too seriously. We read too solemnly. A lot of literatures are read with a lot of baggage that we bring to them. Those perceptions get in the way of reading what is on the page. I read an early story, "Incidents at the Shrine," to some friends and they kept laughing. There is a hidden humor. It is a stylistic humor, tucked away in a tone of voice. I don't laugh on the page. I am a pokerfaced writer.

Guignery: In a letter to Gustave Flaubert in December 1875, George Sand wrote: "You produce desolation and I produce consolation." Would you say you produce desolation, consolation, a bit of both, or neither?

Okri: I like to go to the roots of things. That means upsetting. It means pulling out from under people the world as they perceive it to be. It means creating texts that undermine the world as we perceive it. I am constantly undermining. The world has to be undermined for us. We take too much for granted. The amount we take for granted is absurd. The wreck of our history is because of the amount we take for granted. Even with our thoughts.

From one thought to the next, we take too much for granted. We ought to be slower, and humbler, and much more aware of the gaps between things. To reassure the reader about the world is to do them real violence. It is to say to them: "The world is as you think it is. Please carry on in the same old way." That is a recipe for disaster. We should be giving aesthetic shocks. If we are not giving aesthetic shocks to readers, then what on earth are we doing? Fairy tales are like life, but in oblique ways. We need to be super-interpreters of the world and of reality and of everything that happens to us, in order to make sense of this world. One has to be a destroyer in some way, but a beautiful and creative one. But one should not appear to be.

Guignery: Talking about the new generation of Nigerian writers, in particular Helon Habila and Chimamanda Ngozi Adichie, you refer to their awareness of "the social responsibility of literature" and to the status of the writer as teacher and social critic (thus echoing Chinua Achebe's seminal text "The Novelist as Teacher") (Kapur). Most critics see you more as a dreamer, a griot, a shaman, especially in your later works. Do you see yourself as a teacher and a social critic as well?

Okri: The social critic role is a part of my writing. It is part of the literary tradition in Nigeria. It is an important role. It makes writers coshapers of the society of which they are a part. Somebody has to hold the politicians to account. Somebody has to call them out. Writers are eminently positioned to do that. But there are many other important roles. Each writer chooses the way that can best refract their sensibility. The shaman aspect is connected to this sense of magic. The root of consciousness is magical. People keep saying, "Why do you go on about magic?" and I say to them, "Look at the world. Look at anything. Anything that you're doing is already a magical act of consciousness." The world, as it is, is not the world that we are seeing. We create the world in accordance with our faculties. We are performing an act of magic. It is the root of consciousness itself. We can't help it. We assemble from elements in the air, color, form, and dimension. To perceive is a magical act. We can't get away from that. I am someone who is fascinated by the conundrum of reality. Social criticism, shamanism, literature, all of it are part of the great conundrum of what reality is and our place in it. History, suffering, Myth are all implicated in this.

Guignery: You said in an interview and you've showed in several essays that you have your "quarrels with Nigeria" (Deandrea 56). Do you have your quarrels with England as well?

Okri: One of them is what I said about Myth. Another is the nature of teaching. Something has gone strange with the way children are taught. It has to do with the prevailing philosophy. Education should not be influenced by a prevailing philosophy. It is dangerous when a country goes through an intense religious phase, and all of its teaching becomes intensely religious. Then it goes through an atheistic phase, and all its teaching becomes atheistic. Education should transcend intellectual vogues. It ought to be one place that receives the best of our interrogation, and not the worst of our passing philosophies.

Guignery: You wrote the script for the film *N: The Madness of Reason* (2014) by Peter Kruger. How did your collaboration with the director develop?

Okri: Firstly I should say that Peter Kruger is a genius of a filmmaker. He had the idea to do this film about a French man who went to Africa. He was maybe the first encyclopedist of the continent, in a systematic sort of way. Peter Kruger wondered: "How am I going to tell this story?" He didn't want to do a biopic. He came to me initially to write the script, about seven or eight years ago. When he told me about the story, I knew it was going to take a long time to do this film. I said, "It's going to take you seven years, Peter," and he said, "No, it won't. I'll do it in two years." I said, "No, it's going to take you seven years." I was just about to embark on *Starbook* and I needed all my energies. So he went away, the years passed, he got some money together and did some filming in various parts of Africa, and then came back after exactly seven years with these astonishing images. When he went filming, he read his way through my work: *The Famished Road*, *Astonishing the Gods*, early stories . . . . The premise of the film is about this man who is already dead. It tells the story after his death. A young Ghanaian writer, Nii Parkes, when he saw the film, said, "This film is soaked in Ben Okri's world!" Anyway, he shot all these wonderful images, and didn't know what to do with them. He came back to me, showed them to me and my agents. After about twenty minutes I said, "Peter, I know exactly what to do with this." I knew exactly what to do. I went away and I soaked myself in the images again, and I wrote about twenty-five pages of poetry.

The world is not made by knitting things. A world is made in the spaces between things. The mind is a storymaking machine. A redreaming way of writing may enable one to create a very unique world. We worked really closely together. It was a double process. He had to think as an African, and I had to think as a European. There was a changing of places. Also I wanted to undermine the "heart of darkness" theme. There was a danger that it might have a "heart of darkness" theme. I had to pull it away from that. It is interesting what certain words can do when you drop them into an ocean of images. They can transform things. It was a great education.

Guignery: The film is a reflection on one's need for definitions and categorizations. It is rather paradoxical as you, as a writer, have always tried to avoid definitions, avoid being put in categories in terms of literary genres or critical approaches. How did you feel about that?

Okri: The film sets up the question: "Can you define the world?" There are two great tensions in the film. How to tell a story after death. And how can you be an encyclopedist in a world in which it is impossible to define anything. Where does that put you? It puts you in an ironic position. It becomes doubly ironic to use French or English to describe that reality.

Guignery: The film also conveys the idea of incompleteness. It's called *N* because the man dies having only reached the letter N.

Okri: Incompleteness is a human condition. We mostly die unfinished.

Guignery: I am wondering whether one could consider this film, *N: The Madness of Reason*, and your latest book, *The Age of Magic*, as companions.

Both titles appear quite oxymoronic, and although the quest of the characters in both works is very different, they could also be related: they are all on a journey once again. Would you agree that they could be seen as companions?

Okri: They are companions, one in a terrestrial, the other in an intellectual sense. They are also complementary views of history. *The Age of Magic* is about history as consciousness. *N: The Madness of Reason* is about consciousness as history. I flow in and out of these two things: the social role of the artist and the nonsocial role of the artist. It is important that the artist has these two spheres to flow in and out of. If the artist is only a social artist, then they contribute to the perception of the world as this fixed and immutable thing. They contribute to a lie. Yet we must have social responsibility. We live in society. We live in a world in which politicians make mistakes, in which people are victims of bad policies. We live in a world in which we can do something with the power of our pens. The fact is that we have the power to affect history, not as much as we like, but to the degree that actually we can create a bit more happiness for people on this planet. It is possible to relieve the suffering that people needlessly experience. We can do something. But the artist should not be locked into only that role. It is also our role to awaken readers to the mythic dimension of our lives. We participate in time, but we also participate in timelessness. Without this sense, we can't begin to have a measure of tranquility or confidence about being here.

Works Cited

Deandrea, Pietro. "An Interview with Ben Okri." *Africa America Asia Australia* 16 (1994): 55–82.

Ismail, Adilah. "Ben Okri? One hat worn many ways." *Sunday Times* (Sri Lanka) Feb. 12, 2012. Web. May 14, 2015. http://www.sundaytimes.lk/120212/Magazine/sunday timesmagazine_04.html.

Kapur, Vikram. "Reality is not in the realism." *The Hindu* Jan. 28, 2012. Web. May 22, 2015. http://www.thehindu.com/features/magazine/reality-is-not-in-the-realism/article2839716.ece.

Okri, Ben. "Our false oracles have failed. We need a new vision to live by." *Times* (London) Oct. 30, 2008: 30.

Vogel, Saskia. "Interview: Ben Okri." *Granta* April 7, 2011. Web. May 22, 2015. http://www.granta.com/ New-Writing/Interview-Ben-Okri.

Wilkinson, Jane. "Ben Okri." In *Talking with African Writers*, 76–89. London / Portsmouth: James Currey / Heinemann, 1992.

Ben Okri Q&A: "I Can't Live without Good Conversation, Or Love"

New Statesman / 2018

From *New Statesman* Sept. 19, 2018. Reprinted by permission of Mohammed Fasi.

New Statesman: What's your earliest memory?

Ben Okri: Getting lost in the middle of Nigeria. I was a baby and I just walked or crawled away from home. It nearly gave my mother a nervous breakdown. But I was found hours later. I've enjoyed getting lost since.

NS: Who are your heroes?

BO: My childhood heroes were characters in books and comics. My adult heroes are people who face life bravely, who keep on regardless of opposition and criticism, and who believe in humanity.

NS: What was the last book that changed your thinking?

BO: *The Inner Chapters* by Chuang Tzu. The highest thing a book can do is not to change your thinking but expand your consciousness. Thought is easily changed, but an expanded consciousness sees truly, clearly, for itself.

NS: Which political figure, past or present, do you look up to?

BO: Mandela, Obama, and Lincoln. You can never really say how good a leader has been till some time has passed. It is still perhaps too early to assess Obama or Mandela. But you measure not only by what they did, but the circumstances of their achievements.

NS: What would be your *Mastermind* specialist subject?

BO: The art of living.

NS: In which time and place, other than your own, would you like to live?

BO: The time when we truly will not judge people by the color of their skin, their eyes or their money, their gender, their family, their class, their religion, etc.

NS: What TV show could you not live without?

BO: I can happily live without TV, but I can't live without good conversation or love.

NS: Who would paint your portrait?

BO: Hockney once offered to paint my portrait after I wrote him a poem-portrait. But he proved hard to get hold of. David, name the place and I'll bring the face.

NS: What's your theme tune?

BO: Bob Marley, "Redemption Song."

NS: What's the best advice you've received?

BO: "Follow your light." My father and mother both urged it, and it guides me always.

NS: What's currently bugging you?

BO: The dividedness of the left. The left could be changing the world for the better for good people. Instead they allow others to fuck up the world, through their disunity.

NS: What single thing would make your life better?

BO: The ability to sleep at will, like Napoleon.

NS: When were you happiest?

BO: When my daughter was born.

NS: In another life, what job might you have chosen?

BO: Poet, novelist, essayist, playwright, dreamer. To work with the roots of reality, to speak to people in the deepest part of themselves, to be able to sing of change, that's the one for me.

NS: Are we all doomed?

BO: As long as we remember the fundamental magnificence of what it is to be human, we will overcome evil, transcend disaster, and create, from our worst crisis, surprising new chapters in this amazing human story.

Ben Okri on His "Unavoidably" Political Poems

Ushnota Paul / 2019

From *The Telegraph* (India), March 9, 2019. Reprinted by permission of Ushnota Paul.

We are at the Jaipur Literature Festival being held at Diggi Palace. It's a bitterly cold afternoon in Jaipur. We find Ben Okri—who won the Man Booker Prize in 1991 for his book *The Famished Road* in his usual mysterious mood, wearing his signature beret. His wife Charlotte is busy running around their little daughter Mirabella, who's a handful.

Right after his session with fiction heavyweights like Andrew Sean Greer, Vikram Chandra, Sebastian Barry, and Tania James as copanelists—talking about "Where Does Fiction Come From?"—we caught up with Ben Okri for a chat.

Ushnota Paul: Ben, your latest novel, *The Freedom Artist*, seems to be in the tradition of George Orwell's *1984* and Franz Kafka's *The Trial*....

Ben Okri: That's a perceptive insight. It's unavoidable . . . I'm probably writing that tradition amongst others. There's also a tradition of Voltaire's *Candide*, there's a tradition of Robert Louis Stevenson—writers who write fairly dark fables about strange times, partly quest fables and partly question fables. I think we are living in a Kafka-Orwell time, I think we are living in a time when truth is upside down, a time when it's hard to know what to believe, a time when a lot of things are in doubt, a time of troubles, a time of national disasters. I feel we are in the brink of something, I don't know what, but it feels like it.

Paul: Would you call it a dystopian fiction?

Okri: I don't like the word dystopian, it gives a wrong impression. But I know what you mean. Yes, it's roughly in that territory, but I wouldn't use the word dystopian. I do know where you're coming from.

Paul: You won the 1991 Booker Prize for *The Famished Road*. How would you describe your journey thus far?

Okri: When I won that prize, then it was just an extraordinary surprise. I was just pleased to be shortlisted at that time. And anyway, I didn't write the book for prizes, I wrote the book to touch people, to change people, to transform people, to transform myself. I wrote the book because I had a great story that I wanted to tell. On the day that I won the prize, I remember being stunned and a little bit afraid.

It changed my life, really. It really did. I went from selling two thousand copies of a book to selling hundreds of thousands of copies and continue to sell as many copies. It gave me languages around the world, gave me a lot of opportunities to travel, brought me a lot of friends. But it came with a heavy responsibility as well.

Paul: Your poem "Grenfell Tower" written about the fire in London's Grenfell Tower in June 2017 had so much angst and anger hidden in it. What propelled you to write it?

Okri: There was a tower of twenty-four stories in London where the poor live. That bent down because they put this cladding around it. This tower has been there since the sixties, but since it's for the poor, of course, there's no fire alarm, one staircase for twenty-four floors, no fire extinguishers . . . nothing. So, it caught fire and blazed for three days while the whole world watched. It had a huge impact on people. I live nearby and by the second day, you could smell burning flesh. Seventy people were burnt to death in it, many of them were told to stay in their rooms. I was just so moved and outraged and angered by it that I wrote this poem in July . . . it's not something that I normally do. But then suddenly I found myself pulling on a great African tradition, of poets who react to contemporary outrages on the people.

Paul: You also write poems with hard-hitting greater political statements. How do you balance that—making a statement while writing poetry?

Okri: Sometimes. I don't think the poems are statements. Not all my poems are political but the poems that are political are kind of unavoidable. I just couldn't be writing about flowers and feeling bad about the fact that no one, you know, affirmed me on that particular day, while a tower was burning and people were burning in there . . . . What was I going to be writing about during that period of time?

Paul: You apparently don't discuss your work in the writing stage because you're a little superstitious as a writer?

Okri: Yes, absolutely. I think it's just bad luck to talk about your work while you're writing it. A lot of writers do and it doesn't do them any harm . . . but that's my superstition. I have got a few.

Paul: So you're not going to tell us about what you're working on next, right?

Okri: Of course not. But if you really want to know, I can make up a fake project for you. This is the time of fake truth, so why not a fake project? I'm writing about the mysterious autobiography of the moon, in the first person [*laughs*].

Paul: You're one of those few writers who's a novelist as well as a poet. When you have an idea, how do you know which way it should go?

Okri: Well, the idea tells you where it goes. Some time when I was very young, I had an idea for a poem but it really was an idea for a novel but I couldn't tell the difference. Also, once I had an idea for a novel that really was an idea for a poem. But that's because I was really young and inexperienced. But when you have an idea it tends to come with a form. It's very rare that you have the itch for a poem and then you write a play, because a poem is usually a very contained, mysterious soundscape in itself.

Paul: What's your writing process like?

Okri: Well, it's very simple. With a novel, I manifest half the ideas, and if the idea is full and rich you start writing it immediately. And if the idea is not full and rich, if it's just a scratch or a hint, then I leave it and let it grow inside me. But you don't want to overdo that because you could be stewing it for the rest of your life. And at one point, I just take a deep breath and leap. When I take that leap, on the very first day when you're writing the very first sentence of that novel, it's frightening. Because you could just start in the wrong direction, you could start in the wrong tone and you wouldn't know it for a long time that it's not right.

Paul: Do you read reviews of your work?

Okri: I used to read reviews a lot, I don't so much anymore. My friends tell me about them. When I was much younger, I used to read the reviews and gosh, it used to take such a long time to get it out of your head and I decided that I don't want that anymore. Just write the book. Some of the best reviews are the responses of my readers.

Paul: What did you read as a child that shaped you and your thoughts?

Okri: I loved reading fairy tales when I was a kid. I used to love myths and legends of this world as a kid and I couldn't stop reading about them. There was a time I kind of knew the legends of almost every country, I used to just read them. I also loved reading those early Greek tales. I read Homer and people like that really young and then I just graduated into reading from my father's library.

Paul: Is there a favorite writing corner in your house?

Okri: No, it changes with every book. I handwrite the entire draft... it's magical to handwrite. It feels like I'm really taking ownership of the book.

Paul: How long does it generally take for you to finish a novel?

Okri: It depends. If it's a long novel, it could take you up to seven years. If it's a short novel, it could take you a year.

Paul: So would you call yourself a very patient writer?

Okri: Yeah, absolutely. You cannot write well without patience... because writing is a mysterious activity.

Paul: Some of your poems have titles that are taken from old poems. How much of an influence....

Okri: [*Cuts*] Give me an example.

Paul: I think P. B. Shelley is a big influence in your writing.

Okri: Yes, okay [*smiles*]. There are not many places to get titles from but other poets, especially great poets. See, the thing is, what you want in a title is exactly what you want in a good poem. You want few words that suggest an infinity of possibilities. That's what poetry does. And a good title has to have the concentration and clarity of a good poem... it's very difficult. And where are you going to find it if it's not other great poets? Where else would you find it if it wasn't old books like Bhagavad Gita or the Bible? Sometimes I make up my own titles but they are very difficult.

Paul: You have been compared with Salman Rushdie in the past. Do you agree with that comparison?

Okri: No, I don't agree. I think we are very different writers. Yes, he's more operatic than I am. We come from slightly different writing traditions but we have similar things at the heart of what we do. And I think those similar things have to do with the similarity of our cultures... the fact that we both come from great poetic storytelling cultures. So the aesthetics of our cultures are interestingly similar but the way we write is very different. All you have to do is put a paragraph of Rushdie next to a paragraph of Ben Okri and you'll see the difference immediately [*laughs*].

But inside the swirl of our storytelling where one story becomes another story, that's our tradition... that's what we do in Africa. African storytelling is like the sea... take the river that goes into the sea that goes into the ocean. That's how all my books are... it starts with a trickle that goes into a stream that goes into a river that goes into the sea and it just keeps branching out like that. The storytelling tradition that I come from, we believe that if you touch one thing as a storyteller properly, you touch God.

Paul: Which is your favorite Salman Rushdie book?

Okri: Ah, that's such an unfair question [*laughs*]! I still have a soft spot for *Shame*. I mean I love *Midnight's Children* but I think *Shame* is the book where his aesthetics, his opera, his clarity, his anger fuse together the most.

Paul: Who are your favorite authors?

Okri: I think we'd all have been really poor without Homer.

Paul: And your all-time favorite book?

Okri: I would choose two all-time favorite books—*Don Quixote* and the *Odyssey* by Homer.

Ben Okri Interview: We Can Ascend Mountains

Marc-Christoph Wagner / 2019

Louisiana Channel, Aug. 2019. https://channel.louisiana.dk/video/ben-okri-we-can-ascend-mountains © Louisiana Channel, Louisiana Museum of Modern Art, Denmark. Printed by permission of Louisiana Channel and Marc-Christoph Wagner.

The World Now

Ben Okri: The essence of our world right now is transitioning. We're moving from one thing, slowly into another. The new thing that we're moving into is, I feel, possibly quite dangerous for humanity, for most people on this planet. And this is a time when language has to join, has to help to create—for want of a better phrase—a new army of light, a new army of rebalancing, a new army of truth, because what we need right now more than anything else is truth. We've had plenty of fake news. We've had plenty of alternative facts. This is a time for new truths.

Literature

Okri: You see, that's why literature and language are so important because they're intimately related to consciousness. And literature at its most powerful helps to shift the axis of an age, for the very simple reason that it shifts the access of our consciousness, of each person that reads it. If you can imagine reading *Crime and Punishment* around the time that it was published, or reading *Don Quixote* around the time it was published, to read it for the first time . . . . They are books—and there are many other books like that, *The Outsider* by Camus, *Things Fall Apart* by Chinua Achebe—these are books that when you read them, you're beginning in one kind of consciousness and one kind of state of mind. By the time you've finished, you're in another. You're subtly changed, enriched. That's one of the most powerful things that literature does. It's not rhetoric, it's not trying to persuade you into something that you are not. It's adjusting your mental lens so that you see the world in a new way, clearly, for the first time.

Marc-Christoph Wagner: In this book [*The Freedom Artist*], you describe the world as a prison, a prison that has been built for generations and generations, and you describe [how] the hierarchy in essence is ourselves. The people discover that they are the hierarchy. So [is] what you say that they live in a false consciousness, and the way to kind of wak[e] this up can be words, can be literature?

Okri: Well, living in a false consciousness, living in a slightly darkened consciousness is, in many ways, the long story of humanity. We go through ages when we have a new orientation about how the world can be. There are mental revolutions, there are social revolutions, there are cultural revolutions. And by revolutions I don't mean the upturning, overturning of society, I just simply mean the turning over of the mind, so that we see what we're capable of being, anew. And we're harborers of prisons. We really are. We harbor prisons of ideas about how society can be. We harbor prisons of ideas about what we are as human beings. Gender prisons, race prisons, tribal prisons. All kinds of prisons we have inside our heads and our consciousness. And we need to be progressively freed from many of them, to be able to realize our potential as human beings, and as citizens in our society to the fullest. So not only literature [can do it]: art can do it, dance can do it, politics is eminently—when it's most enlightened—in a powerful way to do it. Politics because of deeds and laws. Literature, dance, music, art because of how it affects our consciousness, because of how it makes us aware of how much freer we can be, and how, in a way, we are primarily, each individual, the cocreators of our world. We really are. Literature at its best empowers that, strengthens that.

Literature in Your Upbringing

Okri: Well, if I'm really honest, literature was always a kind of unconscious part of my upbringing. Books were always there. I didn't primarily want to be a writer when I was a child. I wanted to be a scientist. I wanted to be a composer. I wanted to be a painter. To be a writer came quite low on my list actually. It wasn't even there in a way. But a series of crucial things that happened in my life, the intersection of history and me, I think, began to change all that. If I was going to sort of start to mention the changes, I would say coming back from England to Africa when I was a child was a real, extraordinary awakening for me, because it made me aware, in reverse, that no culture has an absolute view on looking at the world. My love of language was planted in me [by] my father, who was a lawyer, spoke beautifully and loved Latin [and by] my mother, who was a great storyteller, an enigmatic storyteller. But also at school, I loved literature without knowing that it was literature. I just loved what it did, the sounds, the images.

History

Okri: History and its impact on me: the Nigerian civil war. I was a child when it broke and erupted right in the middle of my family. And as a young child still I saw death. I saw people being shot. I saw neighbors, good people, suddenly becoming manipulated by the ethos of the times, and changing overnight. But above all, I saw death. To see death at eight is a real awakener, because you're aware, from very early on, of the strange, apparent finality of life. And I began to ask questions, and those questions began to sound like thunder in my spirit. Social questions, political questions, questions of the individual and reality. That's where it started. Poverty afterwards. Some homelessness afterwards. They just deepened. And one day I began . . . I was painting, and one day I just thought I should write, about rainfall. It was raining outside. So long story (I'll make it short), but I made an astonishing discovery which is that when I wrote, *I* disappeared. Ben Okri vanished. I just went straight into this thing called writing. I was in that place, and then I came back out and the poem was written. And I thought: Wow, that has to be the most miraculous entry into another state of consciousness to have experienced outside of any spiritual practice.

Wagner: I have the feeling that you might have a broader understanding of literature than we know it in the Western world. We have very much our tales and books and so on, but in Nigeria, maybe in many parts of Africa, you have also this oral tradition of storytelling. You have the real world, you have the more kind of spiritual world, so there are many layers coming together and you find that in your books as well. How would you describe for me how this kind of multilayered way of telling stories, living stories, has formed your view on literature, and how is that translated into your authorship?

Okri: That's a very important question, because when I was learning to write, I read the books that were available in my father's library, that he brought with him from England. And so I read all the classics, as we know them. But when I began to write, I became aware—slowly, over a period of time, it wasn't immediate—that there was a real gap between the world as it was described by many of the books I'd read, and my African reality that I grew up with, which is a reality that involves the reality of storytelling, of myths, the realm of the ancestors, the realm of the gods, the realm of the unborn, and this so-called everyday quotidian reality. And one lived and experienced all of these different realities *at the same time*. It's very, very important that I stress that. Of course, this multilayered experiencing of reality is slowly fading because of the impact of—you can call it globalization, or you can call it the modern contemporary universal reality, or "worldwide" rather than "universal" reality. But it's still there.

So when I came to write, after my second novel, I became so aware of this gap between the world rendered by people like Jane Austen and Dickens—great and wonderful writers that they are—and this African reality with all its levels. And I felt it was impossible to go on without finding a new way to write, that would capture all of these levels of reality that I'd grown up with and that were natural to many people's way of looking at the world, to capture all those levels of reality, *at the same time*. Not to write and talk about one reality, describe it and then another reality, which would lead to a very swollen and indigestible text. Because actually, when we experience the reality, we experience it all at once. So I spent years just trying to find a new tone which will have all of these realities and suggested ways, at once. And that was maybe one of the biggest literary experiments, and it was a great laboratory I had to go into, of just working on going back to language, and taking it apart and seeing how . . . . And after that, my writing then became this constant question of investigating what reality actually really is, and how much of it is inflected by our consciousness. And that then led me to how we affect reality. And that then led me to where I am now in *The Freedom Artist*: looking at how figures of power alter our reality by altering our myths, by altering our beliefs, by altering our sense of our history. So they bend our reality and change, literally change who we are and what we can accept, and thereby create a new kind of very dangerous normalization. But it really begins with operating on how we experience reality through myths and through stories. So it's very important that the storyteller analyses in stories just how this process of the manipulation of humanity is being done, right now, as it was done in the 1930s and 1940s.

The Perception of Reality

Okri: I wouldn't say that people in the West are narrowing their perception of reality. What I would say is that the West, because of its success in the manipulation of the material world—evident success in the making of cars, and airplanes, and stuff like that—then proceeds to assume that the way it perceives reality is the universal, and the only way to perceive it. That is its narrowness: the assumption that this way of looking at the world [is the only one], that things are only what you can see and touch—*only*—which is tremendously powerful because it has given rise to this incredible rationalism that's enabled the manipulation and the shaping and the creating of new kinds of things, as it were. But that way of insisting that the things that you can see and touch are the *only* realities, that's the mistake, because there are other realities, there are other people's realities in different parts of the world. And their realities include the things that you can see and touch and also the things that you don't see and touch, invisible things, presences, thoughts, the dead, the unborn . . . . This may or may not be true, but science at this moment does not have the equipment to prove that it's not true. And so reality as we perceive it really finally *is* reality as *we* can perceive it through our consciousness, which is to say through our beliefs. To insist on one belief system as being the only way of seeing the universe is not only narrow. It's a kind of mental, cultural and spiritual tyranny, which has incredible implications for storytelling, and for relationships with one another, and for our relationships with nature, our relationships with the environment, because it means that we're constantly waiting for the evidence of the destruction that we have done, before we believe that we have done any destruction, but by then it is too late.

So we need a new kind of understanding of reality, to understand how we affect it negatively and positively. In short, what I'm trying to say is that we need a wider worldview. We need one that includes what we know to be true and what works for us, but one that also includes what other people know to be true and that works for them, and to respect that, and to be open to that, in terms of the broad possibilities of what it is to be human. That's where literature is very powerful. You have an old oral storytelling tradition of Africa and India and the Middle East, that suggests new ways, richer ways of looking at the world. We need that, desperately, because this narrowness, this very limited way of saying what reality is, is slowly killing us. I'll give you one very simple example of the Europeans who came to Africa and brought with them this very specific idea of farming, that you cut down all the trees. You cut down all the trees and you know it's a farm. We've since discovered that actually, that was the worst thing you can do, you could actually do the farming without having to destroy the trees. The two things can coexist, but you need a new relationship with reality, a new relationship with nature, a new respect of nature—the visible and the invisible part of nature—in order to begin to see this. Just a small example.

Wagner: You mentioned that nobody and no culture has this universal truth. [. . .] I was thinking, in your novel, the mountain plays quite an important role. You go up there, you're part of the society, but you go up and you get a viewpoint that gives you some kind of overview. And then I was trying to connect that a little bit to your biography, because—and I might be wrong—but you have grown up with two worlds, at least: Nigeria and London. And maybe this has led to an observation of the world that you see the one in the mirror of the other, and maybe you don't feel part of one culture. I mean, in Nigeria you might have been seen as the one from Great Britain with a privileged father, and in London you might have been seen as somebody from Africa, in this generalization of a Black person in a white culture. Would you say that this upbringing between two worlds has given you something that can be compared with the observable perspective of that mountain, that you are a part of those societies, but you're able to see them from a distance?

Okri: I am surprised you think that I've lived only between two worlds. I would say I've lived between at least five worlds. There's Nigeria, Africa, which is a constant part of my sensibility and my worldview. Europe, which is where I've lived these many years and written and thought. But there's also the world of books. That's a world. That's a constant world. It's a fluid world. It's a rich world. It's a world as powerful in its influence on me as this living world. In fact I probably spend more time in that world than in any other. Then there's the world of dreams. Then there's the world of conversations with people, from all cultures, constant conversations. And then there's a world—for want of a better phrase—the slowly swirling, unifying world that we're all part of. So I don't think it's really so distinctive as just Africa and Europe, because even in Africa you're reading, so the literary world is available to you. In the African world, Europe has made an important invasion into its sensibility, but even in Europe, Africa is there. I understand what you're trying to say about not being entirely part of one or the other gives you a third space. But I think that third space is available to anybody of sensibility, anybody who has a deep hunger for new possibilities of their art or their spirit. Absolutely. You have writers like Chinua Achebe who attained the level of world-class art growing up in Nigeria, listening to the stories of the land, reading the stories of the world. We can ascend mountaintops in all kinds of ways. But there's an extraordinary synthesis that happens when you have two cultures, two rounds, two worlds. And at the same time, I think maybe the most valuable thing is a way in which it suddenly makes you suspicious of any overdetermining worldview. The idea that these people here, that there's a way of looking at the world that these people have and that's it . . . . When you're in between, you're like: "No, no, no, there isn't just one way, there are so many ways and none of them are true and all of them are true." And that's wonderful to be kind of slightly liberated—a little bit—from the prison of culture. Cultures are both prisons and liberations at the same time.

The Young Generation

Okri: What would I say to the young generation right now? I would say to the young generation that you, that we, the human race right now, are in an absolute decisive moment of human history. We are on the edge of a cliff. And what is over that cliff, and how deep that is, whether there is any recovery from the fall, nobody knows. I always say that it's quite possible that actually, we've already gone over the edge and now we're living right now in the memory of our prefall. We're falling but we don't know it. I would say that we are in great danger as a species, and unfortunately, you are the ones who are inheriting it. A huge awakening needs to take place, *fast*. An accelerated awakening has to take place, and an accelerated reaction and compensation, in terms of our environment, in terms of our climate, in terms of where we are as a species. It might be too late, but I think the time for sleepwalking is over. I think the time for assuming that time will just go on normally is over. I don't know how one can send the fire of a new awakening of how serious the situation is right now in the world. Citizens all over the world should wake up and seize the responsibility of their citizenship, go out into the streets—whatever form there is of saying "This has to stop." We have to reverse the damage we're doing to ourselves. A new world thinking is needed. A new world thinking is needed! No longer Europe, America.

That's part of the problem. A new *world* thinking is needed. We have to look at the whole world right now as one country, one place, whose collective destiny is in great danger. So we need a new world thinking on immigration, a new world thinking on the economies. What does it mean all these different economies, one benefiting the other, becoming poorer? What the hell is all of that? What's wrong with us human beings? We're on this one planet together, how can we live, go to sleep, wake up, knowing that people just like us are dying for simple things like soap or food? It's ridiculous. There's enough to go around for the whole planet. We need a new world thinking, in literature, in art, in politics, in culture, in our relationships with one another. We need to tear down walls. We're complaining about the wall that gentleman is trying to build in America but we've got all kinds of walls between us as people and cultures and nations. It's ridiculous. This world can be miraculous and manageable for everybody.

Wagner: But in order to do that, to shape this "we," we should overcome our divides, as you say, of race, of countries, of gender. Who can be the translator? Can it be a poem [like the one] that you started with? Because [we] need something to overcome those divides.

Okri: Yes, but I resist asking for one figure, one hero figure to come along and do it for everybody. I think that's a very old and dangerous thinking. Anyway I think that kind of thinking, that kind of mythic-hero thinking worked when you were dealing with groups, small groups. That worked then. Now, everybody needs to be the hero. We need to scatter the idea of heroism and awaken it in everybody, all humans, because if we don't *all* wake up to what it means to stand up and express our voice in a positive way, if we don't *all* do it, nothing is going to happen. Waiting for one person to do it, that's way too dangerous because, first of all, there are too many forces that can work against and distort what this one person is trying to say, there are too many forces that can undermine it. We need to get into a space where forces can't undermine. We need to go beyond what can be undermined. So it needs to be everybody. It needs to be the world. We need to all wake up. Yes, you can feel my passion.

The Past Is a Changing Entity

Isabelle Rüf / 2020

From *Le Temps*, Feb. 15, 2020: 36. Translated from the French and reprinted by permission of Isabelle Rüf.

Winner of the Booker Prize in 1991, the Nigerian author is honored by the Pulloff Théâtres for a play he wrote during a writing residency at the Ledig-Rowohlt Foundation castle in Lavigny. He welcomed us there to talk about his work and his career.

On this February morning, the sky over Lavigny is shaken by British turbulences. Did they follow Ben Okri, who arrived the day before from London to attend the world premiere of *Madame Sosostris, the wisest woman in Europe*? Now the author is having breakfast with his family in the castle of the Ledig-Rowohlt Foundation. In 2016, he worked on this play during a writing residency. Now he is back, but this time a tiny child is trotting through the empty corridors. Three years old, a magical age: "Why are we growing up?" her father sighs. "This residency has been an important moment for me, in this wonderful landscape."

Behind the Mask

Sophie Kandaouroff, who looks after the guest authors, directed *Madame Sosostris* at the Pulloff Théâtres. "She did a fantastic job. Bringing the complexity of the play to life in such a small space, while respecting what I wrote, is a performance. Sophie has given the party its sparkle and deep mystery."

But who is this lady, "the wisest in Europe"? The seer appears in T. S. Eliot's *The Waste Land* and before that in Aldous Huxley's *Crome Yellow*. "She is a very ancient figure, from ancient Egypt. She belongs to the great esoteric tradition, like Madame Blavatsky. Here she appears as the attraction of a masked party organized by two female friends in the woods. But she forfeits the party and it is a disaster. One of the two friends takes her place. At first it's a comedy. She is questioned about couples, about betrayals, it is the eternal story of the broken heart, of lost love, which runs through all literature since Dido's lament.

Then the questions widen, touching on the deepest unexplored condition—who we are, beyond our appearance, who our loved ones and friends are. How does the hostess become Mrs. Sosostris behind the mask? What is reality?"

It could be a Shakespeare comedy: "Absolutely. I love his mystery plays—*A Midsummer Night's Dream, Twelfth Night, As You Like It*. Theatre is where the European tradition—Calderón, Pirandello, Ionesco—meets my African roots. These roots are in me, they have never left me. There, in everyday life, you never know where reality is. It is important that the party takes place in the forest, a place where worlds mix."

Ben Okri was born in 1959 in Minna, central Nigeria. His father was Urhobo, his mother Igbo. He grew up between Africa and Britain, as his father, a lawyer, studied. As a child he saw the devastating effects of the Biafran civil war (1967–1970). A Nigerian government scholarship enabled him to study at Essex University.

"I left mainly to write. In Nigeria, I couldn't make a living from my pen. Now I can, I've opened the door. It takes time to become a writer. At first, I wrote out of indignation at the misery of Lagos, the slums, the ghettos, the marginalization. I wrote articles and essays, but then I realized that the message was best conveyed through stories. When my mother wanted to teach me a lesson, it was always through a tale, a fable. Later on, my universe expanded to a wider philosophical and spiritual dimension. Spiritual, please note, not religious."

When the scholarship was cut, the young man experienced hardship, nights on the street or in the metro, fights, hunger. "It was a hard experience, but it had very positive effects. I learned how unforgiving the world is. It was a good lesson in reality for the young romantic writer that I was."

In 1991, *The Famished Road* won the Booker Prize. The hero, Azaro, is a spirit-child who has chosen to remain in the visible world. This vast novel intertwines the levels of dream and reality that are at the heart of African culture. It remains at the heart of Ben Okri's work, even though he lives in England and claims the right for African authors to deal with something other than the famines, social injustices and corrupt regimes that afflict their continent, as is too often expected of them.

He who studied comparative literature writes in the presence of authors from all over the world. "Our perception is too compartmentalized, we need to open up the field; in this field, translation is invaluable, as long as there is no common language for the whole world. This is not likely to happen for another hundred years, at the rate we are going. When I was growing up, I spoke three or four local languages out of the hundred or so in Nigeria. You can't do otherwise in a big city where your neighbors come from all over the place."

He himself forged his imagination in what he calls "the visible books," all the Western literature that saturates his works—poetry, novels, theatre: the *Odyssey* and the other great mythological stories, the Old Testament, "this great reservoir of stories," the *Thousand and One Nights*, *Hamlet*. But just as much in "the invisible books," the African oral tradition, his mother's tales. "There are now some very great Nigerian authors—the theatre of Wole Soyinka, the work of Amos Tutuola, and among the youth, too."

The Illusion of Freedom

Madame Sosostris says that the future is written but the past can be changed. Can it? "But look at Brexit, Trump, the whole political world is just that," Ben Okri snaps, pretending to spin a Rubik's Cube in his hands. "The past is not an immutable block of cement, it is a changing entity. Like the moon, we only know one side. Kings and dictators have always transformed it to manipulate us by giving us the illusion of freedom. 'Make America great again.' Great 'again,' on what model? This is what my latest book is about: by mythologizing the past, we create the conditions for the future that is imposed on us. It is our responsibility to show how we are being manipulated."

Isabelle Rüf: Where do you write?

Ben Okri: It's changing. Essays have to be written at the table, in my office. For other genres, I have to be standing, walking around my living room, barefoot. Often I write, always with a pen, on any medium—bank receipts, small pieces of cardboard—which I then gather. I have to be in a state of play, literature is a game.

Rüf: When do you write?

Okri: In the middle of the night or at dawn. Everyone is asleep. There is more creative oxygen available. And I can feel the dreams of all those sleeping people. But more and more, it moves to the morning. I like its freshness, its clarity. Sometimes I still get up in the middle of the night to feel that energy.

Rüf: What books have shaped you?

Okri: *Don Quixote.* When I went into that book, I was one person, I came out another. Not many books have that power.

Rüf: Why do you write?

Okri: Because that's how I feel connected to existence. It is as necessary as loving, breathing, living. You can't do it any other way.

"Courage Is a Luxury"

Katrien Steyaert / 2020

From *De Standaard* (Belgium), April 11, 2020. Translated from the Dutch. Reprinted by permission of *De Standaard*.

Since he looked death in the eye as a child during the Biafran War, Ben Okri has been shaken up. The Booker Prize winner pleads louder than ever for an awareness on a collective level. Everyone has to deal with their complicity in history. But this is a golden opportunity.

Josse De Pauw stumbles on his wooden leg to the prow of the ship. Once his character, Captain Ahab, claimed his place there but today the man is a shadow of who he was. His beard is grey and tangled, his jacket worn. When he talks, he sounds toothless or drunk on grog. What a contrast with Nobulumko Mngxekeza, the South African soprano who performs the role of Queequeg. Hired as a harpooner, she must obey the authority of her swaggering master, but she does not hesitate to pierce Ahab's all-consuming hunger for revenge—on the white whale that cost him his leg. Sometimes she does this in English, sometimes in Xhosa.

It is a Monday afternoon, before the new coronavirus has the world in its grip, and Ben Okri (61) is attending the last rehearsal of *Moby Dick, at last Queequeg speaks*, an adaptation of Herman Melville's classic by the Ghanaian Belgian director Gorges Ocloo. For Ocloo, a rising star in the Flemish theatre world, the two main characters are like Europe and its old colonies: a demented old man who clings to a bygone world, and his nurse who demands her voice. On Melville's ship, Ahab and Queequeg never exchanged a word, but now they communicate, in the belly of the whale.

"Gorges may not have known it beforehand, but I am one of the most enthusiastic readers of *Moby-Dick*," says Ben Okri after the rehearsal. The Nigerian British author wrote the libretto for the jazzy opera at Ocloo's request. Since winning the Booker Prize for *The Famished Road*—at thirty-two, he was the youngest winner ever—Okri has been one of Africa's most important voices. He has written acclaimed novels, poems and essays, was inducted into the Order of the British Empire and had conversations with Toni Morrison and Salman Rushdie. Bill Clinton, on his first visit to Africa, quoted extensively from Okri's award-winning novel, which inspired Radiohead for the song "Street Spirit."

"We give Queequeg a strong voice," Okri says. "No one has ever done that to us. In the original Queequeg is a prince, in our story she is a woman. And for the first time she says to Ahab, 'I'm on this ship too, so I have a right to know where you're taking us.' What would happen if every individual today held those in power accountable? Would we then also all sail on the rocks, as we are now threatening to do?"

Katrien Steyaert: Will masterpieces such as *Moby-Dick* continue to provide answers to the questions raised by new times?

Ben Okri: In addition to fifty thousand other themes, *Moby-Dick* highlights the relationship between Europe and its colonies, and by extension that between Western and non-Western cultures. I find it too obvious to repeat that this relationship is problematic. Look at the deaths in the Mediterranean, at the policies of European countries about it, at Brexit and some of its feeding grounds, at the underrepresentation of migrants in governments and the media, and there is no doubt: institutional racism is everywhere.

Steyaert: Over a year ago, a UN commission of enquiry pointed out that problem to Belgium in relation to people of African descent.

Okri: Anyone who takes the trouble to observe properly will see the problem. But I am not interested in shouting about this racism or in saying that Europe has the greatest difficulty in dealing with its history. What interests me is the moral, philosophical, economic and spiritual opportunities that Europe is missing. I mean, you can argue about the past until you see blue, but you cannot change it. What we can do is educate ourselves and see how we can grow. We are all accomplices, but it doesn't have to be a burden. It is like a golden opportunity for each of us to become braver and more human. When we face up to what we have done and where it has brought us, we will finally make real progress.

Steyaert: How do you see the role of politicians and governments?

Okri: If policies continue to portray immigrants as someone to be feared, people will continue to shy away from them or make up arguments against them. With spiritual and intellectual courage you can teach citizens how to move on from their past. "These facts we have on our conscience, but afterwards we have also tried this and that, and from there we can go forward"—you hear it far too little today.

Steyaert: Surely there are sincere attempts at decolonization? Flemish universities pay attention to it or set up compulsory courses on interculturalism.

Okri: But it is all so timid. In Great Britain, the first mainstream history books about the European presence in Africa only appeared last year.

Steyaert: Can apologies to ex-colonies offer solace?

Okri: If you put a bullet through someone's mother's head and then apologize, what is the point? We have to go far beyond the symbol. Awareness, truth, education, that's what we need. If you have apologized, you do not have to pass on the truth to future generations. I am taking on the role of psychologist of history here, but I have to. It is part of what the novelist does.

Steyaert: The artist as therapist for society?

Okri: Indeed. We have to accept that it is very uncomfortable to look back on our past, but if we don't, the wound will start to fester and we will slowly turn into monsters. If cultures are to treat each other with respect, we must redefine our notion of civilization. It starts by questioning our values. Why does the history of Western civilization begin with the Greeks, when the Babylonians had already given us so much? Why do we measure civilization only by the skyline we have built or the airplanes we have invented? The West is obsessed with everything tangible. That is why Melville's whale is such a great image for the fatal flaw at the heart of the capitalist vision. C. L. R. James, the great philosopher from Trinidad and Tobago, once said that he discovered his socialism while reading *Moby-Dick*.

Steyaert: For Ocloo, Ahab stands for, among other things, the one per cent richest with their relentless hunger for more.

Okri: That is one possible interpretation. For me it's also about the obsession with yourself, with value and with power. In that sense, I find Queequeg an extremely interesting character. She is a redeeming figure thanks to her ability to see things through. Not that I want to put all the weight on the shoulders of minority voices. The responsibility lies with the vast majority of us, who are between the Queequegs and the Ahabs. We too often forget that we can help shape the world, by voting, but also by questioning much of what we take for granted. True civilization is not just about inventions or economic success, but at least as much about how people are raised, taught and judged. It is about how happy children are, how the elderly are cared for, how the ancestors and the unborn are honored.

Steyaert: The latter is important in Nigeria, where you spent part of your childhood.

Okri: Certainly, but it applies to all true ancient civilizations. They are much broader than the traditional Western view, in which it is easier to treat others unfairly. When the Europeans went to Africa and India to get raw materials and sugar, they did it under the guise of bringing civilization. But the Indians had already built temples when the Europeans were still dressed in raffia.

Steyaert: You also point out how colonizers in Africa cut down entire forests for their idea of arable farming.

Okri: In this way, they encouraged deforestation. Is that so civilized? As long as we don't dismantle this concept of civilization and keep embedding it in the minds of our children, we will gradually turn the next generations into monsters.

Steyaert: Returning from England to Nigeria made you realize that there is no one culture that has the absolute view of the world, you said at the Louisiana Literature Festival this summer.

Okri: When you live in multiple places, you get distrustful of dominant worldviews. Maybe they are all true, maybe none of them are true. That insight is liberating. But I already had the idea of multiple realities through the stories my mother told me about ghosts. They were so enchanting that I still reflect on their meaning. When you hear a story like that, suddenly the possibilities of the world are a lot wider.

Steyaert: In 2016, you gave a TED talk on the importance of stories.

Okri: Literature can subtly change our system. By bringing in compassion, doubt or playfulness, a book, but equally a performance or a piece of music can slightly tilt our ideas. For example, I hope that the audience of *Moby Dick* feels that we are all on a ship—a metaphor for a family, business, nation or the whole society—and that we should all dare to ask questions like Queequeg.

Steyaert: Is this why, in your latest novel *The Freedom Artist*, you write that we may be in a storm of truth or revelation these days?

Okri: Exactly. In that novel I address, among other things, what happens when books die. Austerity measures in Britain over the last ten years have wiped out dozens of libraries and at least 250,000 books. In the light of the future we are heading for, reading is crucial. Because the fewer people who do, the fewer people who construct their own authentic truths, the more people who are more easily manipulated.

Ben Okri on Perception and Illusion

Deborah Treisman / 2021

From the *New Yorker*, Feb. 1, 2021. © Condé Nast.

Deborah Treisman: Your story in this week's issue, "A Wrinkle in the Realm," revolves around a man who notices that women suddenly seem afraid of him and cross the street to avoid him. You don't mention the man's race, but the experience he describes is familiar to many Black men in the US and, presumably, in Britain and elsewhere, too. Do you think of the story as one about racial identity or fear?

Ben Okri: The fascinating thing was to write a story about something without naming it, in such a way that the story speaks about it more strongly than if it had been named. I began with an experience that, over time, had become ground into the fabric of reality that is absorbed as a part of living. This is when it becomes most insidious. It eats into the psychic cavities. After a long time, I sought a way to write about it at a slight remove, so that the distortion that it wreaks on the soul would become more evident through the absurdity of the strategy my character develops for dealing with it. The story is also about perception—how we perceive the way we are perceived.

Treisman: Is there something speculative about the story? Why is it titled "A Wrinkle in the Realm"?

Okri: There is also a speculative aspect to the story, in the idea of taking an image and wandering off with it through the anguish of the human heart to where it intersects with humor. The story is called "A Wrinkle in the Realm" because, in that universe, where people respond irrationally to what they see, something has been glimpsed. The world is governed by perceptions that have a greater force than laws. But they are illusions. The wrinkle is the momentary revelation of that illusion. We are in such a time now. The disparity between the police responses to the Black Lives Matter march on Washington and to the pro-Trump attack on the Capitol is one such wrinkle.

Treisman: The story describes, among other things, the psychological toll of living in a society that views you as different or threatening. It made me think, for obvious reasons, of Ralph Ellison's *Invisible Man*. Was the story inspired by another work, or by a specific experience?

Okri: The story was inspired not by another work but by life itself. But the difficulty was how to refract it in a new way. I wanted the story to have a neutral tone that would allow the action to get stranger and yet feel more normal. The inflections of Kafka, the thematic insinuations of Ellison hover over the tale. But it is also written in the tradition of the old-fashioned contes, those stories in which strangeness blurs the real, like the late tales of Melville, the brief notations of Hawthorne . . . .

Treisman: Your protagonist takes comfort in hiding his face behind a mask. Was the story written during the coronavirus pandemic? Did our new regime of mask wearing trigger the idea?

Okri: The story was hijacked by history. Or it's probably truer to say that, between the conception and the execution, history walked into the story. I'd been carrying the notion for years, and then I found a way to write it. And then the pandemic brought mask wearing. I kept my tranquility because the extreme nature of the masks in the story is hinted at in one or two details. A writer can only accept the accidental gifts of history. They are sort of grace notes. But it is strange when reality collaborates with your fiction. That happened to me in a more significant and disturbing way with my 2019 novel, *The Freedom Artist*. Events in the world made porous the boundaries between fiction and reality.

Treisman: At the end of the story (spoiler alert!), the man puts on a mask that becomes his face. Should we read this metaphorically? Is the mask his real face? Has his reality disappeared?

Okri: Great care was taken to keep that as open and ambiguous—and as clear—as possible. Perhaps the whole meaning of the tale is in that moment when the mask becomes his face. Perhaps there begins the discovery of the wrinkle in the realm. But then please remember that I come from a tradition where the making of masks is a magical, shamanic, and highly spiritual enterprise. It connects the power of the ancestors, the world of spirits, the forces of the universe, and the deflecting of evil. How much of that has influenced the story is anyone's guess. The final mask may be the most real thing in the whole tale, more real than the perceptions of the world. And perhaps the man's reality has changed, become quietly transformed, in some way. The need for invisibility has given way to the greater strength of having found a secret strategy for neutralizing the Medusa gaze of the world.

Treisman: You have a story collection, *Prayer for the Living*, coming out in the US this month. Are those stories connected in any way to "A Wrinkle in the Realm"?

Okri: The stories in *Prayer for the Living* are concerned with the political and spiritual implications of our grasp of what constitutes reality. They blur reality and dream. In the collection, there are twenty-four stories and one poem. Some of the stories are stokus—a form I made up in the aughts, which is an amalgam of the short story and the haiku. Others are long tales. Some are what you might call flash fiction. But all the stories, even the most political ones, are investigations into the nature of reality, which must be the most contested thing in all existence. Our sense of power, our ideologies, our politics, our loves, our fears are all bound up in it. Whether the stories involve famine, the violent deeds of Boko Haram, the impossible desire to get to Byzantium, or the warping of the world in a quantum thriller, they contest the idea that the nature of reality is ineluctable. "A Wrinkle in the Realm" takes this trope, this examination, to a twilight, fabular plane.

Ben Okri: "Nations Like Ours Have a Hard Time Looking Back Truthfully"

Dorian Lynskey / 2021

From *The Independent*, July 1, 2021. Reprinted by permission of Dorian Lynskey, journalist and author.

On June 14, 2017, Ben Okri couldn't see Grenfell Tower from his home in west London but he could smell it. "I was close enough to smell the fumes and the burning flesh and the burning cladding," he says heavily, four years on.

For three days after the fire, he couldn't sleep. Out of those furious, haunted nights emerged a poem full of empathy and excoriation, *Grenfell Tower, June 2017*, which he published just nine days later in the *Financial Times*. A clip of him reciting it on Channel 4 has since been viewed more than six million times.

"Writing the poem was, I suppose, the cure for this inability to breathe the foul air that this thing was pouring into our lives," he says. "It was visceral. I can't fake these things. The real responsibility is responding to something taking you over that you can't override. Then the second responsibility is making it art."

Okri became a literary star in 1991 when his novel *The Famished Road* won the Booker Prize, making the thirty-two-year-old the youngest ever winner at the time. He has since maintained a roaring flow of novels, stories, essays and plays (his latest work, *Changing Destiny*, opens at the Young Vic on July 9) but he's perhaps now best known as a quotable public poet who commands packed houses with his sonorous voice and distinctive beret.

A Fire in My Head, his first poetry collection in nine years, compiles verses on subjects including Barack Obama, ethnic cleansing in Myanmar and the murder of George Floyd. While his fiction comes at politics aslant, his poems are much more emphatic. Jeremy Corbyn quoted him in his debut conference speech as Labour leader and Okri responded weeks later with a stirring poem called *A New Dream of Politics*: "We live in times that have lost / This tough art of dreaming."

In 2018, he edited an anthology of inspirational political writing, *Rise Like Lions*. "Poets turn a lens on something," he says. "We give a voice to something."

When he speaks of Grenfell, Okri says as a startling aside, "I could detect burning flesh in that smell, because of certain earlier experiences." He was born in Nigeria in 1959, moved to England as a baby and returned home in 1967, just as the country was tipping into civil war. As the child of a mixed marriage, he narrowly avoided being shot by a militia because he spoke the wrong dialect.

When Okri came back to England in 1978, he came alone. After the Nigerian government defaulted on his scholarship to Essex University, he was thrown on to the streets, too proud to ask his parents for help. He remembers sheltering from the cold in Tube stations and doorways, writing and reading Joyce and Dostoevsky.

"I hate to say it, but I did have a somewhat romantic idea of my art. I really did believe that the artist has to experience all the dimensions of life: the roughness and the wonder. So I took what happened to me as part of my living apprenticeship."

Even once he got off the streets, it was a long time before he could make a living from writing, but he refused to consider a plan B. "I'd chosen a way. Why would I crack up at the first chill, the first challenge, the first frost that comes along?"

He has a poet's habit of revising lines as he speaks, scrolling through options until he finds the right words. "The only thing that made sense was writing. Everything else was nonsense."

When he wrote *The Famished Road*, he says, "Nobody was interested in African literature in the mainstream. Nobody gave a damn." Only after it won the Booker, sold a remarkable half a million copies and attracted fans from Bill Clinton to Thom Yorke, did he feel the burden of expectation. The role of literary spokesman for an entire continent was not one he wanted.

"I always was, and still am, a little bloody-minded. I'm aware of where I'm coming from, and the great literature and spirit voices of Africa, but for me it was always literature without any prefix attached to it. I was always going to go my own way. It's only by going one's own way that one really gets anywhere."

Nonetheless, he has become the kind of well-known writer whose opinions carry weight. Even with an audience of one, he can deliver a soaring peroration. The current conservative backlash against an honest accounting of Empire provokes a barn burner.

"Nations with big histories, especially histories that have to do with the domination of others, have a hard time looking back truthfully," he begins. "People are twisting themselves into unimaginable knots to make out that nothing happened in the past that was in any way troubling to anybody. They have to do a kind of book burning to expunge all the facts to make that narrative stick. It's just not possible. It looks not only pathetic but guilty."

He mentions the great abolitionist William Wilberforce. "Imagine if he had been a Boris Johnson–type figure who denied what was happening. No! Bigness of spirit is what contributed to change. I don't see cause for defensiveness. I just see cause for acceptance, courage, truth and going forwards."

I wonder, then, if he had any doubts about accepting an OBE in 2001? "I did. It's a complex process, and I sympathize with both sides, but the people who live here have given their love, their blood, their time, their sweat to this land."

If all the immigrants and children of immigrants reject honors, "It will look, from a historical point of view, as if they never really made a contribution." He would change the name, though, to shed the burden of Empire. "It weighs the nation down and makes it difficult for it to go forward nimbly into the future."

Okri is a future-facing character. *Shaved Head Poem* casts the coronavirus pandemic as a warning sign that something has to give. "It's not an accident that we're living in a period when things are happening to the human race at a rather alarming rate. These things are not happening because nature woke up one day and said, 'You know what? I'm going to give you a good beating.' We have to face the fact that we have a hand in it. We want to eat our cake, and eat it again, and still have it."

One word that becomes a regular drumbeat in *A Fire in My Head* is "new": new ideas, new modes of expression, new ways of living. It's why Okri is always moving from form to form. "Yes, I am fascinated by the search for the new, because our experience of life is so ungraspable. It's like wrapping water."

He's still working on *Changing Destiny*, a new adaptation of the four-thousand-year-old Egyptian poem "The Story of Sinuhe." "It should be as well-known as the *Odyssey*. It prefigures many of the concerns of the twenty-first century: identity, culture, migration." In the autumn, he'll publish an ecological fable for children called *Every Leaf a Hallelujah*. He even appears alongside Skepta on the final album by the late afrobeat drummer Tony Allen.

Few authors write as much, and as widely, as Okri but he bridles when I say that. "You're looking at all the different things, but I want to draw your attention to the one thing at the heart of it, which is a dialogue with life in all of its shadings: political, cultural, environmental . . . I'm constantly looking for new ways to capture what it is to be alive." He's swept away by the thought of it.

"It's so fascinating, it's so strange, it's so mysterious. My god!"

In Conversation with Ben Okri

Rosemary Gray / 2021

Madibaland World Festival of Books, online, Nov. 18, 2021. Included by permission of Rosemary Gray, Professor Emerata, Department of English, University of Pretoria. Orcid: 0000-0002-6583-4319.

The original interview was shortened and edited by Ben Okri in 2022, with Rosemary Gray's permission.

Rosemary Gray: Thank you, Ben, for your willingness to declare the festival open and to be interviewed yet again. It is a great honor. My questions pertain to the overarching abstractions of story, freedom, truth and poetry. In your recent novel, *The Freedom Artist* (2019), you write: "In the oldest legends of the land, it is known that all are born in *prison*" (346). By contrast, you also write: "In the new reality, all are born into a *story*" (ibid.). My first question pertains to this last idea of story. How does the new reality of being born into a story enable us to live in [an inferred] freedom?

Ben Okri: It's a wonderful question. Being born in prison is in itself a story. It is a story tinged with death and limited possibility. Where there's limited possibility, there is antistory. But when you live in a world of story, you live in a world of possibilities. This is a world of alternative possibilities and the ways the imagination impacts on life. We're always escaping into story. The thing about stories is that, though varied, they have a rigorous logic. The act of storytelling implies within itself the possibility of transformation. To escape from the world as a prison into the world as a story is a first step in liberation. It means being able to tell one's story. Being able to live one's story. Being able to define oneself in accordance with one's imagination. It's a liberation that we're all striving for in one form or another.

Gray: When you wrote that "all are born in prison," were you thinking of the Platonic notion of the cave, of the shadow world of illusion, of the real and the really real? And if so, what are your views on the possibility of escape from such perceived imprisonment?

Okri: Plato's notion of the cave was in my mind when I conceived the novel. But the idea of imprisonment was more existential than that. The prison in the novel is part of the fabric of life as we all live it. It is so much a part of the fabric that we don't even see it. So it is an invisible prison. Maybe it's the greatest prison of all because we're unaware of it. We don't see the bars. The story had to be cast in this extreme form. This is where we find ourselves, where we have to ask the extreme questions. We've gone past the point where we ask ordinary questions. We're at a stage in human history when it is time to get fundamental. And for me, this was a fundamental question. What are we living in? Are we living in true freedom? Are we living in a simulacrum freedom? Are we living a lie? Do we live in a fiction? Are we in a fiction imposed on us by power structures? Are we living in a deception and an illusion? We assume that we're living in freedom, but when you actually look at the world and look at our condition, we find out actually that we're not free at all. Maybe we are in more prisons than we're aware of. It's time to ask these questions.

Gray: I think perhaps that in *The Freedom Artist* you tend to suggest that it's fear that keeps us in that prison, in a cave. It operates to keep us in line. My next question is related to that: how is your freedom as a writer being affected by our posttruth society, the society in which lies and fictions are seemingly all too often accepted as truth?

Okri: We are living in strange times where the margins between truth and lie, fact and fiction, have become blurred. This blurring has had some profound effects. It really does mean that you no longer know what the boundaries are around your life. It also means you no longer "get" it. It casts doubt over your sense of reality. It undermines your sense of history. It undermines your sense of the present. It undermines your condition as a citizen. It undermines the foundations of your thought. It undermines what you assumed about the world. It renders the citizen powerless and confused and afraid and bewildered. Therefore it makes it easier for us to be manipulated and bullied. By tampering with the fabric of truth, everything else is tampered with. Then the powers that be find it easier to cast its terrifying webs over our lives. The most important thing we have to do is to contest "truth." In climate change conversations, they talk about "rewilding." In this moral domain, we need to be contemplating the truth. We need to start thinking seriously about ways we can bring back a sense of what is truth and what is a lie. Take the way it affects climate change. It's very easy for people to say: "Most of the facts are not facts."

Failure to contest the lies renders us incapable of doing anything to change the situation in which we find ourselves. This puts us in an accelerated journey towards catastrophe. We have to go back to the basics and ask ourselves what the truth is all over again, as if we're starting from the beginning. That's the damage done to our moral universe over the last ten years. It's been a profound damage. It's affected journalism. It's affected whether we believe events or not. Take the January 6 attacks on the Capitol in America recently. There are people contesting whether it really did happen. But to reshape narration is not a new technique. The technical stuff of narration is older than politics, older than history, older than power. But it's been reapplied with terrible force in our times and with sinister leakage into our lives.

Gray: In *Rise Like Lions* (2018), your lovely collection of poetry which is a tour de force of poetry through the ages, you imply that freedom is alchemical. This suggests that it is more spiritual than physical. Does this have to do with one's state of consciousness, perhaps? And if my assumption is correct, would you like to elaborate on the alchemical nature of freedom?

Okri: It's a difficult question. Any time the ultimate question is mentioned a certain amount of puzzlement arises in the minds of most people, because it seems to be a fabled thing. But when I speak of the alchemical nature of freedom, I'm not speaking only of a spiritual conversion. I'm speaking also of a physical one. The thing about alchemy that everyone was interested in and knows about is the transformation of the ordinary into the extraordinary, base metal into gold. That is what freedom does. It transforms every aspect of our lives. Going for a walk, reading a book, looking at the sky, falling in love, falling out of love, "going in." Once you put freedom in it, everything is enriched. Freedom goes straight to the core of what it is to be human. It makes all things flower. Just going for a walk with a sense of freedom, and the experience flowers into all kinds of possibilities and joys. But take freedom away from the simplest thing, and everything collapses. Everything dies around you. If you take away freedom, then going for a walk takes on the possibility of death. Looking at the stars becomes tinged with fear. Freedom is that element in the consciousness that really opens us up to the world and opens us to ourselves.

Freedom is alchemical. It brings the gold of consciousness into ordinary life. This is why freedom is so invaluable in lands where writers and artists fight for freedom and defend it and think of it as the first condition of being human. Deep rage rises in those who feel their freedoms are being encroached upon or suppressed in any way. That is because freedom is what most defines our humanity. To the degree that our freedoms are stripped from us is the degree to which we are being dehumanized. This is not a theoretical thing. It is not a mystical thing. This is something that people are prepared to die for. A thing worth fighting for. A thing people wage wars for. People give up their lives so their children and their nation can be free. A nation is only free if it continually fights threats to freedom. Then it is free to grow in all sorts of ways. Free to make mistakes. Free to screw it all up. Free to grow. Free to learn. Free to take steps sideways. Free to go at tangents. Everything is possible once freedom enters the equation. But when freedom is not in the equation, there is only one thing that we care about. And that is how to attain freedom, how to embody it. The alchemical nature of freedom gives life its splendor. Even if it is the splendor of living in a hovel. At least it is your hovel. It is your freedom, your consciousness. It means you can still go out and shout to the sky. You can protest or rebel. Freedom is priceless.

Gray: My next question has to do with your expertise as a poet. I know you are a world-renowned poet and justifiably so, but I want to come back to that same collection, *Rise Like Lions*. You state in that collection that, "Ultimately poetry transcends. It speaks beyond. [. . .] It gathers all our inner states, the core of our being, and it takes us beyond" (181). Would you like to comment further on how poetry "takes us beyond" for those who are not familiar with your works?

Okri: I say the same thing about poetry that I say about freedom. They have many things in common. They have the same alchemical power. Is the question "how does poetry take us beyond?" What a metaphysical question. But poetry takes us beyond our limitations. Something strange happens with poetry. Really good poetry meets you where you are. It comes to you. And with a touch, it dissolves the chains that you didn't even know you had in your mind. Poetry gives the mind wings. But it speaks to you where you are. When I say it "takes" one beyond, I mean it takes you to where you are. This is "beyond" because awareness is transcendent. We are not often where we are. This is another way of saying that poetry deals with truth. It seems to do so through the devices of exaggeration, metaphor, simile, intensity. But what is the goal? To *bring* you to a state of truth, not to *tell* you truth. But maybe it's the truth of what we are. It's very hard to say how it does that.

Because poetry does not really address us in particular ways. I'm thinking of the opening lines of Okigbo's *Labyrinths*:

> Before you, mother Idoto,
>   naked I stand;
> before your watery presence,
>   a prodigal
>
> leaning on an oilbean,
> lost in your legend.

What is the presence here? What does it mean to be lost in a legend? How does this bring us to truth? I don't know. I think it has something to do with the clarity of the language. Something to do with a submerged mythology. Something to do with the rhythm of the language. The way the language of poetry is close to the bone of experience. That line carries within it a silent injunction to stand naked before the mysteries of life. Stand naked before one's condition.

But the world deals with illusions and feeds them to us. We carry these limitations. We carry these fears. We carry this sense of ourselves as being creatures in history rather than agents of it. But poetry, because it deals with truth and freedom, reminds us that we are more than all of that. Poetry takes us beyond our limited selves into our fuller selves, if only for a moment. But that moment is enough. That glimpse is sufficient.

Gray: It was indeed a metaphysical question, and you've given a metaphysical answer. I know that as an artist the creative juices flow continually in you, in an everflowing stream and I wondered how the coronavirus pandemic has affected your writing.

Okri: It had a big effect on many of us. It had a very sobering effect on me. The world got shut down. People died and continued to died. It created a sense of fear, a sense of something we have not yet experienced before. It reminded me of growing up during the civil war. The sense of crisis, of living in some kind of a bunker. The sense of not being able to go out and having to be very careful. The sense that every breath could bring death into your body. The early days of the pandemic were quite terrifying for many people.

But for me as a writer, it did that strange thing that happens very rarely. It brought back that proximity of death which wakes me up. That's a fundamental part of my consciousness. It's part of how I relate to the world.

Anything that goes anywhere near reminding me of the proximity of death has that awakening effect on my consciousness. It brings me to this sense of existential survival. Like everybody else, I hunkered down and shut the doors and kept things very tight. I worked slowly and steadily. That lockdown was good for many writers, in certain ways. I'm used to having my freedoms curtailed but not curtailed like that. I missed the world. But the concentration that this gave me was amazing. I didn't write any differently. I didn't write much more, though I had more time in which to write. But I was aware of a kind of a new focus, an awakening around the edges of my mind.

Gray: Could you share with us what you've been writing about or what you've been working on at present, about the great fun of writing a book for children, the exciting thing about changes in genre, perhaps?

Okri: I've always switched genres. I really don't perceive of genres as genres. For me, it's all about the forms that a particular question takes as it becomes a creative world. I try to find answers in the work. Or at least I see where the questions lead me.

It's been a busy year. I've brought out a book of poems, the first in about nine years, called *A Fire in My Head*. It is a collection of my political poems. I've been writing political poems for a long time now. Actually, I've been writing political poems all my life. But these are particularly concentrated political poems. Poems about Grenfell Tower, Notre Dame, George Floyd. There's even an oblique poem about Brexit.

Then I also brought out a book of stories called *Prayer for the Living*, I happen to love the story form. The short story is the most rigorous literary form after the sonnet. People take it too much for granted. A good short story is hard to write. A good short story redefines the universe, in every sentence. I carry short stories in my mind for a long time. The short story is the highest kind of laboratory work. I mean this in terms of form. You are not often given an opportunity to ask a question and to find ways of framing that question perfectly. Short stories are more about perfection than almost any other form I know. The way it is told, its tone, is central.

Then I had my first play produced in many years. *Changing Destiny* was performed at the Young Vic. It is based on a four-thousand-year-old Egyptian poem. That was very difficult, as you can imagine. Plays and short stories are difficult to do well. It was the first play that the Young Vic performed coming out of lockdown. It was tough to do it for all sorts of reasons. It was quite a strain on actors rehearsing the plays, under lockdown conditions. But the result was amazing.

The most recent thing I've published is *Every Leaf a Hallelujah*. It's an environmental fable for children and adults, from 5 to 105 years. It was a challenge to write a children's book after *The Freedom Artist*.

Gray: I want to ask you about another poem. You mentioned the disaster of Notre Dame and you wrote: "We fight over cabbages while / Our souls perish in open view" ["Notre Dame Is Telling Us Something," *A Fire in My Head*, 2021, 12]. It reminds one almost of the adage of Nero fiddling while Rome burns.

Okri: That's it; that's the tone of our times, isn't it? Here we are. The earth is cooking and we're worrying about all sorts of silly things.

Gray: That is one of the most salient things: what matters, what doesn't matter. And how do we distinguish between them? We are fussing and bothering about silly little things that are minuscule really in the grand scheme of things, rather than considering the "now," considering being mindful, considering being grateful for what we have.

Okri: Or even considering the contributions that we can make so as not to escalate the climate crisis. There are not enough conversations about the role of the writer in this crisis. These are environmentally challenging times. I think that writers ought to take more of an interest in this. The climate crisis ought to be at the center of our concerns. We've avoided it and left it to the climate specialists. But this does not concern them alone. This is for us. This is for everybody. We can draw attention to it. We can magnify the understanding of how we can avert a global climate catastrophe. This is one challenge we need to take on. Writers ought to take on the magnitude of this existential challenge. We haven't got a choice. The magnitude of the environmental crisis is one of the things that I'm concentrated on at this particular moment.

"Write with New Urgency": A Conversation with Ben Okri

Anderson Tepper / 2022

From *World Literature Today* 96, no. 4 (July–Aug. 2022): 26–28. Reprinted by permission of Anderson Tepper.

Author of *The Famished Road*, among other books, Ben Okri has never been a run-of-the-mill writer. He has been hailed as "a literary and social visionary," and his oeuvre—novels, plays, poetry, haiku, stories—probe essential truths of our times. Creatively, he is as restless as ever, reimagining and expanding his literary landscape. Earlier this year, two new works—an edition of his 1995 quest novel, *Astonishing the Gods* (featuring a new introduction), and the eco-fable *Every Leaf a Hallelujah*—were published in the US by Other Press. Here, he speaks about invisibility, consciousness, and the lifesaving powers of literature.

Anderson Tepper: In your introduction to *Astonishing the Gods*, you explain how the book poured out of you in the summer of 1993. Tell me more about what prompted it.

Ben Okri: The truth is I had been carrying the germ of the idea of the novel since I was a child. I had always wanted to write a story about a person who arrives on a mysterious island. Later I became fascinated by the ancient trope of invisibility. It is there in fairy tales and legends. In Nigeria, in certain traditions, individual disappearance, return, and transformation are linked. Then a strange incident happened to me. It was a racial incident, and it ignited the third link in the magic chain of inspiration. Suddenly I knew who these invisible people of the island were and why they were invisible. The book was written the way it was because of a technique I learned from late Renaissance art, a technique that is also there in the best of traditional African art. And because of the indirect way it's written, a few people read the novel the wrong way. They thought I was celebrating self-annihilation or some form of social abdication. A few incisive questions would have revealed other layers. *Astonishing the Gods* had to be written the way it was to be true to its themes. The real question now is, "What are its themes?"

Tepper: What was it like to revisit the book today, and why publish it in the US now?

Okri: Books are seldom what we think they are. If they are any good, they reveal aspects of themselves not comprehended before. Invisibility is little understood. In a world where everything visible is celebrated, people don't understand that invisibility is the precondition for true creativity. Writers are mostly invisible when they write. We only see them when the work is done. In the night things grow unseen. In the mind ideas germinate unnoticed. The common aspiration is to be seen.

But there is another higher invisibility where thought is prepared, where the best work is done, and where true transformation occurs. I think this new paradigm is much needed now in America where there is a kind of arms race of visibility, leading to exhaustion and stress and depletion of the creative and spiritual faculties. I believe there is a reason this book has taken twenty-seven years to come to America. There is a mysterious destiny in books. When a book like this appears in a land, that is when it is most needed. *Astonishing the Gods* is in America at the right hour. These things happen due to an underlying power greater than individuals. It is perhaps the power of culture itself.

Tepper: Like the book's hero, you "set out to find one thing, but found another." What did you discover in the process of writing?

Okri: One of the great things I discovered is that sometimes a book wants to write you, and you should have the humility to let it. But also you must always be ready for when a really deep dream, a big work, needs your aesthetic, your humanity, to come into being. Most books we write, we choose, we determine. But every now and again, for reasons beyond our immediate understanding, a book wants to write you, wants to borrow your hand and your nervous system. Such books reveal their true value over the unfolding years. We think they are one thing, but they turn out to be another. And they go on changing with our changing needs. They are mercurial. They slip through your fingers. They adapt themselves to time.

Tepper: Did this book lead you in a new direction as a writer?

Okri: I'm not sure that books work that way, that they lead on to something else, that they are links in a chain. I think the spirit engages in what it is deficient in, what it needs. Or the spirit operates in what it has too much of, its excessive strength, its repletion. So the work is more cyclical, more contrapuntal, even more call-and-response. The next stage of what *Astonishing the Gods* opened up as a possibility came much later. And even then I am not so sure. I think *Astonishing the Gods* is a rare egg. It stands alone in my body of work, a fable about its own secret purpose. And as for new directions, I am taking them all the time. You have to remember that *The Famished Road* was a radical new direction after the early novels and books of short stories.

Tepper: *Every Leaf a Hallelujah* is a collaboration with artist Diana Ejaita. Tell me how you worked together and how your daughter, Mirabella, "accompanied" you on the journey.

Okri: The difficult thing was to dream up a story that was environmental in its heart, a fable about courage, animated by a desire to keep alive the love without which no struggle, no campaign, ever truly succeeds. There were two ways to work with Diana. Either she comes up with images that I am inspired by, or I write a story that she illustrates. I had already done the first way with the wonderful paintings of the Scottish artist Rosemary Clunie. We worked on a book together called *The Magic Lamp*. It's one of a kind. She made twenty-five paintings over ten years, and I wrote twenty-five accompanying stories over the next five years.

I wanted something different with Diana. So I went off and sought a dream. I went back in spirit to the forests of my childhood. I wandered in parks. Then the story began. Mangoshi, the seven-year-old heroine, came to me. I wrote it over several months. Every day my daughter wanted to know how it was going. When it was finished I sent it to my publishers, and together we chose Diana Ejaita as the illustrator. She loved the story. She was in Ouagadougou at the time. She went to the forests there. Also, she was pregnant with her first child, and she made the illustrations with the sense of this new life growing in her. Hence the wonderful fertility of her drawings. The important thing was that we left her in complete freedom and trusted her artistic instincts. But I did share one small secret with her. When she sent in the illustrations, we gasped with delight.

Tepper: You wrote an essay for *The Guardian* in which you argue that artists must reckon with the world's dire climate situation and engage in "existential creativity." What does this require?

Okri: The demands are purely personal. I offered them to the public only to share where my thoughts and convictions have taken me. If we understand what is happening to the planet, and therefore to us, and if we love this earth and our life on it, then we simply would not be doing most of what we do. There is too much waste. We use up far more energy than we need. We pollute too much. We are overdrawn on the bank of our environmental future. What one does depends on one's conscience, one's understanding. But the way we live is no longer sustainable, and each day we contribute to the suicide of our civilization. One does not want to preach, but disaster is staring us in the face. What does it demand of writers? That they use their voice to draw attention to this ongoing catastrophe, and that they write with new urgency. How can one write the same way if one knows that we are drifting toward a terminal condition of the earth?

Tepper: What sort of work have you been concentrating on lately?

Okri: Last year I had a new play produced at the Young Vic, in London. Called *Changing Destiny*, it is set in ancient Egypt and was directed by Kwame Kwei-Armah. I've had three plays performed in the last three years. *Madame Sosostris* was staged at the Pulloff Théâtres in Switzerland to full houses. And this year there's a musical play touring Belgium and the Low Countries called *Moby Dick, at last Queequeg speaks*. Yes, it is the *Moby-Dick* story, but told from Queequeg's point of view, and so it's about race, immigration, abuse of power, identity, and leadership.

In these last few years I brought out quite a wide range of works. *The Freedom Artist* came out in 2020. *A Fire in My Head*, my first book of poems in nine years, came out last year. It is a volume that has some of my strongest political poems, including "Grenfell Tower, June, 2017," a reading of which on the Channel 4 Facebook page has been watched a staggering 6.7 million times. It's an important volume for me to bring out now. Then there was a volume of stories called *Prayer for the Living*, which contains some of my best short stories.

Tepper: I was thrilled to hear you speak at the Booker Prize ceremony, thirty years after *The Famished Road* helped open the way for a new generation of African writers. Are you especially encouraged by the vitality of this work?

Okri: The new generation of African writers are conquering the world on their own terms. One can now quietly say that African literature is among the most powerful in the world. And *The Famished Road* helped that explosion. Winning the Booker was vital to this, but I think the real surprise is that the novel continues to live, continues to grow. It has been called magical realism, animist realism, fantasy, spiritual realism, African realism, and so on. It is none of those things, or it may be all of them, plus some other -isms too. It has just been reissued as an Everyman Classic, the first African novel since *Things Fall Apart* to achieve this status.

The thing about all my books is that you ought to come to them with a fresh mind. I don't do what has been done before. I do new things and I find new ways. Literature ought to wake us up to the miracle of life and being and the possibilities of mind and consciousness. Literature ought to help make us agents of change, ought to wake us up to our essential freedom, the freedom to make this world as we want it. We can't do this if we see the world in the same way that led to the world being as it is, hurtling toward environmental crisis and the shrinking of freedoms and the slow loss of selfhood. We need a new consciousness to make a new future. Literature ought to be that new consciousness.

Ben Okri on the Ambiguity of Reality

Deborah Treisman / 2022

From the *New Yorker*, Sept. 12, 2022. © Condé Nast.

Deborah Treisman: Your story "The Secret Source" envisions a country that has somehow doctored its water supply to make its citizens docile and agreeable to whatever the government proposes. How did this idea come to you?

Ben Okri: A number of conflicting impulses led to this story. One is a sense that friends of mine have that our reality is doctored. And, to some degree, it is. Things are constantly being added to our water. In some countries, fluoride is added. Things are added to our food. Persuasive reasons are given for this. But there are concerns about whether these additions are actually good for us. Certain authorities maintain that fluoride can negatively affect the pineal gland. Descartes considered this gland the seat of the soul. Then I encountered various people who believe that many aspects of modern life are tampered with in order to make citizens more docile. Their belief has an impact on their day-to-day lives. I've met people who felt the same way about vaccination, including a doctor. One of these people died recently of the very thing he was refusing to protect himself against—COVID. Then it occurred to me to write a story about the consequences of believing something at a time when the thing you fear seems to have become a reality. I wanted to explore what happens when reality becomes its own conspiracy theory. I am fascinated by the perceptual structures of a generation's belief system.

Treisman: Britain, where you live, is suffering from a real drought at the moment. Did that provide a kind of dystopian setting in which to write this story?

Okri: This is the second time now that real life has hijacked one of my stories. It happened first with "A Wrinkle in the Realm," a story the *New Yorker* published last year. Back then, it had to do with masks. Now it has to do with droughts. In both cases, the stories were written before the events. I'm not sure what to make of this. The current drought will now play into the story, becoming part of it. Still, the story is not about the drought but about something larger and more sinister, the manipulation of scarcities caused by a climate emergency and an indirect examination of why passivity seems increasingly to be the default position of the populace. Is this natural, or is it caused? I do not much rate the anticipation of future events in fiction. Contingent prophecy is really a sideshow in the deadly serious game that is literature. And the purpose of "The Secret Source," if one can speak of a purpose in so complex an art as that of the short story, is to reveal our uncomfortable truths and perhaps hint at our unsuspected resilience.

Treisman: Your characters Fisher and Venus and their flatmates aren't affected by the water in the same way as other people. Why not? Why do they question, when the scientists and academics in the story don't?

Okri: They are affected by the water, which is why they're able to be aware that they are. Perhaps because of their youth, they are more aware of the dimming of their minds. Also, they are inclined to the periphery of things, which perhaps gives them an unconsciously questioning attitude. Besides, once they realize what's happening to them, they break the first seal of the spell that has been cast on them through the everyday ordinariness of water. In a book of poems that I wrote about the new millennium, "Mental Fight," I spoke of the need for an antispell against dark enchantments cast on us by power. How to break the hold that ideologies have on our minds has been one of the themes that's engaged me for most of this millennium so far. Without knowing it, Fisher and Venus represent an antispell generation, trying to free themselves from the lies that imprison them, even if their attempt is possibly fatal.

Treisman: Fisher and Venus seek out a "secret source" of pure, uncontaminated water. At the very end of the story, you leave open the possibility that they find one; you also leave open the possibility that what happens is all a dying hallucination. Why does that ambiguity appeal to you as a writer?

Okri: The ambiguity had to be there because reality itself is ambiguous. How can we ever know it? Do we know for sure that the air we breathe is killing us, with all its pathogens and pollutions? And, even if we are right, is it not also possible that our rightness is tragic? The deeper you look into the big questions of life, the murkier things get. Certainties are complicated by the unintended meaning of events. And those meanings go on changing. It seems to me that reality is perfectly explicated in the wave-particle ambiguity at the heart of quantum physics itself. As is the mind. In the story, both readings are true at the same time. But it is you, the reader, who choose what is true for you. The great value of ambiguity is not avoidance but an amplification of the essential unknowability of reality.

Treisman: Is there another possible interpretation of the ending?

Okri: There are many other possible interpretations. There is the grail interpretation. There is the psychoanalytic interpretation. There is the generational one. And, of course, there is the political dimension. I think, in these times, everyone dreams of a secret source—of energy, of truth, of power. It says something about the disillusionment prevalent in our world. Water in the story can stand for many things. But I think symbolism is never so powerful as when the thing is the thing it stands for, when water stands for water. Not what water symbolizes but water itself. When we begin to perish for lack of the thing itself, which nourishes language and provides the ultimate symbol of essentialness, we are in a dire place indeed.

Treisman: Should we read "The Secret Source" as an allegory? A cautionary tale? A fable? Is it part of a story cycle or collection?

Okri: The story is a slice of reality, a fable, a satire, a cautionary tale, an immaterial finger writing a warning on a wall, a cry in the dark, a good old-fashioned piece of speculative fiction in a tradition as old as *Candide* or *The Decameron*, tales that we tell one another in the twilight of strange times. It is of a piece with the kinds of writing I am doing right now, like my forthcoming novel *The Last Gift of the Master Artists*, which reimagines life in Africa just before the slave trade, or my novel *The Freedom Artist*, which came out a few years ago. The story itself will be in a collection of stories, poems, and essays called *Tiger Work*, which comes out next year and directly and indirectly tackles environmental themes.

Ben Okri or the Aesthetics of Suspicion

Vanessa Guignery / 2022

Vanessa Guignery: In your novel *Starbook*, the narrator remarks: "A good conversation was a work of art" (100). For this volume, we have collected a number of interviews, some of which are called conversations. Which differences do you see between a conversation and an interview?

Ben Okri: A conversation is freer and less intrusive. It can be more playful. An interview tries to catch a reality that cannot be caught in that way. We, as writers, take a long time over our sentences. We work carefully at the things we say. An interview rarely allows you the freedom to do that. It pins you down to the moment, to the errors of the moment, the limitations of the moment. A conversation is truer to how we communicate with one another, to how we communicate our truths. I always prefer a conversation to an interview.

Guignery: I seem to understand that you don't particularly like rereading the interviews you gave.

Okri: Does anyone recognize themselves in interviews? Maybe it's the flawed nature of the interview as a form. Maybe it is an imperfect way of communicating what someone is really like. Maybe our views are complex and nuanced but the interview fixes us to one moment. Maybe our truths are elusive. There are two kinds of interviews. There is the question-and-answer variety. It tries to be objective, but no one speaks so perfectly all the time. We all have our hesitancies, our searching for the precise words to express our thoughts. And anyway, most writers, if they are any good, write better than they speak. To read in print some of one's response to a question is like seeing oneself pulling faces in a mirror. Then there's the form of the interview where you are paraphrased, sometimes with prejudice, sometimes with sympathy, but always from the interlocutor's point of view. This one is not about what you are saying. It is about how you are perceived at the time. The first one is objective and oddly untrue. The second one is subjective and possibly judgmental. But a conversation is like going for a nice walk in an interesting neighborhood with someone you like.

Guignery: In your biographical note on your website, you're presented as a cultural activist. What do you mean by that?

Okri: A cultural activist to me is somebody who uses culture to advance the struggles that they believe in. I wouldn't chain myself to a railing. I wouldn't glue my hands to a painting. That's not the kind of activist I am. But I would write the most explosive thing I could think of as a way of getting across a strong feeling I have about the environment or about racial injustice. It is using culture as one of the weapons in the liberation struggle. But this is one strand of my artistic practice.

Guignery: Do you feel you have used culture as a weapon more forcefully in the last few years?

Okri: It's something I have always done in different ways. Some moments in history require a stronger artistic response. It is part of the tradition of African writing, because of the conditions out of which African writing came: protest against colonialism and afterwards against bad governments. The writer was always seen as one who bears responsibility for drawing attention to things going wrong in the land. We use writing as a weapon. That was always part of it. Then I came to England and found that it's not part of how it is perceived in the West at all. The term "cultural activist" is a good cover for being a legitimate fighter on behalf of justice.

Guignery: I feel that you were already "fighting" in your early work but maybe in an indirect way whereas some of your recent work is more direct.

Okri: I'm not sure about that. Some of the poems in *An African Elegy* are direct, some are indirect. My novels are always indirect. Many of the poems in *A Fire in My Head* are political poems. Some are not. People notice the political ones because they are published in newspapers and address issues on everyone's mind. But they don't notice the quieter ones, the love poems, the Shakespeare poems, the poems on art, on fatherhood. Because of its brevity poetry is good for protest. You can say something strong and true in a short space. Literature has always been direct or indirect, an art that speaks through mirrors, or one that attacks an injustice frontally, that holds governments up to scrutiny or ridicule. It's been there since Sophocles or Aristophanes. As long as there have been injustices done to citizens, there has been an art that responds to them. When times are really bad, art becomes more direct. It wants to speak clearly. You don't paint a *Mona Lisa* when your land is going up in flames. You paint a *Guernica*. I've just swung more, in a few of my work, towards this more direct method, this holding up the pennant. But that is just one aspect of what those works do. Just as within the more indirect works there was the presence of the direct, so in these more direct works there is the presence of the indirect, of unseen aesthetic dreams.

Guignery: You regularly collaborate with artists, painters, film directors, dancers, or composers (Rosemary Clunie, Charlotte Jarvis, Avish Khebrehzadeh, David Hammons, among others). Is this association with other artists and art forms essential to your creation?

Okri: I see all of the arts as one great river and I love collaboration. I get a lot of strength working with a dancer, with a composer. (I did a collaboration with Tony Allen and Damon Albarn of Blur in a track that came out last year.) I find it fruitful. It's something that is part of the great tradition. Cocteau collaborated with Picasso. Cocteau drew, wrote plays, performed. Harold Pinter was an actor. Miles Davies painted. Jazz always worked with poetry. For me it's *the* great tradition.

Guignery: In your collaborations with artists, does inspiration circulate both from their work to yours and from your work to theirs?

Okri: Yes, it works both ways. David Hammons told me about a work that he did that was inspired by a short story of mine called "Incidents at the Shrine." And I will soon publish a short story that is a fugal response to his great conceptual work called "Blizz-aard Sale." Rosemary Clunie has done many paintings out of my books. I have made stories out of her paintings. I have done dance and poetry combinations with Charlotte Jarvis. Dance came out of the poetry and poetry out of the dance. The poem existed before the music we made for it with Tony Allen and Damon Albarn. For me it should flow in all directions because it is all the same energy. A line of poetry by T. S. Eliot should be able to inspire and *has* inspired drawings and paintings as much as he was inspired by Stravinsky. I find that the great periods in literature also tend to be great periods in art, periods when the spirit of collaboration and of expression is very strong. We are all trying to express in the particular language of our art something that is inexpressible but that shows a feature or an aspect in another of the great arts. It doesn't surprise me that T. S. Eliot in the *Four Quartets* was inspired by Beethoven's quartets. And Beethoven himself was inspired by Goethe. So where does it start and where does it stop? It is a constant circulation.

Guignery: The biographical note on you in the book of paintings by Avish Khebrehzadeh indicates that you have "a secret life as a painter." Could you talk about this?

Okri: I tell the story that on a certain day, in Lagos, at the threshold of my artistic life, I made a decision to draw what was on the mantlepiece and to write a poem. Before that I had been painting, I had been drawing, I was going to be an artist. But I had to choose between art and literature. I knew I couldn't be good at both at the same time. I had to make a decision. Michaelangelo is the only one I could think of who was did both well. He was a great artist, but he's not a Dante. But then who else is? I had to choose and I chose literature. But art never left me. It has only been kept secret. These last many years I have been collaborating with the Scottish artist, Rosemary Clunie. Some of the fruits of this will be seen in our exhibition in London called *Firedreams*.

Guignery: You performed T. S. Eliot's *The Waste Land* at the Marylebone Theatre on November 11, 2022 to mark its centenary. It's a poem that is marked by a polyphony of literary voices. Are you particularly interested in this polyphonic dimension?

Okri: What I love most about this polyphony is that it's a democratic one. Strangely enough, this goes against the perception that people have of T. S. Eliot. We don't think of him as someone who was greatly sympathetic in his work to the working classes or to women. He inclined towards the elite. But *The Waste Land* is populated with women, with the working classes and with other voices. It has all these levels of society and different linguistic registers, tonally harmonized. *The Waste Land* is great poetry and great theft, some of the best artistic theft of the twentieth century. How do you steal artistically? How do you steal with genius? Look at *The Waste Land*. That's how you do it. Performing it and learning it was a great way to be in conversation with Mr. Eliot.

Guignery: Can you talk about your experience of learning the poem?

Okri: I learned all the lines by heart. It was hard at first. It felt like a difficult poem to learn but the more I learned it, the simpler it became. Eliot is a great poet and his inner rhythms help me to remember the lines. When I read it at first I was not aware of these inner rhythms. But things connect. It's like a great painting. One part of the painting is not isolated from another part. It's extraordinary to live inside the poem.

Guignery: Your play, *Madame Sosostris, the Wisest Woman in Europe*, performed in Lausanne in February 2020, is inspired by a character from *The Waste Land*. However, Madame Sosostris is absent from the play. Instead we find characters playing roles in a masked ball, a sort of *mise en abyme* of theatre but also a reflection of the way in which we all play roles in our lives. Is this notion of role-playing and what it says about our fluctuating identities important to you?

Okri: I'm not sure we know who or what we are. We constantly weave in and out of identities throughout our lives. We are different at thirty than at ten, different at twenty than at forty. Those early personas become strangers to us. I know friends who today are formally dressed, but in their twenties were anarchists with spiky hair. You see them today and you wonder: what happened to the anarchist with red and yellow hair? It's in there somewhere. Just one of several inner identities. Masks often reveal the true face. Costumes often liberate secret aspects of the personality.

Guignery: In the play, are the characters able to reveal more about themselves because they are donning costumes?

Okri: They think they conceal, but reveal by concealing. They think they're operating under the mystery of their costumes, but their costumes subvert what they're doing. Masks, by covering one aspect, allow often the most contradictory aspect to be unveiled. So a cautious woman becomes the wisest and the most expressive. Odd reversals are at work.

Guignery: Madame Sosostris is a figure from ancient Egypt and your play *Changing Destiny*, first performed at the Young Vic in July 2021, is also inspired from ancient Egypt, more specifically a four-thousand-year-old poem entitled "Sinuhe." In the play, the soldier Sinuhe runs away from Egypt when the Pharaoh dies because he thinks people will believe he is part of the conspiracy and will be killed. The play is a meditation on identity, guilt, the loss of home, the nature of exile and homecoming. Did you feel that these themes resonated very powerfully with our contemporary world?

Okri: More than that, I felt it was a precursor of *Hamlet*. Throughout the poem Sinuhe does not know whether he was one of the conspirators or not. He does not know whether what he did led to the death of the king. Not knowing and being torn by that—that condition of the mystery of the consequences of our actions and how our actions sometimes are veiled from us—was fascinating. It was very modern. Pirandello would have resonated with that. Absurd theatre would understand that. But this aspect was there four thousand years ago when they had more stable identities than we do now. There is also the theme of power and what you do with a leader who has become a tyrant. That is a big question. Ancient societies were scared of killing kings. In Egypt the pharaoh was a god. But deicide is of our century. It is of our time. And then there are themes of exile and migration. That was a revelation. It gave me great faith in the power of poetry and art, that while being sunk in their time they can continue to speak to us all the time.

Guignery: In 2020, you wrote the script for the opera or musical play *Moby Dick, at last Queequeg speaks* directed by Gorges Ocloo. In Melville's

Moby-Dick, Queequeg is a man but in the opera, she is a woman. How was that choice made?

Okri: It was understood from the start that that was going to be the case. It seems I have been working with gender fluidity for a while. In *Changing Destiny*, originally played by two people, a man and a woman, the roles were reversed every other night. This way both played all the roles. On some nights the Pharaoh was a man, on others a woman. With the female dimension in the opera *Moby Dick*, another layer is added to the text. But it was really a way of looking at those big *Moby-Dick* issues: the state, the tyranny, the individual, power, powerlessness, responsibility, obsession, evil, colonialism, resistance. Big themes. four-thousand-year-old themes. In fact, *Moby Dick* is in many ways a bigger and more symbolic version of the original of *Changing Destiny*.

Guignery: And what is the significance of "at last" in the title?

Okri: In *Moby-Dick* we all know that Queequeg speaks but not really. Melville speaks for Queequeg. There's a whole trope in modern diaspora literature that looks at Western texts where the Aborigines, the people of the land, don't speak. There's a whole trope going back to *Robinson Crusoe* or *Heart of Darkness* or *L'Étranger* where the white characters do all the talking and the Black characters are being spoken to and spoken for. There is the need to allow those who are silent to speak. This is a text in which those who are silenced in literature get to speak for themselves. And when they speak something else comes into view, something beyond rancour, something that balances all that silence, something like a song, an ascending voice and vision . . . .

Guignery: In your theatre adaptation of *L'Étranger* by Albert Camus, you also thought of the voice that doesn't speak. The Camus estate didn't agree to let you have the unnamed Arab speak in the play but when the play was performed at the Coronet in London in September–October 2018, the audience could watch a short film by Iranian British artist Mitra Tabrizian called *The Insider*, in which we hear your text. In it, the Arab is given a name (Mamoud) and speaks.

Okri: Yes. I managed to circumvent the Camus estate's interdiction. Catherine Camus wasn't happy that I attempted to make the Arab speak, even outside of the play. But she couldn't do anything about it because we're in the territory of my freedom. The text is now in my book of poems, *A Fire in My Head* ["The Insider," 63–65]. I like these migrations. It was part of a play, then a monologue in a film, and then it becomes a poem. I love those migrations that operate throughout the different dimension of texts. Things that can't live over here will find life over there.

Guignery: *L'Étranger* is a very important text to you. Why did you wish to turn it into a play seventy-five years after it was published?

Okri: It's a different text from *The Waste Land* but they have something in common. Camus enters into the spirit of working-class characters. He gives them a strong clear voice. He reveals a void in their quotidian lives. He gives them sensuality. And yet he's able to use that voice to explicate this philosophy of the absurd. Could he have managed that with the middle and upper classes? What Camus did was to get that voice and that class to express underlying conditions of his times. *L'Étranger* is only about a hundred pages, but it manages to distil the mood of our troubled century. We feel it to this day. That is no ordinary achievement. It is like discovering one of the fault lines in the human spirit at a given time in history, and then being able to isolate and identify that psychic crack. It's also a precise and elegantly written book. (I was in conversation at the French institute with Kamel Daoud who wrote a response to it [*Meursault, contre-enquête*]. He said he found *L'Étranger* boring. That remark inversely hints at the strength of *L'Étranger*, for Daoud's book exists in its shadow.) *L'Étranger* is a great little book. Novels of six hundred pages don't get to the place it reaches. Its enduring influence is mysterious. Camus's artistry amplified a focal point of what went wrong with humanity at a junction in history.

But *L'Étranger* is also an inherently dramatic work. I sensed that straightaway. Camus was also a playwright, and I felt it would make for a powerful play. It had never been staged as a full play before. It had mostly been done as a monologue. We gave it the full treatment at The Coronet in London, with a cast of eighteen, many from the community theatre, and its entire run sold out, with people queuing for tickets. The run was extended and still it sold out. It could have run all year. The interest in it was so great. This proved that the power of the work was not just in its art. Camus in that work put his finger on something that speaks to us even when it migrates from its native medium of the novel. I think he hints at the terror of a life without light. He points to the danger of the darkness waiting for us if we lose the qualities that make life meaningful. The emptiness is real, and if it engulfs you then casual murder is as easy as genocide or a meaningless war. Unknowingly, he illuminated the unexpected consequences of life without moorings. With Nietzsche's "God is dead," a vast emptiness crept into the world. And humanity is not great enough to fill that void. The emptiness that makes you kill a man and the emptiness that makes you kill a whole people is the same. The consequence of that emptiness haunts our future, in our destruction of our environment. The deserts in our heart become deserts in history.

Guignery: Some of your poems collected in *A Fire in My Head* have a powerful political tone, like "Grenfell Tower, June 2017," the poems on Boko Haram, on the Rohingyas or on George Floyd ("Breathing the light"). These poems evoke tragic moments but also often include a hope for transformation. Do you feel that poetry can bring some form of consolation?

Okri: Consolation is a strong word. But a lot of poetry does bring consolation. People in prison have been sustained by Shakespeare's sonnets and all kinds of poems. The consolation of poetry is not always in its more overt messages. It might be in its secret messages, its deeper truths. In all of my direct poems there's also a secret dimension. The consolation of poetry could also be in the pattern of sounds and imagery. There's something consoling about imagery. For images take the mind somewhere else. They don't take the mind into an obvious condition of action or pain or anger. They take the mind to somewhere more contemplative, a distillation of feeling. But if poems achieve consolation that's great.

This revealed itself more with the Grenfell Tower poem. The reading I did was seen by six million people on the Channel 4 Facebook page. It's a strange fact that six million people, as a way of wanting to engage with this tragedy, watched this poem. If you go to the physical site now, the tower itself is covered over. It has the image of a green heart at the top and there are plans to demolish it. In a sense, they're trying to physically and visually remove it from our consciousness. You can't actually see the burnt tower anymore. It's been masked over. There's a costume over it. What the poem does is to keep the burnt tower there as a mental fact. Regardless of what happens. To keep it so it's there, preserved: the fire, the place, what was done, what was not done. To have it as a memorial, a constant reminder to increase our vigilance, our sense of social justice. This is what poetry can do but doesn't do often.

Poetry misses a lot of power when it is denied a political dimension. There's been a way of talking about poetry in the West that does give an impression that poetry only has one kind of role or possibility. T. S. Eliot himself did not know how to deal with the Second World War in poetry. He wrote a short attempt at a war poem. But a poet like Neruda has no problems in talking about the disappearances in Chile and the great injustices done in Latin America. Walt Whitman was celebratory as well as political.

Dante was also a political poet in *The Divine Comedy*. The *Aeneid* is a political poem about empire. The establishment always tries and covers up what poetry is doing, under the name of art, or pure poetry. Most of the time it's not true at all. Political poetry is seen a lesser species of poetry. Somehow impure. But I don't agree. Poetry is never pure. It is always doing something. And doing nothing is itself a kind of statement. The notion that poetry can't be political is part of the ploy of the establishment, whatever that establishment is, to limit the power of poetry, to discourage it from entering the fray, from joining the great battles of freedom and consciousness that are at the heart of every society. They prefer that poets keep quiet and practice their art silently in their corner and never bring the force of their art to bear on the consciousness of their times. Fortunately most poets have a conscience and can see what is going on and are sufficiently mature in their art to know how to use it to speak to their people when the need arises. After all poetry takes place in the world and derives its vitality from all of life. We know Shelley felt he had no choice but to write what became the great poem about the Peterloo massacres. He was not even in England when the massacres happened, but he responded anyway. We know that Byron used poetry in a political way and that the young Wordsworth was an extension of the French Revolution. Poetry too has all kinds of mansions.

Guignery: Is it important for you to put some hope, some light even in the most tragic situations?

Okri: I don't put the light in there. The light is there already. It's just that I see it. Other political poets prefer to highlight just the tragedy, but I think the tragedy is stronger for the fact that it is never just tragedy on its own. There is always this other element, the light of the human spirit. It's always there in whatever debased form in which you see it. It's there and we have to name it as well. We don't want to do a Queequeg with the human spirit and its suffering conditions and not give it a voice. We don't want to suppress the many-sided truth of tragedy, which is what we do when we say "This terrible thing is happening, we have to focus on just that." We want our tragedies pure and unmitigated. They are more powerful because they are impure, because there is still that light. It may be brutalised, but it's there.

Guignery: We talked earlier about important writers for you such as T. S. Eliot or Albert Camus. Can you talk about your fascination with *Don Quixote*?

Okri: *Don Quixote* is one of my favorite works of literature. I read it first in my twenties. I read it every day when I was going to the BBC to do a program I was presenting on the radio. I travelled in the daytime by tube.

Reading *Quixote* was my consolation. It was my escape. It was my healing. It was my homeland. It's the first book in which I could track the blossoming of something in me. I was one kind of person before I read it and I could feel myself changing under the impact of this book and by the end of it I was another person. I was another kind of writer. It's the first book in which I was conscious of a transformation during the act of reading.

Guignery: In "Don Ki-Otah and the Ambiguity of Reading," included in the anthology *Lunatics, Lovers and Poets: Twelve Stories after Cervantes and Shakespeare* (2016) and in your collection *Prayer for the Living*, Don Ki-Otah comes into a printer's shop and reads his adventures written by "[s]omeone called Ben Okri" who "claims to be writing [them] from oral history" (207). Why did you choose to imagine this scene?

Okri: The scene parallels exactly what happens in *Don Quixote*. For the anthology, we were all meant to write a story about the works of Cervantes or Shakespeare. They died in the same year. I chose that printer's shop because of the magic of reading. That moment in *Don Quixote* is the most modern. I don't know how writers do it, how they anticipate the future, anticipate movements of the human mind, movements within literature itself. It's almost as if they create it in advance. The closest the classics came to this idea of a text in which the writer is written was the *Aeneid* when Aeneas arrives in Carthage. He listens to the songs of Troy and his own adventures. He hears himself being mythologized. Between the *Aeneid* and *Don Quixote* a great revolution had taken place: the invention of the book as a cultural artefact, as a complete reality in its own right.

When Don Ki-Otah goes into the printing shop, the ambiguity is whether he in fact does read what is printed or whether he imagines it. Imagining what we read is a modern propensity. We read on top of what we're reading. We're always doing that. Two people who have been leafing through a newspaper might say: "Ah, there was a coup! Did you know there was a coup?"

"Apparently there were two coups."

"But the newspaper says there was one coup."

"There was another coup, but they didn't print it in the papers. The journalists didn't know about it."

And the next one might say: "Ah, then there were three coups."

They treat reality with suspicion. They treat the establishment with suspicion. They feel that what is told to them is always a fraction of what actually happened. To get a sense of what really happened, you need the additional quality of your own imagination and an understanding of how power operates in your land. So it's not just what you read. It's also your imagination and your understanding that is overlaid on that reading.

What I'm talking about here is not orality. And it's not rumor either. Though rumor is a dimension of it. Rumor itself has a communal imaginative quality. What I mean is that we've been able to imagine what really happened but we've not been told. Reality is constantly censored and sanctioned and packaged for consumption. This does not happen here in England to the same degree. People tend to believe what is written. There's a bit more of a belief in what is written. You open *The Guardian* and you read that Prince Charles did this and that. You think: "Ah, he did this and that!" But nobody says: "He did this and that but is it possible that he also did that and this?" I wanted that element, a different layer. You could call it the aesthetics of suspicion.

Guignery: One of the characteristics of Don Ki-Otah is that he reads very slowly and *"Read slowly"* is a phrase which has appeared at the start of all of your books for a number of years. Can you talk about that?

Okri: It is now part of my literary aesthetics. You're the one who helped it take a definite form in the *Callaloo* magazine feature that you did on me. It was the first place that published a whole essay on the aesthetics of reading slowly.[1] I think reading slowly is a new kind of reading. I often say that if you read a bad book slowly, it's made worse. If you read a good book slowly, it's not made better but it's more bearable. But if you read a great book slowly, you multiply its world. There are books that owe their reputation to their having been read fast. They were written to be read fast. Their effect is in the blur of their reading. When you go contrary to the reading instruction implied in the writing you come up against another book, sometimes one not as good as the same one you read fast. I have made sure that even in the texts where I suggest that you read them slow, if you disregard my suggestion and read them fast or at a normal pace, the book you then read still approaches what I intended. But you'll get much more from them read slow. Reading slowly is more than immersion. It's a complete empowerment of one's own imagination. I think we read too fast. The thing about reading fast is that we make approximations in our reading. We whizz past that which was carefully built up. We miss the music and the subtleties and often the quiet miracles of construction. Some sentences in great writers are not to be believed in the marvel of their composition. Some passages and some pages are as exquisite as passages by Bach or Beethoven or Mozart, magical feats of linguistic truth and beauty. Passages that could awaken the deep wisdom and joys of the soul. We rush past them in the fever of narration, trying to get to the end. I have said this before, but I don't write just to get you to the end, but to experience eternal moments wherever you are in the text. You ought to be able to do that, be transported on any page, to get ultimate pleasures of reading in mid book. The purpose should not be to want to rush to the end but to sense the beauty and all the possibilities of being in this moment now. Reading should be like life. Do we in life want to rush to the end, to get to the end of our life's narration so quickly? No. We want to linger, to drink in the depths and surfaces and majesty of being, the miracle of existence. That's also what reading should be like. So that when you do come to the end it should be an unprecedented experience, like one's own death. But what a grandiose meditation!

Back to the dangers of reading too fast. We notice less, and what we notice is more impressionistic. But when we read slowly we live in the moment. Then reading approaches the condition of living. We notice more and we live in that world. Slow reading creates more worlds, more realities.

Guignery: Invisibility is a recurrent trope in your work. In *The Freedom Artist*, an invisible world coexists with the visible world. Do you think that the invisible world is where some form of freedom can be found?

Okri: I have a whole network of ways of perceiving invisibility. I have an ongoing dialogue with the possibilities of invisibility in my work. It doesn't stop. It began as an aspect of liberation but it's become all kinds of other things. We don't properly understand invisibility. We think it's just absence, or the unseen. There's a deep misunderstanding about this. The things that are the most invisible are the things that are visible. We don't see what's right in front of us. In that sense reality *is* invisible to us. Perhaps the most visible things are the things that we don't see, the things that we imagine, the things that we fear, the things that we desire. It's all inverted. It's all topsy-turvy. It has to be questioned. But we have to find a way to question it in a way that can be understood in language even if the brain misinterprets. And so in the imaginative way we engage with visibility there has to be subversion. Visibility needs to be subverted, because it is never what we think it is. If you don't add the element of subversion, you will not quite get what I'm really saying.

Guignery: That element of subversion is present in *The Freedom Artist* and in your short story "The Secret Source" [*New Yorker*, September 19, 2022] where some individuals decide not to abide by the rules of society. Do you feel that resistance is necessary to question reality?

Okri: Resistance is built into almost all of the great philosophical and religious traditions. Nietzsche missed that aspect about Christianity. The original documents of Christianity constantly question reality. Many of the proverbs of Jesus are a complete turning upside down of reality. But then when Nietzsche was talking about Christianity, he wasn't talking about Jesus. He was talking about the institution of the church. All the great philosophical traditions come with a doubt and resistance, from Plato to Schopenhauer. Again it comes down to reading. Anyone who has looked at life honestly will tell you that reality is there to be read. But to read something is already to say that what you're seeing is not quite what it is. You need to interpret the codes that are in front of you. So reading in a sense already brings with it an act of subversion. It's subverting the surface of things in order to interpret what's happening on the inside. It's a soft subversion.

Guignery: "The Secret Source" and *Every Leaf a Hallelujah* confirm your interest in environmental issues which young generations are very much aware of. Do you feel that literature can be one of the modalities through which more people can become aware of climate emergency?

Okri: Literature has been doing that all along without our being aware of it. It would be interesting to know the fairy tales that Greta Thunberg and her generation read. The fairy tale tradition was always environmental. Ancient myths and legends were environmental because they warned against tampering with nature's harmony. They say: "Don't mess with the rivers because something bad will happen. You will offend the gods or the goddesses or the nymphs of the rivers, of the trees." This is the reason why forests and rivers and mountains have deities. It was a way of saying that they are sacred places, and that if you mess with them, if you tamper with them in some way, you will pay the price for it. Environmentalism is inside storytelling already. It was always there from the beginning, from the oldest tales you could tell. The fairy tales always say to us that not only should you not mess with nature, but you should not mess with human nature. So, not only environmentalism but also cultural environmentalism and moral environmentalism are always there in stories. Stories are there to help us regulate our relationship with the environment, with our own internal environment, to help us know when we are misaligned, when we are out of harmony. It would be interesting to investigate the invisible storytelling dimension of why people suddenly revolt.

Guignery: *Every Leaf a Hallelujah* is your first children's book.

Okri: Yes, although I say it's for the ages of 5 to 105. I wrote it for the children in all of us.

Guignery: Did your becoming a father incite you to write this book?

Okri: I'd always wanted to write a children's story. I'd always felt I'd be a natural, but I never got round to it. I got to fifty and still hadn't done it. And then I got to sixty and still . . . . But I think you do need a reason. I told my daughter many stories, but I forgot to write them down. Two weeks later, I would say: "These were good stories. What were they again?" I had forgotten. That wasn't so good.

Guignery: But you wrote this one down.

Okri: She was a great help. I began to write it and then she made it her job every day to come and ask me if Mangoshi had saved the forest yet. She was my storytelling policeman. Writing a children's story is harder. It is harder being simpler. It is harder telling a story indirectly directly. Children are easily bored with the obvious. It has to be true imaginatively.

Guignery: Fifteen years after its publication, you revised *Starbook* (2007) and published *The Last Gift of the Master Artists* (2022), which is more compact that the original. In interviews, you explained that you wanted to put more emphasis on slavery which you felt that some readers of *Starbook* had missed. Was the deletion of some passages a way to make the slave trade theme more visible?

Okri: Most people did not get the slavery element in *Starbook*. Many of them still took it as a fairy tale or as a story with fairy tale elements. They were not hit enough by the foreknowledge of this terrible thing that was going to happen. I had taken the trouble to keep coming back to it in different ways. That's because I wanted to find a new way to deal with the slave trade (which was not just "these people were dragged and taken across," as in Spielberg's film *Amistad*). It is our job as artists to find another way to get people to hear the anguish of these terrible moments in human history. I wanted to find a way that was emotional and that showed it wasn't just people taken from A to B. This A that they were taken from was a rich world. These people had a world. These were not just individuals that were going to be stripped to be sold in the marketplace. What was taken was a whole civilization, a whole world, with all its complex ways of seeing the universe, of managing and transforming reality. I felt that no one had properly foregrounded that. I didn't want to make big claims. I just wanted the earth and the imagination and the spirit of art to do all of that so that at the end when they are taken away, you feel the enormity of it. The slavers were smashing the axis of the world.

Therefore, it wasn't just foregrounding the slave trade. The tonal quality of the whole book had to be such that this would come through. It was also the network of tones and colors and the tranquility of the spirit. I wanted two great elements: the tragedy and the transcendence. These two great Ts had to be there at every point, in every sentence, for you to feel both. How do you have the tone of the tragic and the transcendence in every sentence? It's not easy. But that's what I had to do in *The Last Gift of the Master Artists*.

Guignery: Can you talk about the reasons for the cuts from *Starbook*?

Okri: I cut, but I also redistribute. Whatever I cut is there in some form in the surrounding territory of the rewriting.

Guignery: In *The Last Gift of the Master Artists*, there are more blanks between the sections and between the paragraphs than in *Starbook*. Was this a way to give the reader more space to read slowly and reflect on what's written?

Okri: Absolutely. But I also wanted the reader to feel the presence of gaps. All kinds of gaps run throughout the book: gaps in history, gaps that are disappearances, gaps between people, gaps within people, gaps in the heart, gaps in nature . . . . I realized that I had not aesthetically materialized the fact of gaps in *Starbook*. I don't know why I missed that. I think it's because I felt that it could only be done in the writing. It never occurred to me that it could also be done in the book as an aesthetic object. That alone is a reason to rewrite *Starbook*, to let the gaps show. When you get to read about the white wind, the mind is doing a double thing because you are literally seeing these blank pages.

Guignery: Could you talk about the actual process of rewriting?

Okri: A lot more work went into the rewriting than the writing. I spent longer at it. I typed it all out again, rewrote that, typed that out again and then set it down and went for long walks and asked myself: "What was I originally trying to do with this book?" Sometimes you forget what you were originally trying to do because the book takes on a life of its own. *Starbook* was never the title that the book wanted to have. It only got to be called *Starbook* because I was exasperated. I had exhausted many pages and still I could not find the title for this book. I had all kinds of very fanciful titles and none of them were right. And even when I was rewriting the book, to the very last day, I still hadn't found it. I went for a long walk and came back. I took a piece of paper and said to myself: "You have to really sit down and do the proper aesthetic and spiritual mathematics of this book right now." I had to find my way methodically and then I got it.

Guignery: Was the process of rewriting similar to when you rewrote *The Landscapes Within* into *Dangerous Love*?

Okri: It was much more complex because *Starbook* is a much greater book. I don't want to reduce the importance of *Starbook* in any way in what I have said so far. It was a difficult book to write, but it was a book in which I had to sustain such a high level of inspiration every day. In a way that book broke me. And it took me a long time to recover from the cost of writing it. The novel was an attempt at something that was much bigger in every sense. But first, you need to account for the invisible way in which the book came into being, which is why it's called *Starbook*. It's there in the opening sentence which people now see clearly. They didn't see it before. Everybody now sees that opening sentence: "This is a story my mother began to tell me when I was a child, but didn't finish. The rest I gleamed from the book of life among the stars, in which all things are known." The mother didn't finish the story she was telling you and yet you wrote the rest of the book. It must have been very short, what your mother said: "There was a prince who disappeared one day and we tried to find him. Wait a minute, I'll get something . . . ." And then she goes to the kitchen and never resumes the story which was real. Did she not finish it because of a continuing grief? Was it forgetfulness, or distraction? Or was there a greater, more secret design? Knowing my mother, there was always something more. So we're talking about less than two sentences, and then the other 480 pages you got from the book of life among the stars? I had to deal with the implications of that in *The Last Gift of the Master Artists*.

Guignery: The first sentence of this novel points to the importance of your mother in your upbringing.

Okri: I think my mother's side becomes more evident in a book like *The Last Gift of the Master Artists*. I feel that I've not foregrounded my mother's side as well as I should have. I grew up in Nigeria at a time when most of the writers were very left-wing, so I felt somewhat quietly discouraged to mention the fact that my mother was a princess. She was from the royal family. That sense of royalty was an important part of my upbringing. When we went to the village, we didn't just go as members of the village, of the tribe. We went back and were greeted as members of the royal family. This has no impact at all on the storytelling aspect of my mother except that, growing up, I was aware of these ancestors of princes and kings and queens. That's why the story of the prince that disappeared made such an impact on me.

Guignery: How important are the unseen and the unsaid in *The Last Gift of the Master Artists*?

Okri: You have to understand that *The Last Gift* came after *Prayer for the Living* which I think is my most important volume of stories. If you read it carefully, you'll see that I'm working a lot with things that are said and things that are not said. Not only in the stokus but in many of the interleaving stories, like "Hail," the one where the guy goes into a framer's shop to get a frame. His girlfriend is next door. There's a baby. The framer is talking to a young man about a painting and the young man says to the framer: "I sold five hundred paintings." This strange ordinary conversation is taking place deep in the story. The narrator is at the window looking out so that's already one plane. Behind him this conversation is taking place. And there are frames everywhere. The girlfriend's outside. She comes into view. She's framed. It's all these frames taking place. The organization of the visible and the invisible, the framing and the not framed—I think my work went into the invisible here more than in any of the novels. I had been working towards it. In *The Age of Magic*, there's a lot of what has already been done with that: framing and reframing, the visible and the invisible, the said and the unsaid, the hinted-at and the not hinted-at, the things that are behind certain structures. And then, farther back in time, there's *Astonishing the Gods*, a little symphony of the unseen.

I brought all of that to *The Last Gift* because it's a book about the secret kingdom of master artists. When I came to write it, I suddenly realized that the master artists are the real heart and meaning of the kingdom. They are the ones that give the kingdom its magnificence, and yet they are not on the surface of the kingdom. The book had to be shaped with all of that in mind, with an awareness that was sculpted in. You can't say everything. Take "The Burghers of Calais." If you don't know the story and you see one figure like this and another figure like that, you don't know what it is. But Rodin had to take the story out and leave the gestures there as pure forms. That's what I had to do.

Guignery: *The Last Gift of the Master Artists* is also a book about art, about the power of art and the role of artists in society.

Okri: It's also about what art is. But it is not what the West thinks of as art. It's a very different definition of art. Somebody gave me a wonderful reading of *The Last Gift*. I thought: Good, I've done my work in such a way that you can bring these readings that even *I* may have unconsciously intended but not consciously put there. That reader said: "Ben, what you seem to be saying is that the true art of government at its best also has to be a work of art. Because the Prince has to go below the surface and find the tribe of artists and then bring back what he has learnt into the art of governance." I thought that was a beautiful reading. I've always believed that politics should be capable of being a work of art. For art is not just a manipulation of words or materials. It is also the shaping of civilization.

Guignery: Is there a topic which hasn't been addressed in previous interviews and that you'd like to talk about?

Okri: The one thing that's missing in most of the interviews is that I never get to talk about either my present or my past or my changing philosophy of writing itself.

Guignery: How has it changed over the years?

Okri: It has changed a great deal. Perhaps my writing has become more spiritual. Not that it is inclined towards spiritual subjects, but that it is engaged in reverberations. There are more silences in my writing now. For me, writing was never just about sentences, stories, themes, plots and characters. It was always about the mystery of the word. What the word does. The word in itself, in its abstraction and its specificity. How words make worlds. Not because they make them but because they suggest them. When I was much younger I never knew how to make silence a part of the amplification of the writing. As I've gotten older, I've come to realize that every word, in its right place, has a strange power but you have to allow the space for amplification to happen. Otherwise the word comes up against another and the amplification stops.

Guignery: Do you think your work as a playwright may have had an influence on this evolution?

Okri: That's a different aesthetic. There's the verbal dimension. A lot of what happens in a play can't be written down. It can be suggested. The really skillful writers know how to suggest it so that the director will go in the direction that was indicated for them and not in another one. You learn a lot about the unspoken from theatre but the place to really learn it is in the short story. This is not always the case, of course. Maupassant, Hemingway, Mansfield were great writers of short stories, but didn't excel in the theatre. Fitzgerald was not a good playwright. On the other hand, Chekhov's plays grew out of his mastery of the short story. There are very few novelists who are also great playwrights. Hugo, perhaps; Voltaire, perhaps not. Turgenev wrote at least one enduring play. Think of Flaubert, Dickens, Tolstoy and one might be tempted to conclude that the novelistic mind and the theatrical mind are almost antithetical. Looking at the other side is just as interesting. How many great playwrights were truly good novelists? Not many. Shaw tried, Ibsen didn't, Miller abstained, Soyinka wrestled, Pinter dipped a toe in, and Stoppard dabbled briefly.

Guignery: And yet you write both novels and plays.

Okri: That's because I come from the short story and the poem. Those are my roots. They both deal in suggestiveness. Writing plays was one of the earliest things I did. It took me a long time to understand how to do it. I am still learning. I want to write plays differently. I have a whole aesthetics of playwriting. That is another conversation altogether. Most of these different areas in which I work is because I have a quarrel with the orthodoxy. By this I mean the way in which a form gets to be codified. It is presented as being the only way to express the world through this form. They did it for all the genres. There's an idea of what the play should be and you see hundreds of plays like that. But I am interested in other possibilities.

Guignery: Are you writing a play right now?

Okri: I want to find a way to reimagine tragedy. This is very challenging. Perhaps even impossible. That's good. Maybe in five years, we'll have another conversation about this.

Note

1. Ben Okri, "Some Aphorisms." *Callaloo* 38, no. 5 (Fall 2015): 1042–43.

Ben Okri on Manipulating Reality

Katherine Hu / 2023

From *The Atlantic*, Feb. 15, 2023. Reprinted by permission of *The Atlantic*.

Katherine Hu: In your short story "The Third Law of Magic," an artist sells snowballs at a market. We get a clear view into his motivations for the show, which take on a philosophical weight as they accrue. When do you choose to focus on your character's thoughts instead of their actions?

Ben Okri: Part of the story's tension is precisely in the contrast between the character's exteriority and interiority. You think you see one kind of person, but when his inner world is expressed, that limited perception explodes.

Interiority is most powerful when it moves with the dynamics of the story. This is another way of saying that perhaps, in a story like this, there are three levels of stories going on. One is the overt story, the quest for a new art form to express that which is almost impossible to express. The second is the story of the journey through the city and the way the city reveals the potential of the quest. The third level of narration is internal.

There is a story going on inside all the time that's different from the story going on outside. I am fascinated by that. The inner story drives the outer, and the outer story fuels the inner. But all the stories are part of the overarching one in a symphonic way.

Hu: The story evokes a piece of performance art by David Hammons known as *Bliz-aard Ball Sale*, an event that has since faded but lives on in stories. How does your reimagining play into Hammons's original mythmaking?

Okri: One aspect of David Hammons's genius is the generation of mythic fractals. His art encompasses aesthetics, race, politics, magic, dislocation, and identity, among others, but even more so it creates rumors, gossip, tales, and exaggerations in the minds of his audience.

An artist's work does not always tend towards myth; a work can be great and yet not generate much mythology. But Hammons specializes in the secret art of mythmaking. Isn't generating myth a higher kind of aesthetics? *Bliz-aard Ball Sale* is the audacious act of making art out of ephemerality, disappearance, rumor, and the posthumous existence of that which was not widely experienced when it existed. It is the gift of Houdini.

I am fascinated by the way life distills into myth. For me, writing is an act of resurrection and magic. It too brings back to life that which few people noticed. It too raises from the dead. Its greatest realm is not the world but the vast kingdom of the human mind. But this story is not a reenactment of Hammons's *Bliz-aard Ball Sale*, but a dream woven around it, the way Charlie Parker might take a theme and wander off into his own world, giving us two gifts in one: the fragrance of the original, and a spare, enchanted reverie.

Hu: The pure, unadulterated wonder of the young boy when he sees the snowballs is one of my favorite parts of the story. You describe it in such vivid detail. Do we tend to complicate innocence, or is it inherently complex?

Okri: I am glad that moment moves you. It was important to the story that it was the boy who grasped, without thought, without undue complexity or critical analysis, the wonder of the work. That is exactly what art at its purest is meant to do, to stop our breathing and our thinking. It ought to cut through all the emotional baggage, all the neurosis, all the overthinking and reach right into the spirit to awaken us to something that transcends what can be expressed in words.

Innocence is much more complex than it seems. It is why brilliant people can do things which are the fruits of tremendous thought but which, when experienced, appear to have the incomparable genius of childhood itself. It was once said that all great things are, at heart, simple. There are two kinds of innocence: innocence of spirit and the innocence of wisdom. I am not sure which of the two is more complex.

Hu: In putting a price on snow and scouring the city's waste, the artist exposes contradictions in capitalism and consumer culture. These contradictions hint at larger questions about how value is ascribed in society. Is there an alternative means for us to derive and create value?

Okri: There has to be an alternative way for us to derive and create value. If not, we as a species are irredeemably doomed. If value can only come from the ever-escalating arms race of competing demands, if it can only come from money, then this exposes its fundamental contradictions. Value ought to be related to being and consciousness. In real terms, the sight of one's child in a moment of unique happiness ought to be greater in value than a fur coat. The joy one feels in the presence of the one we love ought to be greater in value than a new car.

This is not to say that the car and the coat are without value. But then what value can one place on that which we pay so little attention to, which we forget to celebrate—the sheer invisibility of one's good health or one's sanity or the safety and well-being of one's family? Civilization has to move towards the higher value of consciousness, of being. Otherwise we are in grave danger of commodifying the priceless while conferring unnatural value on the worthless.

The time will come when we will value peace more than gold, when we will value the happiness of the many over the ecstasy of the few. Our society will only ever be as great as what we value. We have to reevaluate before it is too late, before we start unknowingly worshipping death.

Hu: How does "The Third Law of Magic" fit into your work more broadly?

Okri: It continues my interest in what constitutes reality. This has always characterized my work. I have always felt that if we have a proper grasp of what reality is, we will better know what to do with this tremendous gift of life, this infinite energy compressed into a mortal frame. I think all literature at its best tries to do that.

Reality is all we have to work with, but we don't really know what it is. The truth about reality is that its subdividable aspects can yield results which can be faithfully replicated while we remain completely in the dark about its other aspects or the whole itself. This is odd, for it gives us the illusion of control, when in fact what we have is merely the control of contingent conditions. Therefore, much of our confidence is provisional. One can be wrong and yet some things we do seem to work. One can be right and yet some things that we do appear not to work. Often it is a matter of perspective, of time, of truths concealed from us.

This paradox of reality is at the core of a novel of mine called *Astonishing the Gods*. In *The Freedom Artist*, reality can be manufactured for a people to such a degree that it invades their own realities. In *The Last Gift of the Master Artists*, the realities of a whole people are about to be altered by the white wind, but the dreams of the master artists continue to endure. This short story places the law of magic within the realm of the real, and hints that the ultimate magic is reality itself, the most unknowable magic of them all.

Hu: What distortion of reality have you been most intrigued by recently?

Okri: The most outrageous distortion of reality that I have witnessed recently is where an event that took place before the world's gaze has, slowly—with suggestions, with countertheories, with insinuations of secret forces at work—been made to look as if it wasn't the very thing the world actually witnessed. It took the dogged collation of recorded facts, eyewitness statements under oath, and visual evidence to slowly reestablish to the world what it originally witnessed.

This is a very strange thing to experience in one's lifetime—where powerful forces can make you doubt what you experienced. It makes one feel that if they can do that, they can do anything. It all comes down to manipulating reality and how reality is then perceived. We need to advance the art of decoding reality and interpreting what power does to reality, if we are to protect our freedoms and our future.

Hu: You work in a range of media, and your writing takes many shapes. What projects are you working on?

Okri: My next book is a suite of stories, essays, and poems around the theme of climate change called *Tiger Work*. It gathers all my writings on the subject. Both strength and beauty of spirit are required to draw attention to the specter hanging over us, one that we live with as if it weren't there. We carry on each day as we did the day before, but each day we bring nearer the conditions we fear. A radical act of mass consciousness is needed to awaken us to the tremendous responsibilities of the moment.

My novel, *Dangerous Love*, was published yesterday. In September, Other Press will also be publishing a play of mine set in ancient Egypt called *Changing Destiny*. I am additionally working on a book of essays, a new play, and a short novel about resisting tyranny, texts that I hope to thread with the wonder of being here on Earth.

Index

abiku, 10, 11–12, 13, 14, 15, 45, 48
Achebe, Chinua, xiii, 20, 24, 30, 68, 70, 98, 104, 105, 125, 129, 130, 131, 132, 133, 144, 161
Adventures of Huckleberry Finn, The (Twain), 103, 110
Aeneid (Virgil), 45, 201, 202
Africa, 15, 16, 30, 71, 74, 77, 79, 80, 81, 104, 107, 108, 111, 126–28, 131, 132, 160, 169, 170
African aesthetic, 16, 102–3, 131, 142, 153
African literature, 9, 20, 21, 26, 42–43, 48, 50, 53, 128–29, 131, 175, 188, 194
Albarn, Damon, xxi, 195
Allen, Tony, xxi, 176, 195
Arabian Nights/Thousand and One Nights, 16, 130, 165
Arcadia, xiv, 63, 65, 70, 135, 138
Aristotle, 3, 57
Armah, Ayi Kwei, 20, 37, 90
art, 8, 15, 21, 25, 55, 60–61, 63, 64–65, 68, 75, 76–77, 79, 81, 85, 91, 119, 174, 194, 201, 209
artist, as figure, 7, 8, 24, 44–45
atomization, xiv, 9, 29, 143
autobiography, 6, 7, 25
Austen, Jane, 3, 89, 107, 108, 132, 158
awakening, xv, 147, 157, 161, 162, 183
Azaro (*The Famished Road*), 11, 12, 13, 15, 43–44, 50, 89, 104, 109–10, 111, 113, 114, 115, 116, 164

Bacon, Francis, 96, 109, 143
Beautyful Ones Are Not Yet Born, The (Armah), 37
Beowulf, 16
Biafran War, 24, 25, 49, 157, 164, 167, 175
Bible, 35, 63, 153, 165
Blake, William, 84
blindness, 17, 21, 23
Bliz-aard Ball Sale (Hammons), 195, 212–13
Booker Prize, xii, xiii, xx, 47, 50, 51, 151, 167, 174, 188
Borges, Jorge Luis, 14, 116
brevity, xiv, 95, 96, 124, 143, 194
Brexit, 165, 168, 183

Camus, Albert, 109, 132, 138, 143
Candide (Voltaire), 150, 192
capitalism, 21, 28, 32, 112, 169, 213
Catcher in the Rye, The (Salinger), 120
Cézanne, Paul, 84, 85–86
chaos, xv, 7, 8, 17, 21, 22, 24, 28, 32, 33, 40, 41, 42, 63, 66, 84, 127, 135
Chekhov, Anton, 133, 140, 210
Christianity, 35–36, 39, 90, 92, 204–5
climate change, xv, 161, 179–80, 184, 187–88, 191, 215
Clunie, Rosemary, xvi, xxi, xxii, 187, 195, 196
Coetzee, J. M., 47, 90, 131

colonialism, 14, 26, 29, 35, 38, 40, 70, 90, 105, 113, 127, 168, 170, 176, 194, 198
compression, 27, 95, 109, 142, 143
consciousness, xiv, xv, 9, 11, 12, 17, 25, 27, 29, 109, 110, 111–12, 114, 116, 120, 134, 145, 147, 155–56, 189
consolation, 22, 43, 144, 169, 200, 202
conversation, xi, xvii, 60, 149, 160, 193–94, 96, 209, 211
Crime and Punishment (Dostoevsky), 133, 155
Crome Yellow (Huxley), 163
cubism, xiv, 77, 97, 135

Dante, 45, 49, 196, 201
darkness, 8, 21, 22, 29, 30, 51, 88, 146, 199
death, 11, 12, 33, 136, 157, 182–83
Defoe, Daniel, 50
dialogue, xi, 27, 55, 58, 61, 64, 65, 68, 84, 89, 95, 100, 114, 127, 128, 177, 204
Dickens, Charles, 3, 49, 130, 158, 210
discipline, 9, 61, 140–41
Divine Comedy, The (Dante), 201
Don Quixote (Cervantes), 133, 154, 155, 166, 201–2
Dostoevsky, Fyodor, 132, 175
dreams, xi, xv, 10, 14, 23, 26, 27, 31, 63, 64, 77, 80, 95, 97, 108, 139–40, 141, 160, 173
dystopia, 150, 190

echo writing, 110
education, 38, 49, 86, 121, 127, 141, 145, 146, 168, 169
Ejaita, Diana, xxi, 187
Eliot, T. S., 23, 195, 196, 200
Ellison, Ralph, 69, 172
enchantment, 84, 120
England, xix, 10, 19, 26, 31, 49, 100, 107, 132, 137, 145, 157, 160, 164, 175

environment, xv, 161, 187, 192, 200, 205
Europe, 77, 80, 81, 82, 99, 146, 160, 167, 168, 169

fairy tales, 152, 205, 206
Flaubert, Gustave, 132, 140, 141, 144, 210
Floyd, George, xv, 174, 183, 200
folktales, xii, 4, 54
Forster, E. M., 66
freedom, xv, 21, 22, 61, 64, 65, 68–69, 83, 87, 89, 94, 105, 117, 125, 156, 165, 178, 179, 180–81, 189, 191

García Márquez, Gabriel, 43
ghetto, 4, 5, 6, 19, 39, 100, 111
Greek classics, 3, 4, 16, 130, 152

Hamlet (Shakespeare), 165, 197
Hammons, David, 195, 212–13
happiness, 23, 106, 138, 147, 149, 213, 214
Hawthorne, Nathaniel, 172
Head, Bessie, 20, 131, 132
Heart of Darkness (Conrad), 198
Hemingway, Ernest, 104, 210
history, xiv, xv, 14, 15–16, 26, 31, 35, 36, 44, 54, 70, 77, 92, 103, 104, 106, 108, 111, 112, 113, 114, 115, 117, 138, 145, 147, 157, 158, 161, 169, 172, 176, 179, 206
home, 136–37
homelessness, 9, 19, 157, 164, 175
Homer, 16, 48, 49, 50, 57, 58, 117, 152, 154
hope, 18, 56, 201
human spirit, xii, xiv, 15, 61, 77, 78, 82, 90, 93
humor, xv, 28, 29, 143–44, 171
hunger, 9, 116–17, 161

illumination, 21–22, 30, 58
imagination, xii, xiii, 3, 25, 26, 27, 45, 50, 65, 77, 136, 178, 202–3
infinity, 7, 11, 12, 16, 28, 75, 92

influence, 9, 20, 31, 48, 52–53, 71, 153
innocence, 8, 28, 213
inspiration, xiii, 4, 71, 83, 84, 172, 187, 195, 196, 197
interpretation, xvi, 26–27, 36, 38, 40, 57–58, 61, 72, 191–92
Interpreters, The (Soyinka), 38–39
invisibility, xii, 17, 105, 134, 173, 179, 185–86, 204, 209
Invisible Man (Ellison), 69, 133, 172

James, Henry, 104, 109
Jarvis, Charlotte, xxi, 195
journey, 10, 30, 69, 105, 115, 126, 127, 135–36
Joyce, James, 31, 104, 115, 132, 175
Jung, Gustav, 41, 111, 139

Kafka, Franz, 150, 172
Khebrehzadeh, Avish, 195
Kruger, Peter, xxi, 145–46
Kundera, Milan, 95

Labyrinths (Okigbo), 17, 182
Lagos, xix, 6, 7, 19, 20, 40, 102, 111, 164
language, 9, 20, 28–29, 49, 50, 104, 105, 132–33, 165
Leaves of Grass (Whitman), 103
literary genres, xiv, 96–97, 98, 100, 109, 122, 124, 143, 152, 183, 198, 210; aphorism, 95, 143; essay, 94–96, 100, 109, 124; fable, 4, 9, 150, 164, 192; novel, 9, 11, 46, 52, 109, 122; play, xiv, 183, 210–11; poetic essay, xiv, 94, 100, 143; poetry, 45, 52, 94–95, 96, 100, 108, 109, 121–22, 123, 124, 143, 151, 153, 181–82, 200, 201; short story, 9, 27, 100, 109, 183; stoku, xiv, 106, 142, 143, 173
loss, xv, 71, 72, 76
love, 21, 42, 70, 74, 100

Madame Koto (*The Famished Road*), 11, 12, 13–14, 112, 113, 114
magic, xv, 54, 65, 74, 80, 82, 91, 101, 119, 120, 135, 145, 213, 214
magical realism, xiii, 43, 48, 52, 102, 133, 188
masks, 30, 172, 190, 197
Maupassant, Guy de, 140, 210
Melville, Herman, 69, 167, 169, 172, 197–98
memory, xv, 26, 31, 148
Moby-Dick (Melville), xxi, 69, 167–69, 188, 197–98
Montaigne, Michel de, 96, 109, 143
Morrison, Toni, 132, 168
Mum (*The Famished Road*), 111, 112, 113
music, xiii, 14, 29, 73, 83, 85, 108, 119, 156
myth, xi, xiii, xiv, xv, 4, 9, 13, 23, 48, 49, 79, 92, 93, 101, 102, 103, 108, 112, 113, 115, 134, 138–39, 143, 145, 152, 158, 212–13

names, 36–37, 113
narrative voice, 27, 28, 43, 110
nature, xiii, 33, 83, 160, 205
Neruda, Pablo, 124, 200
Ngũgĩ wa Thiong'o (James Ngugi), 20, 131
Nietzsche, Friedrich, 199, 204–5
Nigeria, xii, xix, 7, 8, 10, 19, 20, 30, 46, 49, 57, 80, 105, 145, 148, 160, 164, 175

Ocloo, Gorges, xiv, xxi, 167, 169, 197
Odysseus, 4, 63
Odyssey (Homer), 16, 63, 136, 154, 165, 176
Okigbo, Christopher, xv, 17, 24, 45, 131, 182
Okri, Ben: aunt, 112–13; biography, xii, xix–xxii, 3, 19, 39, 48–49, 51, 83, 100–101, 111, 156–57, 160, 164, 175, 182, 208; childhood, 3, 95, 105, 148, 169, 187, 213; cultural activist, 194;

daughter, xxi, 163, 187, 206; father, xix, 3, 6, 19, 49, 130, 143, 149, 157, 158, 164; fatherhood, 149, 194, 205; *Firedreams* exhibition, xvi, xxii, 196; mother, xix, 4, 19, 131, 143, 149, 157, 164, 170, 208

Works By: *An African Elegy*, xx, 194; "An African Elegy," 45; *The Age of Magic*, xv, xxi, 135, 136, 137, 146–47, 209; *In Arcadia*, xv, xx, 63, 73, 105, 135, 137, 138, 143; *Astonishing the Gods*, xx, xxi, 56–57, 70, 93, 105, 185–87, 209, 214; *Birds of Heaven*, xx; "Boko Haram," xv, 200; "Breathing the Light," xv, 200; *Changing Destiny*, xiv, xxi, 174, 176, 183, 188, 197, 198, 215; "In the City of Red Dust," 22, 32, 34, 41; "Converging City," 31–32; "Crooked Prayer," 28; *Dangerous Love*, xvi, xx, 54, 55–56, 57, 58, 70, 133, 137, 207, 215; "Disparities," xix, 31, 35; "Don Ki-Otah and the Ambiguity of Reading," 202, 203; "The Dream-Vendor's August," xx, 33–34; *Every Leaf a Hallelujah*, xiv, xxi, 176, 184, 187, 205–6; *The Famished Road*, xii, xiii, xiv, xx, 10–18, 43–44, 45–46, 47–48, 49, 54, 78, 89, 98, 102, 104–5, 108–17, 131, 133, 135–36, 137, 144, 151, 164, 174, 175, 187, 188; *A Fire in My Head*, xv, xxi, 174, 176, 183, 188, 194, 198, 200; *Flowers and Shadows*, xiii, xix, 5, 6, 19, 20, 24, 27, 28, 30, 35, 39–40, 42, 49; *The Freedom Artist*, xv, xxi, 150, 156, 158, 170, 172, 178–79, 183, 188, 192, 204; "Grenfell Tower, June 2017," xv, xxi, 151, 174, 175, 183, 188, 200; "Hail," 208–9; "A Hidden History," 26, 31; *Incidents at the Shrine*, xiii, xix, xx, 6, 9–10, 27, 99, 101–2, 103, 131, 133, 142; "Incidents at the Shrine," 9–10, 32, 144, 195; *Infinite Riches*, xx, 98, 105, 137; *The Landscapes Within*, xiii, xvi, xix, 6, 7–9, 24, 25, 27, 30, 31, 36–39, 41, 42, 49, 55, 101, 137, 142, 207; *The Last Gift of the Master Artists*, xvi, xxi, 192, 206–9, 214; "Laughter beneath the Bridge," xix, 25, 28, 41; *Madame Sosostris, the Wisest Woman in Europe*, xiv, xxi, 163–65, 188, 196; *The Magic Lamp*, xxi, 187; "Masquerades," 30; *Mental Fight*, xx, 83, 122, 191; *Moby Dick, at last Queequeg speaks*, xiv, xxi, 167–69, 188, 197–98, 201; *The Mystery Feast*, xxi; *N: The Madness of Reason*, xiv, xxi, 145–47; "Notre Dame Is Telling Us Something," 183, 184; *The Outsider*, xiv, xxi, 198–99; *Prayer for the Living*, xiv, xxi, 173, 183, 188, 208; *Rise Like Lions*, xxi, 175, 180, 181; "The Secret Source," xxi, 190–92, 204, 205; "In the Shadow of War," 25; "Shaved Head Poem," 176; *Songs of Enchantment*, xx, 54, 57, 98, 105, 137; *Starbook*, xiv, xvi, xx, 67, 70–76, 78–79, 81, 93, 106, 135, 146, 193, 206–8; *Stars of the New Curfew*, xiii, xx, 27, 45, 72, 103, 133; "Stars of the New Curfew," 23; *Tales of Freedom*, xiv, xx, 106; "The Third Law of Magic," xxii, 212–14; *Tiger Work*, xxii, 192, 215; *A Time for New Dreams*, xiv, xx, 94–97, 114, 121, 124, 143; "To Katya, aged seven, in a bomb shelter in Kyiv," xxii; *A Way of Being Free*, xx, 83, 94, 100; "When the Lights Return," 21; *Wild*, xiv, xx, 122, 123, 142;

"Worlds that Flourish," 32, 33, 40;
"A Wrinkle in the Realm," xxi,
    171–72, 190
oral tradition, 29, 40, 43, 142, 157, 159,
    165
Orwell, George, 150
Outsider, The (Camus), xiv, xxi, 155, 198,
    199

painting, xiii, 23–24, 39, 42, 83, 110, 115,
    119, 120, 142, 156, 157, 195–96
perception, xv, 8, 9, 10, 14, 15, 16, 17, 22,
    23, 25, 30, 89, 102, 108, 115, 121, 134,
    140, 159, 171
Picasso, Pablo, 43, 77, 84, 195
Pinter, Harold, 195, 210
Pirandello, Luigi, 164, 197
Plato, 3, 89, 130, 178–79, 205
Plutarch, 109
point of view, 27, 28, 43–44, 105, 110
politics, xv, 20, 28, 42–43, 49, 72, 74, 95,
    103, 151, 156, 168, 173, 174–75, 183,
    192, 194, 200–201
postcolonialism, xiii, 22, 52, 126, 132
poverty, 9, 111–12, 127, 157, 162, 164
power, 22, 26, 103, 158, 191, 197, 198
prison, xv, 156, 161, 178, 179, 191

racism, 168, 171, 185
reading, 4, 27, 38, 58, 62, 110, 119, 120,
    155–56, 170, 202, 203–4, 205
realism, xv, 31, 42, 46, 48, 84–85, 86, 88,
    134, 188
reality, xv, 10, 14, 22, 23, 24, 25, 27, 29,
    30, 31, 42, 43, 48, 49, 88–89, 102,
    103, 104, 106, 108, 109, 111, 114, 116,
    119, 121, 134, 140, 141, 142, 158, 159,
    172, 173, 179, 190, 191–92, 203, 204,
    205, 214–15
redreaming, 26, 139, 140
regeneration, xiv, 74, 75, 80
religion, 27, 32, 35, 62, 75, 145, 164

repetition, 29, 115
responsibility, 5, 36, 43, 50, 53, 60, 61,
    69, 87, 90, 127, 132, 144, 147, 151,
    161, 169, 174, 194, 198
rewriting, 55, 206, 207–8
riddles, xiii, 11, 16, 142
river, 9, 17, 45, 104, 105, 109, 117, 121, 122,
    139, 153, 195
road, 10, 14, 15, 45, 104, 105, 117, 136
Road, The (Soyinka), 10
Robinson Crusoe (Defoe), 198
Roman classics, 3, 4
Rushdie, Salman, 153, 154, 168

satire, 29, 45, 49, 192
seeing, 8, 22, 36, 93, 97, 103, 113, 119–20,
    121, 204
Shakespeare, William, 9, 62, 104,
    128–29, 130, 132, 164, 194, 200
Shelley, Percy Bysshe, 153, 201
slavery, 70–72, 76, 77–78, 176, 192, 206
social criticism, xv, 4, 5, 102, 127, 145,
    164
South Africa, 64, 80, 125, 126
Soyinka, Wole, xiii, 10, 17, 20, 24, 39, 45,
    68, 90, 105, 129, 131, 132, 165, 210
spiral, 115
spirit-child, xiv, 12, 15, 43, 48, 104, 105,
    108, 110, 113, 114
spiritual, as realm, 54, 60, 61–63, 64, 65,
    92, 133, 157, 164
spirituality, xv, 35, 75
Stevenson, Robert Louis, 150
story, 4, 65–67, 69, 131, 132, 170, 178
"Story of Sinuhe, The," 176, 197
storytelling, xiii, 48, 67, 85, 131, 142,
    153–54, 158, 178, 205
stream of consciousness, 31, 47
suffering, xiv, xv, 13, 15, 21, 44, 45, 54, 78,
    80, 90, 100, 138, 145, 147
symbolism, 23, 24, 26, 37, 40–41, 138,
    192

Tempest, The (Shakespeare), 111
Things Fall Apart (Achebe), 70, 98, 130, 155, 188
time, xi, 77, 79, 115, 141, 147
titles, 23, 30, 38, 153, 207
Tolstoy, Leo, 132, 133, 210
tradition, 43, 57, 68–69, 85–86, 89–90, 104, 112, 113, 114, 132
tragedy, 105, 201, 206–7, 211
truth, 23, 39, 155, 170, 179–80, 181–82, 191
Tutuola, Amos, 17, 165
Twain, Mark, 3, 103
Twitter, xi, xiv, 142–43

universality, 30, 64, 65, 128, 129–30, 159
utopia, 63, 69

Virgil, 45, 49
voice, 29, 102, 110–11, 168, 196, 198, 199, 201
Voltaire, 150, 210

war, 24, 25, 78, 157
Waste Land, The (Eliot), xxii, 163, 196, 199
Whitman, Walt, 200
writer, role of, xv, 26, 45, 145, 147, 169, 194
writing, 4–5, 20–21, 23, 73, 101, 118–19, 121, 152, 153, 157, 158, 165–66, 175, 182–83, 186, 210

Yeats, W. B., 20, 122

About the Editor

Photo by Zulfikar Ghose

Vanessa Guignery is professor of contemporary British and postcolonial literature at the École Normale Supérieure de Lyon in France. She is the author of monographs on Julian Barnes, B. S. Johnson, Ben Okri, and Jonathan Coe, and the editor or coeditor of some fifteen collections of essays on contemporary British and postcolonial literature. Her latest monograph is *Julian Barnes from the Margins: Exploring the Writer's Archives* (Bloomsbury, 2020) and she edited a special issue of *Études Anglaises* on contemporary Nigerian literature (2022). She is the author of *Seeing and Being: Ben Okri's "The Famished Road"* (2012) and the editor of *"The Famished Road": Ben Okri's Imaginary Homelands* (2013) and of a special issue of *Callaloo* on Ben Okri (Fall 2015).

www.ingramcontent.com/pod-product-compliance
Lightning Source LLC
Chambersburg PA
CBHW030106170426
43198CB00009B/508